# THE GLOBALIZATION SYNDROME

## TRANSFORMATION AND RESISTANCE

*James H. Mittelman*

PRINCETON UNIVERSITY PRESS　PRINCETON, NEW JERSEY

Copyright © 2000 by Princeton University Press
Published by Princeton University Press, 41 William Street,
Princeton, New Jersey 08540
In the United Kingdom: Princeton University Press,
Chichester, West Sussex
All Rights Reserved

*Library of Congress Cataloging-in-Publication Data*
Mittelman, James H.
The globalization syndrome : transformation and
resistance / James H. Mittelman.
p.   cm.
Includes bibliographical references and index.
ISBN 0-691-00987-2 (cloth : alk. paper)
ISBN 0-691-00988-0 (pbk. : alk. paper)
1. International economic relations.   2. International relations.   I. Title.
HF1359.M58 2000
337—dc21      99-039631      CIP

This book has been composed in Sabon

http://pup.princeton.edu

Printed in the United States of America

1   3   5   7   9   10   8   6   4   2
(Pbk.)
5   7   9   10   8   6

For Linda,
Alexandra, Jordan, and Alicia

# Contents

# List of Tables

# Preface and Acknowledgments

THROUGHOUT my studies, I have puzzled over why so many millions of people are marginalized in the global political economy, or even downwardly mobile, while others have the good fortune to experience upward mobility. Of course, cutting a trajectory is not a matter of fortune in the sense of sheer luck, whether good or bad, but rather of a combination of material and historical conditions, agency and strategies, power relations, life-ways, and evolving structures. This book tackles the problem not so much from the perspective of different national experiences, but by attempting to develop a globalization framework. It began with a broad and insufficiently focused question, one that I sought to sharpen several times over: Why does globalization enhance the lives of some people and diminish those of others? The effort here to come to grips with this issue draws not only on the work specifically undertaken for this book, but also builds on almost three decades of my prior research, much of it in Africa and Asia.

During the course of the fieldwork for this book, I held appointments at the Institute of Southeast Asian Studies in Singapore (1991); the Department of Sociology, the University of the Witwatersrand, Johannesburg, South Africa (1996); and the Institute of Malaysian and International Studies, Universiti Kebangsaan Malaysia (National University of Malaysia, 1997–98), where I returned in 1999. From these bases, I was able to fan out to other parts of Eastern Asia and Southern Africa. At the University of the Witwatersrand and Universiti Kebangsaan Malaysia, I had the opportunity to offer ongoing faculty development seminars on globalization, allowing me to learn from colleagues about diverse globalizing processes and different ways of interpreting them. During the write-up stage of this study (1998–99), it was a pleasure and honor to be resident in the School of Social Science at the Institute for Advanced Study in Princeton, where I found an ideal environment for reflection and exchanging views with a group of congenial scholars.

I owe a debt of gratitude to several institutions and individuals. For financial support, I thank the Professional Staff Congress of the City University of New York, the World Society Foundation, the Pok Rafeah Foundation, and the Institute for Advanced Study. The institutes that hosted me in Africa and Asia as well as my home base, the School of International Service at American University in Washington, D.C., played a major role in making possible the research for this book. Although it is difficult to single out individuals among many helpful people, this book could not have been completed without the participation of colleagues who coauthored four of its chapters: Richard Falk, Albert G. Milbank Professor of International Law and Practice, Princeton University, and three former students from my Ph.D. course on "Social Theory in Comparative and International Perspective," Christine B. N. Chin (now Assistant Professor in the School of International Service, American University), Robert Johnston, and Ashwini Tambe. The students in my graduate and undergraduate courses contributed importantly to this book, complicating theories and concepts, challenging me, and introducing new ideas and opposing views. In addition, this book bears the mark of meticulous research assistance provided by graduate students with whom I have enjoyed working: Lucien van der Walt at the Department of Sociology, University of the Witwatersrand; and Aparna Devare, Juliet Litterer, Lauren Mitten, Ashwini Tambe, and Megan Thomas at the School of International Service, American University. Also, at American University, Assistant Dean Joseph Clapper helped immensely with many aspects of this study.

I am indebted to other persons who both facilitated the fieldwork for this book and also made important, substantive suggestions: Glenn Adler, Leonor Magtolis-Briones, Jacklyn Cock, Jorge Emmanuel, Heng Pek Koon, Akihiko Kimijima, Francisco Magno, and Yash Tandon. Apart from those already mentioned, my hosts in the Department of Sociology at the University of the Witwatersrand advanced my thinking about globalization, and I want to acknowledge Belinda Bozzoli, Deborah Posel, and Eddie Webster. In addition, special thanks go to Ishak Shari, director of the Institute of Malaysian and International Studies at Universiti Kebangsaan Malaysia, and my colleagues there, who know the full meaning of offering warm hospitality—particularly Abdul Embong Rahman, Abdul Halim Ali, Clive Kessler, Masrur Karsan, Mohd. Yusof Kassim, Norani Othman, Osman Rani-Hassan, Rajah Rasiah, Sabihah Osman, Sumit Mandel, and Roslina Rosi. At the Institute for Advanced Study, several scholars provided both important suggestions and friendship, and, I owe a debt of gratitude to, inter alia, Kamran Ali, Rainer Bauböck, Steven Caton, Thomas Flynn, Clifford Geertz, Mauro F. Guillén, Evelyne Huber, Nancy Hirschmann, Michael Mosher, Gordon Schochet, John D. Stephens, and Dana Villa.

A number of colleagues commented on preliminary drafts of this book in its entirety or on some chapters, and I acknowledge their key role. Foremost among them is Robert W. Cox, who produced detailed and tough criticism of one of the drafts of the manuscript, corrected numerous errors both of facts and in judgment, and pointed the way forward. For his relentless criticism, understanding, and encouragement, I am especially grateful. James N. Rosenau has been another source of support and advice. Many individuals provided constructive criticism of individual chapters or passages of this book, and I want to recognize, among them, Linda Yarr, Glenn Adler, Björn Hettne, Yoshikazu Sakamoto, Timothy Shaw, Carol Thompson, Paul Wapner, and a superb research team at the National University of Singapore: Kris Olds, Peter Dicken, Philip Kelly, Lily Kong, and Henry Wai-Chung Yeung.

I am indebted to Princeton University Press's anonymous reviewers, who contributed incisive criticism, as well as to Malcolm Litchfield, political science and law editor, and his deputy, Elizabeth P. Swayze, who strengthened my work. I was fortunate to work with Deborah C. K. Wenger, whose careful copyediting added immeasurably to crafting the end result. In addition, over the years, I have benefited from many valuable discussions with my former professor and friend, Kenneth W. Grundy, and two eminent scholars who fell victim to the systemic tragedies of Africa, Aquino de Bragança and Claude Ake.

I dedicate this book to my wife Linda and our three children, Alexandra, Jordan, and Alicia. Without their love, companionship, and unfaltering patience, it would have been difficult, if not impossible, to carry out this work.

None of the people mentioned above are implicated in the final product, for which I alone am responsible.

This book has been several years in the making, and I first presented parts of the arguments elsewhere. Some of the chapters in this book are based on, or select passages are taken from, my previously published essays, but much of the effort here is devoted to bringing the evidence forward, introducing fresh ideas, and deepening the analysis. I have sought to substantially modify, update, and interweave all of the materials into a single fabric. I have added sections to my prior works, rewritten the extant sections, and presented new chapters.

I am grateful to the publishers for permission to draw on my earlier essays, which first appeared in *African Studies Review* in December 1991; *Third World Quarterly* in September 1994, June 1995, and December 1998; *Global Transformation: Challenges to the State System* (edited by Yoshikazu Sakamoto, United Nations University Press, 1994); *The European Journal of Development Research* (coauthored with Mustapha Kamal Pasha; Frank Cass & Co. Ltd.) in December 1995; *Global Governance: A Review of Multilateralism and International Organizations* (Lynne Rienner Publishers) in May–August 1996 and (coauthored with Robert Johnston) January-March 1999; *New Political Economy* (coauthored with Christine B. N. Chin) in March 1997; and my *Globalization, Peace and Conflict* (Penerbit Universiti Kebangsaan Malaysia [National University of Malaysia Press], 1997). In addition, the United Nations University/World Institute for Development Economics

Research commissioned my research on regionalism for a series of books being edited by Björn Hettne, András Inotai, and Osvaldo Sunkel and copublished by Macmillan in London and St. Martin's Press in New York.

Finally, the World Bank and the World Economic Forum have generously given permission to use material from copyrighted works, respectively: "GDP Comparisons for Four Economies: Market Price and Standard International Price Estimates," *Global Economic Prospects and the Developing World* (New York: Oxford University Press, 1993), p. 67; and "Global Competitiveness Index," *Global Competitiveness Report* (Geneva: WEF, 1998), http://www.weforum.org/publications/gcr/98rankings.asp.

*James H. Mittelman*
*Princeton*
*March 1999*

# List of Abbreviations

| | |
|---|---|
| ACP | African, Caribbean, and Pacific (countries) |
| ADB | Asian Development Bank |
| AFTA | ASEAN Free Trade Area |
| ANC | African National Congress |
| ANZUS | Australia-New Zealand-United States (Treaty) |
| APEC | Asia-Pacific Economic Cooperation (forum) |
| ARDL | Asian regional division of labor |
| ASEAN | Association of Southeast Asian Nations |
| CBO | community-based organization |
| CEA | Chinese Economic Area |
| CEC | Commission of the European Communities |
| CENTO | Central Treaty Organization |
| CIDA | Canadian International Development Agency |
| CIS | Commonwealth of Independent States |
| DPRK | Democratic People's Republic of Korea |
| EAEC | East Asian Economic Caucus |
| EAEG | East Asian Economic Group |
| EIU | Economist Intelligence Unit |
| EJNF | Environmental Justice Networking Forum |
| ELMS | Environment and Land Management Systems |
| EPZ | export processing zone |
| EU | European Union |
| FDI | foreign direct investment |
| FRELIMO | Mozambique Liberation Front (*Frente de Libertação de Moçambique)* |
| G-3 | Group of Three |
| G-7 | Group of Seven |
| GDLP | global division of labor and power |
| GDP | gross domestic product |
| GNP | gross national product |
| ICEM | International Committee for European Migration |
| ICP | International Comparison Program |
| IDL | international division of labor |
| ILO | International Labor Organization |
| IMF | International Monetary Fund |
| MAI | Multilateral Agreement on Investment |
| NAFTA | North American Free Trade Agreement |
| NATO | North Atlantic Treaty Organization |

| | |
|---|---|
| NFA | Native Farmers Association |
| NGO | nongovernmental organization |
| NIC | newly industrializing country |
| NIDL | new international division of labor |
| NSS | Nature Society of Singapore |
| OECD | Organization for Economic Cooperation and Development |
| PAGAD | People against Gangsterism and Drugs |
| PO | people's organization |
| PP21 | People's Plan for the Twenty-First Century |
| PRC | People's Republic of China |
| PRE | Economic Rehabilitation Program (*Programa de Reabilitação Económica*) |
| RENAMO | Mozambique National Resistance Movement (*Movimineto Nacional de Resistência de Moçambique*) |
| R&D | research and development |
| SADC (formerly SADCC) | Southern African Development Community (previously known as Southern African Development Coordination Conference) |
| SEATO | Southeast Asia Treaty Organization |
| SEZ | special economic zone |
| SIJORI | Singapore-Johor-Riau (Growth Triangle) |
| SREZ | subregional economic zone |
| TNC | transnational corporation |
| UN | United Nations |
| UNCTAD | United Nations Conference on Trade and Development |
| UNDP | United Nations Development Program |
| UNHCR | United Nations High Commissioner for Refugees |
| WEF | World Economic Forum |
| WTO | World Trade Organization |

# THE GLOBALIZATION SYNDROME

# Introduction

THE MAIN CONCERN of this book is the interplay between the powerful thrust of globalizing market forces, sometimes propelled by the state, and a counterthrust fueled by the needs of society. Above all, the challenge here is to discern globalization's contents—i.e., historical transformations in world order—and the resultant discontents. Then there are specific questions within these basic issues, posed in individual chapters.

In contrast to many of the previous interpretations of globalization, this book is an attempt to present a holistic and multilevel analysis, connecting the economic to the political and cultural, joining agents and multiple structures, and interrelating different local, regional, and global arenas. Given the broad scope of the topic, of course, no single study by itself could be fully integrative, but this volume is one step in that direction. Heretofore, globalization studies have come in different genres. As we shall see, there is a tendency toward economism (a one-sided emphasis on material factors to the extent of indifference to politics and culture, although political commitments and cultural values may be implicit in the analysis). Another is state-centric approaches, also evident in a good deal of cross-national research, which posit that public policies are driving the globalization dynamic. And some persevering forms of area studies insist on particularities and detailed descriptions about the transformations in a given locale without also grasping the linkages to evolving global structures. These three genres do not cover the entire gamut of globalization discourse, but they certainly dominate much of it.

Whereas most of the globalization literature is based on the experiences of the West, my findings are, in the main, drawn from the non-Western worlds. As distinct from other books on globalization, this volume considers, but in no way romanticizes, the voices of the subjects of globalization, including those who resist this trend. Without presuming to speak on their behalf, which would be a pretense of arrogance without license, I explore globalizing processes from the standpoint of those who are hurt by them: trade union movements, people on the fringes of society (in some cases, a bedrock for populist politicians), the unemployed and underemployed in various parts of the world, and the marginalized, especially women and children, in developing countries. Directly, or more often indirectly, they encounter the globalizers: internationally mobile capital and its allies in the state, exporters who balk at restrictive trade practices, local industrialists (to the extent that they are competitive with overseas enterprises), and domestic finance positioned to gain from liberalization and increased access to foreign markets. These groups, in turn, vie with nationalist politicians, inward-oriented bureaucrats, and other prominent protectionists, some of whom are advocates for domestic business adversely affected by transnational flows. In this contest, there are no villains or heroes, but constellations of actors with concrete and conflicting interests in the intrusive transformation under way at a global level, in some cases provoking resistance to it, albeit in very different forms.

The core argument of this book is that globalization is not a single, unified phenomenon, but a *syndrome* of processes and activities. As used here, the term "syndrome" designates a pattern of related characteristics of the human condition, or, more specifically, within the global political economy. Although some critics, on both the left and right, do indeed regard globalization as a pathology, in our context "syndrome" is not meant to convey the medical sense of symptoms of a disease, because globalization is by no means an abnormality. Rather, globalization has become normalized as a dominant set of ideas and a policy framework, while, as I will show, also being contested as a false universalism. Integral to the globalization syndrome are the interactions among the global division of labor and power (GDLP), the new regionalism, and resistance politics. Although these are not the only factors, of course, they stand out as central to the transformations in world order.

The GDLP is the anatomy of the global political economy. Its parts are a spatial reorganization of production among world regions, large-scale flows of migration among and within them, complex webs of networks that connect production processes and buyers and sellers, and the emergence of transnational cultural structures that mediate among these processes. Moreover, globalization proceeds through macroregionalism sponsored by states and economic forces seeking to open larger markets as a means toward greater competitiveness, subregional transborder arrangements, including Asia's "growth triangles" (a term coined by Singapore's Prime Minister Goh Chok Tong in 1989) and "growth polygons," and microregional projects such as export processing zones (EPZs). The power component of the GDLP and in the new regionalism has a counterpoint, for it provokes resistance politics. More specifically, a specific configuration of power, which will be delimited, begets resistance movements as a response to globalization, albeit in nascent form. This configuration also precipitates a search for alternatives that could make the productive potential of globalization serve the goal of equity rather than subject society to the exigencies of hypercompetition with the widening gap between rich and poor and the deterioration of public social policy that neoliberalism (heightened integration in the global political economy) has brought about.

Hence the contradictory nature of globalization: It offers major benefits, including gains in productivity, technological advances, higher standards of living, more jobs, broader access to consumer products at lower cost, widespread dissemination of information and knowledge, reductions in poverty in some parts of the world, and a release from long-standing social hierarchies in many countries. Yet there is a price for integrating in this global framework and adopting its practices. Expressed or tacit acceptance of being encompassed in globalization entails a lessening, or in some cases a negating, of the quantum of political control exercised by the encompassed, especially in the least powerful and poorest zones of the global political economy. In addition, the penetration of world markets and increased polarization on a world level erode cultural traditions, giving rise to new hybrid forms.

## THE CONCEPT OF GLOBALIZATION

Having foreshadowed the theme of this book, let me offer a concept of globalization, at least in a preliminary manner so that it can be built up in the chapters that follow. Although the literature provides many definitions of globalization, there are two main categories.[1] The first of these is to point to an increase in interconnections, or interdependence, a rise in transnational flows, and an intensification of processes such that the world is, in some respects, becoming a single place. Typical of this genre is the following: "Globalization refers to the process of reducing barriers between countries and encouraging closer economic, political, and social interaction" (Tabb 1999, 1). A more expansive, but basically similar, formulation is put forward by the president of the Ford Foundation:

> The term [globalization] reflects a more comprehensive level of interaction than has occurred in the past, suggesting something different from the word 'international.' It implies a diminishing importance of national borders and the strengthening of identities that stretch beyond those rooted in a particular region or country. (Berresford 1997, 1)

This definition is especially useful inasmuch as it captures key features of globalization—cross-border flows, identities, and social relations—but ambiguous about the nature of social relations and silent about hierarchies of power.

A second cut is more theoretical and emphasizes the compression of time and space. Three authors, in particular, have contributed impor-

---

[1] For a list of definitions, see Scholte (1997, 15). Other useful sources are Albrow (1996); Guillén (forthcoming); Held (1995); Held, McGrew, Goldblatt, and Perraton (1999); Kofman and Youngs (1996); McGrew (1992); McMichael (1996b); Rosenau (1997, 78–98); and Waters (1995).

tantly to this conceptualization, although others could be named as well. Distinguishing between place and space, Anthony Giddens holds that the former is the idea of locale, or a geographical (understood in the sense of physical) setting of social activity, whereas with globalization, the latter is structured by social influences absent from the scene. Space is increasingly dislocated from place, and networked to other social contexts across the globe. And the old modes of time (say, seasons or sunup and sundown in agrarian societies) also become separated from space, opening to various possibilities of recombination (Giddens 1990, 18–19). "Globalisation can thus be defined as the intensification of worldwide social relations which link distant localities in such a way that local happenings are shaped by events occurring many miles away and vice versa" (Giddens 1990, 64).

Along similar lines and noting that time horizons are shortened and that it is difficult to tell what space one occupies when it comes to determining causes and effects, David Harvey posits the "annihilation of space through time" (Harvey 1990, 299). Spaces from hitherto remote worlds form a collage, changing not only cultural representations, as in art exhibitions, but also the commodity mix in our daily lives. The marketplace for food, for instance, is very different from what it was decades ago, with local products being supplanted by national and then global goods, transforming consumption patterns and price structures, which are integrated into international trade. Proceeding along this same broad avenue of inquiry, Roland Robertson emphasizes cultural practices and, in matters linked to globalization, a high level of variation. For him, globalizing cultural processes are propelled by global consciousness, but less emphasis is accorded to technology than it is in Giddens's scheme (Robertson 1992, 142–45, 183; Albrow 1996, 98). All three accounts pivot on the notion of time-space relations, and relate globalization to modernity—for Giddens, it is a consequence of modernity—and postmodernity. Giddens's analysis of time-space compression is fundamentally tied to social technology; Harvey's, to shifts in capital accumulation; and Robertson's, to the cultural sphere.

While not rejecting this course altogether, but attempting to go further, I propose a somewhat different concept. *As experienced from below, the dominant form of globalization means a historical transformation: in the economy, of livelihoods and modes of existence; in politics, a loss in the degree of control exercised locally—for some, however little to begin with—such that the locus of power gradually shifts in varying proportions above and below the territorial state; and in culture, a devaluation of a collectivity's achievements or perceptions of them. This structure, in turn, may engender either accommodation or resistance.* Most agents acquiesce, but others attempt to write a script that embraces macroeconomic growth processes and new technologies while linking them to social equity and reform programs. In this scenario, the transformation commenced with market forces, yet political responses to it are of paramount importance. Whereas the market clearly continues to be a motor of globalization, there is an enormous difference between the interplay in initiating and maintaining or undermining this trend. Although politics and market relations have always been intimately related, globalization is emerging as *a political response to the expansion of market power*, both as a form of domination and an emancipatory possibility.

Furthermore, globalization is *a domain of knowledge*, not a fully fledged paradigm but a critical approach that helps to explain the intricacy and variability of the ways the world is structured and, by extension, to assess reflexively the categories used by social scientists to study this distinctive correlation of both integrating and disintegrating processes. A rubric for myriad phenomena, a globalization framework *interrelates multiple levels of analysis*—economics, politics, society, and culture. This frame thus elucidates *a coalescence of diverse transnational and domestic structures*, allowing the economy, polity, society, and culture of one locale to penetrate another.

In this connection, it is worth emphasizing that some champions of globalization and some of its detractors alike engage in economism. Ironically, the base-superstructure construct has resurfaced, this time by purveyors of globalization who bestow uncritical acclaim on neoliberal restructuring. Popularizers of the notion of global trends (e.g., Ohmae 1990; Naisbitt 1996) tend to posit one-way causality and believe that aided by technological advances, marketization itself is transforming the world around us. Rather than overwork the concept of globalization by engaging in an economistic analysis—or for that matter, political determinism, as do realists and neorealists who argue that states, not markets, are driving globalization—and obfuscate the linkages, one must identify specific interactions among its economic, political, and cultural dimensions. Indeed, globalization is a multilevel set of processes with built-in strictures on its power and potential, for it produces resistance against itself. In other words, globalization creates discontents not merely as latent and undeclared resistance, but sometimes crystallized as open countermovements.[2]

## APPROACH

Theoretically, a useful point of entry for exploring the underpinnings of globalization, and for holding together empirical data so that a complex

---

[2] While I was lecturing and writing on globalization's "discontents," unbeknownst to me at the time, two books also picked up on this theme, though quite differently from what is attempted here. See Burbach, Nunez, and Kagarlitsky (1997) and Sassen (1998).

set of materials does not spin out of control, is Karl Polanyi's seminal work. One need not engage in a celebratory reading of his writings to note that they are suggestive of not only a holistic approach to global restructuring, but also the basis of a conceptual reformulation. Although I turn to other master writers, such as Fernand Braudel and Antonio Gramsci, and do not draw exclusively or even primarily on a Polanyian framework, it is pivotal for my probings—a touchstone for ordering concepts that I revisit, criticize, and attempt to extend at several junctures.

In *The Great Transformation* (1957, originally published in 1944), Polanyi explored the socially disruptive and polarizing tendencies in the world economy driven by what he called the self-regulating market, not a spontaneous occurrence but the result of coercive power in the service of a utopian idea. He traced the tendencies in the global political economy that generated the conjuncture of the 1930s and produced—out of a breakdown in liberal-economic structures—the phenomena of depression, fascism, unemployment, and resurgent nationalism, collectively a negation of economic globalization, leading to world war. His notion of "double movement" encapsulated unprecedented market expansion entailing massive social dislocation and a sharp political reaction in the form of society's demands on the state to counteract the deleterious effects of the market. Perhaps similar to the global economy of the 1930s, contemporary globalization appears to be approaching a conjuncture in which renewed liberal-economic structures will generate large-scale political, social, and economic disruptions, as well as sustained pressure for self-protection. The concrete processes analyzed in each of the chapters that follow are an integral part of this contradiction. To examine these processes, it is useful to reach beyond Polanyi's renowned 1944 book, cull his writings that are not as well known, and tease out the implications for the conjunction between the expansion of the market and specific issues centrally related to the GDLP, the new regionalism, and resistance politics.

To focus the analysis, there are compelling reasons why one must delimit the *ontology of globalization*. One can hardly proceed without first indicating the basic units that comprise an existing order. The balance of social forces on the ground is rapidly changing, and thus it becomes important to bring to light potential agents of transformation in diverse contexts. Although the term "ontology" is derived from philosophy and refers to the branch of metaphysics that studies the nature of existence or being, it has come to mean the specific objects of inquiry. These are the parts of world order that interact with one another, and the interactions will be discussed more fully under the rubric of evolving global structures in chapter 1. As the word "evolving" denotes, ontologies are not once and forever, but they are in historical motion. In this connection, it is worth recalling that the French economic historian Braudel suggested that a number of "observation points" be identified for viewing history. Specifically, he posited that axes be established corresponding to "social orders," hierarchy, time, and space. Along these axes, he proposed imagining divergent positions, such as those pertaining to different regions and spatial hierarchies (Braudel 1980, 55; Helleiner 1990, 74). Following Braudel, one may attempt to capture the advent of the ontology of globalization, without in any way fixing it as a static framework:

(1) The *global political economy* may be conceived in a Braudelian manner as a system of interactions on a world scale. Braudel did not make the world economy the exclusive dominant factor in his analysis, but emphasized the entities that interact with it and thus establish global structures. Although several political and economic entities spur globalization, it is especially the rise of the transnational corporation (TNC) that shapes globalizing processes, for the TNC coordinates production and controls operations in several countries, even if it is not the owner (Dicken 1998, 8). However, the large corporation is by no means the only force driving globalization. Notwithstanding their very different positions in the global political economy, states, too, have become agents of globalization, particularly through the neoliberal framework of deregulation, liberalization, and privatization.

(2) In Braudel's sense, *states* are mapped with dotted-line borders, partly permeable, able to regulate transborder flows—a template superimposed on the global economy. In an era of globalization, states—and more properly, the interstate system—are by no means epiphenomena, as sometimes argued, for policies—e.g., those on migration—do set conditions for exit and entry, however imperfectly enforced. Production is organized partly within borders and partly crossing borders in transnational flows. Similarly, migratory movements are partly within borders and partly across national frontiers.

(3) *Macroregions*—the European Union (EU), the North American Free Trade Agreement (NAFTA), and the Asia-Pacific Economic Cooperation (APEC) forum—coordinate capital flows within a spatial unit but also provide access to the globalization process. The formation of macroregions involves a vast enlargement in the size of the market, a restructuring of extant political units, and a reorientation of the full meaning of citizenship. Embedded in the state, national citizenship is less meaningful because of the separation of citizenship and work. Laborers who live in their home country and work in another include border crossers (e.g., residents of France with jobs in Switzerland) and computer-based home workers linked to transnational production processes through electronic means. Macroregions may thus be regarded as loose geographical units larger than a state with some political and cultural bonds, however varied, tenuous, and sometimes contentious. Although globalization of production is a homogenizing force, local cultures

still provide focal points for identity, as well as inspiration and sources of creativity (e.g., in clothing styles, food, and toys) for the assembly line. Cultural boundaries also reinforce the distinctiveness of political and economic groupings.

(4) *Subregional patterns* pull together nodes, intersect states, and enlarge the concept of proximity to encompass factors other than geographical distance. Indeed, historical legacies and economic forces can provide the propellants for the migration of industries, employment creation, and spillovers to other areas as well as demonstration effects. An example of ways to pull subregional entities into a tighter web of globalization is the synergy being established in a transnational triangle known as the Alpine Diamond, which links Lyons's textile and chemical industries, Geneva's financial services, and Turin's automotive base. Having established computer links and business partnerships, these cities are planning high-speed rail connections to reduce travel time between them to less than seventy minutes. Along with Stuttgart, Barcelona, and Milan, Lyons is also part of a prosperous subregion, called the "Four Motors" because they fuel much of Europe's economic growth (Drozdiak 1995).

(5) *Microregions* are evident within the boundedness of sovereign states. For example, Catalonia, Lombardy, and Quebec are relatively autonomous entities relative to the political jurisdiction of states. In addition, industrial districts form a mosaic of highly interdependent economic and technological forces, themselves embedded in a more encompassing network of transactions. The State Council of China, for example, decided that microregions (i.e., EPZs) would be national pace-setters for reform and thus serve as locomotives to power economic growth. It was deemed necessary to make microregional advances so that economic structures will form a "staircase pattern." In Guangdong Province, Shenzen is reputedly China's fastest-growing city and the largest of China's four special economic zones, designated environments driven by overseas capital and participation in the GDLP. Cheap labor—and hence large-scale internal migration—is a crucial factor of production in Shenzen's expanding import and export trade (Mittelman 1990, 66).

(6) With the increase in demand for service sector employment, leading global cities offer new opportunities, especially in "information occupations" and in low-wage jobs. The demand in strategic *global cities* for service employment attracts large concentrations of indigenous ethnic minorities, as well as workers from other regions. Global cities become major actors in their own right, negotiating directly with other players in the global economy, often engaged in transactions without regard to national authorities.

(7) *Civil societies* are also emerging as key actors in the GDLP. Sometimes their activities are embodied in social movements or institutionalized in non-

governmental organizations (NGOs),[3] and in other cases their expressions are latent and not formally organized. The response of civil societies to globalizing structures may emanate from the local or national level, or it may also be a transnational initiative. Under differing conditions, civil societies react singly or collectively to globalizing forces. An important trend is the growth of networks across borders. Whereas some analysts portray networks as voluntary organizations linked in a reciprocal and horizontal manner (Keck and Sikkink 1998, 8), they are understood here as not necessarily taking an organizational form but, more fundamentally, as relational groupings whose members or component parts are interconnected, however tightly or loosely, and which are realized materially at specific junctures in time and space. However constituted, civil-society responses to globalization may be either elitist or populist, atavistic and divisive or constructive and cohesive, elements projecting a vision of an alternative order. The questions of the appropriate form and scale for adjusting to or countering globalization and the relationship between open and latent resistance are issues to which we will return.

Proceeding from Braudel's notion of looking simultaneously from a number of "observation points," each of which provides diverse shadings of the total picture, one may break down the multilevel process of globalization—or, rather, set of structural changes—into discrete linkages. A refrain in this book is "globalization and. . . ." Without neglecting traditional concerns in the social sciences such as "society" (the centerpiece in sociology) and the "state" (pivotal in political science and international relations), attention turns to what might be called people-level globalization: flows partly eluding the realm of state regulation and rooted in economy and culture, including certain shared beliefs and practices, migration, remittances, diasporas, and the parallel economy.

Empirically, it is important to ground a study of changing global structures, for they have not been experienced uniformly across regions, and the reactions vary widely. There is no substitute for understanding the many layers that form a particular sense of time and place. Theory provides an indispensable route to this understanding, but structural explanations also have their contextual limits.

In terms of method, this book attempts to highlight the variation that occurs when globalizing structures meet local conditions. Surely,

---

[3] In keeping with conventional practice, I use the term "NGO," but with reservations. NGO is an unfortunate construct since, by definition, it is a negation, and the frame of reference is solely the state. In fact, with globalization and neoliberal pressures to reduce the scope of the state, the work of many NGOs now substitutes for activities previously performed by the state. Additionally, some NGOs are financially supported by the state and interstate organizations (or corporations). In short, globalization blurs the lines between government and "nongovernmental organizations."

globalization does not pound everything into the same mold. My research strategy is to primarily locate globalizing tendencies in two dissimilar subregions: Eastern (i.e., East and Southeast) Asia is an epicenter of globalization, and Southern Africa constitutes a key node in the most marginalized continent. Encompassing diverse fast-track countries that registered economic growth rates of more than 8 percent per year for a decade (until the onset of the economic crisis in 1997), Eastern Asia has experienced remarkable dynamism. This subregion includes Japan and China, the world's second and third largest economies; the latter is projected by the World Bank to become the world's largest economy, ahead of the United States, early in the twenty-first century. In contrast, the twelve countries of Southern Africa have a combined gross domestic product (GDP) of a little more than one-half of 1 percent of world GDP—about the same as that of Finland—and efforts to extricate themselves from this condition bump up against the structured disadvantages of a globalizing world economy (Davies 1996, 26).

Although it was, of course, impossible to carry out research in all of the countries in the two subregions, this book is built around empirical explorations of varied duration and intensity in Japan, Malaysia, the Philippines, Singapore, and Vietnam, as well as Botswana, Mozambique, South Africa, and Zimbabwe in 1991, 1993, 1996, 1997, and 1998. I selected Japan and South Africa because they are the subregional hegemons; the other countries represent a broad range in terms of inclusion in, or exclusion from, the growth processes and power mechanisms of globalization, and in the robustness of their civil societies. The fieldwork in each country involved multiple visits lasting from two weeks to one year. Following closely related research that took me to the People's Republic of China on two occasions in the late 1980s, I collected documentary materials and engaged in on-site research in the 1990s. I attended meetings of various resistance groups, accompanied them on campaigns, including to a toxic waste dump (Holfontein, South Africa, 20 July 1996), visited lands contested as "ancestral domain" (a term used to underline the relationship between the issues of land rights and social justice), and queried members of civic associations, bankers, lawyers, business people, bureaucrats, ministers, members of parliament, a high court judge, journalists, local scholars, and students.

I conducted more than 100 separate interviews in the above-mentioned Asian and African countries. I say "separate" because in some cases, and to my pleasant surprise, more than one member of an organization unexpectedly turned up for an appointment with a single interviewee and participated in what became a group interview. Structured at the outset and then opening into freewheeling discussion, the interviews typically lasted from two to three hours. With most of the interviewees, it immediately became apparent that the architecture of globalization is too huge to perceive as a whole, but if one moves to a finer scale—more discrete issues—the structures become discernible. Interviewees kindly shared their experiences and observations with me, in some cases for attribution and, in other instances, on condition of anonymity. These individuals were selected with reference to the categories deemed theoretically central to this book, as set forth in chapter 1 (and then extended in chapter 9 on reconceptualizing resistance politics). I sought out, among others, activists directly or indirectly challenging global structures, especially, but not only, those who are pursuing environmental objectives (for reasons best elaborated in the analysis that follows), although they also mobilize around other causes pertaining to social justice. Of course, the proximate issues varied from one case to another, but in all instances involved transboundary problems. The names of the interviewees whose remarks could be attributed, their positions, and the places and dates of our meetings are noted in the list of references at the end of this book; the questionnaire may be found in the appendix.

In addition to the formal interviews, there was ample opportunity to talk informally with many people in international and indigenous NGOs, including what are known as people's organizations (POs) in the Philippines and community-based organizations (CBOs) in South Africa, businesses, government, international organizations, the media, and universities. Stationed in New York City and Washington, D.C., for most of my career, I also sought to take advantage of the opportunity for extensive, on-site inquiry into the central growth mechanisms of globalization, key international institutions, and U.S. foreign policy.

The method adopted here does not entail a systematic subregional comparison or a particularistic account—dense description—of many different national experiences. These are not the aims of this book. Rather, the purpose of visiting the cases is not only to provide evidence to sustain or modify my arguments, but also to raise basic questions about the propellants of globalization and what the consequences might be. Finally, some chapters are of course more theoretical than others, and some are mainly meant to offer illustrative material for examining analytical propositions. Where data are not accessible, or when it was not possible to obtain systematic or comparable evidence, I try to avoid forcing the cross-regional analysis. If there is a compelling illustration or a deviant example from a region outside Eastern Asia and Southern Africa, I forego a measure of symmetry and do not hesitate to invoke it.

Placed within bookends, an introductory chapter on "The Dynamics of Globalization" and a conclusion that extends major points and considers alternatives, the issues fall into three broad categories that correspond to the dimensions noted above. The four chapters in Part I examine the changing division of labor and power: theories of division of labor, followed by discussion of key facets of the GDLP, namely, migration, poverty and gender, and marginalization with a case study of Mozambique—a country at the low end of the GDLP, one that, at this writing, has, by following a neoliberal globalizing strategy, attained the highest economic growth rate in Africa over the past five years, a performance that warrants close scrutiny in terms of the lessons to be derived. Part II, on the new regionalism, consists of chapters on rethinking the concept of regionalism, hegemony and regionalism (an inquiry meant to complement the geoeconomics in globalization studies by also focusing on the geopolitics), and subregional responses to globalization. Part III probes resistance to globalization, and is divided into chapters on the meaning of resistance, environmental countermovements, and organized crime groups (which not only impair globalization's licit channels, but also are playing a key role in setting new rules).

With a topic as broad as the globalization scenario, there are, of course, many other vital issues that could be studied. I have examined some of them more fully in other venues—e.g., finance (Mittelman 1996; Mittelman and Pasha 1997, especially chapter 3) and the military-strategic aspects of security (Mittelman 1994, 1997a)—but additional themes are worthy of consideration. Well aware of my own limitations, however, I find that those that come to mind are either outside my expertise or beyond the scope of what could be undertaken in this project.

To sum up as concisely as possible, what follows is an attempt to explain how globalization bears on major problems of our times. This book emphasizes the interactions between globalizing structures that intersect different levels of analysis in highly, if not the most, dissimilar parts of the world, gauged on a continuum of economic dynamism and marginalization. Integral to the scale of upward and downward mobility in the global political economy are zigzags (as in the Asian economic crisis of the late 1990s) and reversibility. The objective is to explain the systemic dynamics of globalization, myriad consequences, and varied responses.

# CHAPTER 1

# The Dynamics of Globalization

THE MANIFESTATIONS of globalization include the spatial reorganization of production, the interpenetration of industries across borders, the spread of financial markets, the diffusion of identical consumer goods to distant countries, massive transfers of population—mainly within the South[1] as well as from the South and the East to the West—resultant conflicts between immigrant and established communities in formerly tight-knit neighborhoods, and an emerging worldwide (though not universal) preference for democracy. But what explains globalization? What are its causes, when did it originate, and what are its mechanisms? Moreover, where should an analysis be focused, and what conceptual building blocks are required? These questions guide the following discussion, foreshadowing key concepts that will be used in this book.

## WHAT IS THE MAINSPRING?

To examine the pattern of globalization, the choice of an avenue of inquiry is crucial because it sets one's sights on research questions and provides a perspective on data. An appropriate starting point, I believe, is the nature of the labor process and its products on a global level, for conflicts between capital and labor, commerce, and consumer tastes all reflect what is produced and how it is produced. Hence, attention must center on how whole societies and their constituent groups try to influence and adjust to changes in the organization of production.

[1] "South" is a broad term denoting the developing countries, most (but not all) of which are located in the Southern Hemisphere. In conventional usage, the South, then, serves as a descriptive expression and a rough marker, not an analytical category. More than a geographical construct, however, this shorthand is often employed metaphorically to identify the parts of the world, themselves stratified, where, despite exceptions, poverty and powerlessness are most acute. The problems of the South have also become internalized in the "developed" North, which, to be sure, has its own pockets of poverty and marginalized groups: a pattern accentuated by increasing global flows, such as some streams of migration (chapter 3). To emphasize that the South has become a social relationship with worldwide implications—both a cause and an effect of spatial reordering—some authors prefer the term "Global South." Mindful of these considerations, but for the sake of brevity, I will herein simply refer to the South; or for variation in style, use, interchangeably, developing countries or developing world (terms with their own ambiguities).

First, the question of the chain of causality requires careful attention. On the one hand, it may be argued that there is equivalence among the dimensions of globalization. This approach would, however, duck the difficult matter of causality and merely be a form of circular logic: Everything influences everything else. Alternatively, one could diplomatically argue for multiple causality. If so, this tack would also dodge the problem. Not to engage in reductionism, I believe that if one is to delve beneath appearances, it is imperative to draw some arrows between cause and effect.

The acceleration of structural change in world affairs means that competition has been fundamentally transformed from the time when it was delimited more restrictively by transport and communications systems. Competition in the economic sphere—the condition of "the warre of all against all" that Thomas Hobbes attributed to the political realm—brings capital into closer confrontation with other units of capital. There is a new intensity in global competition, evident in corporations' responses to the changing equation of opportunity and loss. Competitive structures are global insofar as decisions taken in one part of the world bear directly on decisions made elsewhere. Seeking market growth and cost savings, firms have pursued technological innovation. It is competition that drives technological change, and not the other way around, a point forcefully argued by John Stopford and Susan Strange (1991, 65, 71), who invoke ample evidence. Indeed, to modify an old aphorism in light of contemporary globalizing tendencies, one might say that competition has become the mother of inventions. Today, competitiveness, or free-market competition, has been elevated to an ideology, and this icon represents an important element in the globalization matrix.

Central to the structural changes in competition is the management of time. A key aspect of the shift from the old Fordist model of mass production, mass consumption toward post-Fordism is the introduction of a much faster system. This "just-in-time" method caters to niche marketing and provides greater flexibility for management, and insecurity for workers. So too the spatial scale of competition is transformed, bound up as it is with the transmission of information through cable, fiber, and satellite links. To be sure, worldwide competition has quickened the rate of technological innovation, altering the configuration of winners and losers.

Social research has helped to flesh out different aspects of the changing dynamics of competition. With capitalists coming into more direct confrontation with other capitalists, the psychology of market participants and business strategies has necessarily shifted. Richard D'Aveni (1994) calls this condition "hypercompetition"—a concerted effort to increase market instability and to establish the uncertainty of operations—or what appears to me to be a type of social Darwinism. Politically, this climate is maintained by the "competition state," whose chief functions are to play an enabling role and prevent market failure (Cerny 1990). At the same time, the autonomy of the state is reduced, constrained, and disciplined by capital. The capacity to provide social protection against market shocks is also lessened, evidenced by the diminution of the welfare state in diverse contexts. In fact, the state itself adopts corporate logic, embracing variants of neoliberal ideology to justify the socially disruptive and polarizing consequences of its policies and subjecting its own agencies to cost-cutting measures.

According to economists Robert Frank and Philip Cook (1995), the Darwinian struggles among firms have given rise to a winner-take-all psychology in which minuscule gradations in talent generate enormous differences in income. Rewards are concentrated in a few hands, such as those of the captains of the software industry. With its interlocking products and popular applications, Microsoft Corporation controls 85 percent of the world's personal computer market, notwithstanding reviews in computer magazines that often assign higher ratings to other products. In the United States, although a star surgeon, a star athlete, or a star CEO is only a tad better than his or her near rivals, the superstars are now receiving a vast multiple of other performers' earnings. The entire national economy can be likened to the National Basketball Association, an American corporate culture that not only embellishes the values of materialism and self-aggrandizement, but also broadcasts them to most parts of the world. From entertainers, models, and designers to other professionals, the top performers in their trade draw far more compensation than do those who are second-best, for small differences in ability are magnified in the wealth generated by profits. Winner-take-all markets have grown because aggressive deregulation lowers barriers, information technology augments the volume of transactions, and markets are more specialized. In this hypercompetitive environment, the new rich are enjoying runaway incomes, the middle class is increasingly stretched to the limit, and large numbers of people are mired even deeper in poverty. The expansion of winner-take-all markets has become inefficient insofar as the addition of more contestants to a market no longer heightens the level of competition or improves the product. Additional players do not draw proportionate rewards, and society loses what they could have earned in other employment. One might investigate whether this structure of inequality is becoming universalized. It would seem to feed the potential for conflict, and does not bode well for future world order.

In terms of a hierarchy of causal factors accounting for globalization, then, the changing conditions of capitalism, especially hypercompetition as a driving force, have created a changed environment. Hypercompetition is accompanied by a restructuring of production, including its spatial reorganization, which, is, in turn, facilitated both by technological advances and state policies. Global flows—labor, finance, trade, information and knowledge, and consumer goods and other cultural products—are thereby accelerated.

Are these cultural products American? Does globalization mean Americanization? Not entirely. True, as the long reach of CNN, McDonald's, and Coca-Cola suggests, globalization is heavily American, but it also comes in other forms, such as the croissant and reggae music. Moreover, like other countries, the United States itself has experienced the disruptions caused by evolving global structures. Although in a different structural position than are other parts of the world, mid-America, too, is shocked by the pressures of hypercompetition, new technologies, and a shifting labor market. As a result, the character and complexion of U.S. cities have changed perceptibly, as have their ways of life.

## THE ORIGINS OF GLOBALIZATION

When did this pattern of globalization emerge? There are three possibilities. It may be argued that globalization dates to the origins of civilization itself and is thus at least five thousand years old. When groups of people first came into contact with one another through conquest, trade, and migration, the globe began to shrink. Urbanization may be regarded as an integral part of this process of intensifying communication and economic intercourse. Religion is another important aspect of this scenario. For example, it is said that Islamic globalization began many centuries before the current idiom of globalization was constructed (Habibul 1997, 111).

Growing out of world-systems theory, a different perspective is that globalization originated with the development of capitalism in Western Europe in the sixteenth century. According to this view, decisive shifts in the relationship between capital and labor accompanied by major technological innovations enabled capitalism to encompass the entire globe. A new type of economy and social relations thus swept the world, deranging precapitalist formations and incorporating the remnants in a very different system whose main feature is the combination of competitive markets oriented to profit maximization, wage labor, and the private ownership of the major means of production.

A third interpretation is that capitalism itself has changed in fundamental ways since its inception. The 1970s marked an important turning point, beginning with deep recession in the Western countries. This downturn had wide ramifications, certainly in many developing countries. By the late 1970s, the hopes of a new international economic order, a reform package proposed by leaders from the developing world, were dashed, and the socialist countries experienced economic shortfalls. The Bretton Woods system of fixed exchange rates collapsed. Many developing countries abandoned import substitution in favor of export promotion in an attempt to secure foreign exchange. Debt structures mounted appreciably, and several countries felt the sting of financial and other forms of market discipline. The new strategies speeded a restructuring of production away from the old Fordist industries and toward more flexible, capital- and technology-intensive operations. With technological advances, the intensification of this trend resulted in the weakening of trade union power, reductions in social expenditure, deregulation, privatization, and an emphasis on enhancing competitiveness: in short, a distinctive balance of forces (Cox 1996c, 21–23).

Which interpretation is correct? Is globalization five thousand years, four centuries, or a few decades old? Does the debate over this historical trajectory come down to the long run versus a medium span versus a more recent constellation of structures? I think not. Viewed historically, globalization may be best understood in terms of its continuities and discontinuities with the past. Of cardinal importance, the temporal and spatial reorganization of production has indeed intensified competition—a hallmark of capitalism, itself born out of anterior social systems—to a new level known as hypercompetition. If so, neoliberal globalization may be regarded as the contemporary phase of capitalism. That is, the period before the sixteenth century may be construed as a time of *incipient globalization*. A second period, from the inception of capitalism in the West until the early 1970s, was an era of *bridging globalization*. Third, the period since the early 1970s comprises *accelerated globalization*, a series of linkages to be examined below.

## THE "MYTH OF GLOBALIZATION" THESIS

Implicit in this discussion is the argument that globalization constitutes an historical turn—indeed, an epochal transformation in world affairs. By no means is this claim generally endorsed, for some observers deny the very existence of globalization. If their contention is valid, this book would not be worth undertaking; it is therefore necessary to respond to those who regard globalization as a myth, and then delimit a series of evolving global structures.[2]

If realism—the dominant approach in international relations—is right that states are the decisive actors on the world stage, there is no need to

[2] Elsewhere (1997a), I have evaluated other critiques of the globalization framework, namely, deconstructive social theory and various right-wing perspectives. The recent upsurge of right-wing populist movements offers interpretations that should not be ignored. They raise pertinent questions about alternative politics in light of the impact of globalization on societies today.

look beyond their own actions and interactions with one another. Implicit in the state-centric perspective is that the ontology is unchanging. If the objects of study are fixed and immutable, there would be no reason to consider globalizing tendencies, especially in the realm of nonstate politics. For others who work in the mainstream, globalization is accommodated to a state-centered approach by transposing this set of processes into a policy question, How do states adjust? They thereby set aside the possibility and implications of structural transformation. This denial is joined by more historically minded scholars, such as Paul Hirst and Grahame Thompson (1996), who claim that the world economy is not truly global, but centered in the triad of Europe, Japan, and North America, also known as the Group of Three (G-3). Taking to task those who advance a strong version of the globalization thesis, Hirst and Thompson present data on trade, foreign direct investment (FDI), and financial flows to show that globalizing activities are concentrated in the developed countries. They also argue that the current level of internationalized activities is not unprecedented; the world economy is not as open and integrated as it was in the period from 1870 to 1914; and today, the major economic powers continue to harmonize policy, as they did before, or at least still shape the flow of finance and economic governance in general.

Their data are useful, if interpreted to show that the optimism about globalization may be unfounded for the underprivileged segments of the global political economy. Additionally, this line of attack on the concept of globalization does rightly warn that it would be an error to exaggerate globalizing tendencies. Empirically, however, the analysis is weakened by the authors' failure to note the strong upward trend in FDI in developing countries in the mid-1990s. Following unfavorable economic conditions in the early 1990s, which produced an FDI recession that ended in 1993, there was a surge of flows into developing countries as well as an increase in outward FDI from developing countries, including interdeveloping country FDI, though mitigated by the Asian economic crisis of the late 1990s.

The United Nations Conference on Trade and Development (UNCTAD) reports that flows into developing countries reached a record level, 39 percent, of total inflows in 1993. Eighty percent of the inflows were directed to ten developing countries, especially to China, followed in rank order by Singapore, Argentina, Mexico, and Malaysia (UNCTAD 1995, 7, 9). Of course, there is considerable unevenness among developing countries, and FDI flows into Africa remained flat in 1993, causing Africa's share of all inflows to developing countries to decline by 5 percent in 1993. Its share plummeted to 3.8 percent in 1996, the lowest since the early 1980s and down from the 1986–90 period (UNCTAD 1997, 56). Moreover, Africa's oil-producing countries accounted for more than

70 percent of total FDI inflows to the continent. But the global trend, at least until the late 1990s, has been for the FDI boom to developing countries to accelerate. It reached $100 billion in 1995 (UNCTAD 1996, xvii). FDI flows to developing countries expanded in 1996, increasing some 34 percent over 1995, to $129 billion; the bulk of overall investment went to industrialized countries *and* to Asia (UNCTAD 1997, xx). South, East, and Southeast Asia received around two-thirds of the total for developing countries in that year; however, the Association of Southeast Asian Nations (ASEAN) economies experienced a substantial drop in the region's investment inflows, from 61 percent in 1990–91 to 30 percent during 1994–96, partially due to stiff competition from other parts of Asia (UNCTAD 1997, 78, 81).

Dealing with the poorer countries, a critical indicator of their insertion into the GDLP is debt flows not only to private lenders, but also to those associated with structural adjustment programs required by international financial institutions—at bottom, a way of disciplining states. These transactions are part of a massive $1.5 trillion in capital flows that now circulate the globe *each day*. (Global capital flows are apart from the real economy, i.e., goods and services, which also constitute transfers across borders.) Although financial integration is touched on, these indicators receive insufficient attention in the negative argument that globalization is a myth. So too, in the attack by Hirst and Thompson, the changing global division of labor is not systematically explored. The decline of Fordism, a system of production and consumption that began in the U.S. automobile industry, and the shift toward the need for a more flexible work force under post-Fordism have direct implications for the reorganization of people's livelihoods and thus their modes of existence.

One might also look at worldwide tourism, which generates jobs, offers foreign exchange, and shapes mental images of peoples and places, all profoundly affected by lower fares, more routes, and technological advances. Two decades ago, when the world population totaled 4.4 billion, 287 million people went on international trips. In 1996, with a global population of 5.7 billion, 595 million tourists traveled. It is estimated that by 2020, 1.6 billion of the world's 7.8 billion people will go abroad (Crossette 1998, drawing on statistics compiled by the World Tourism Organization). Another alternative indicator is cross-border mergers and acquisitions. The value of these transactions doubled between 1988 and 1995, to $229 billion (UNCTAD 1996, xiv). It is noteworthy that during the last two decades, the volume of world trade grew at twice the rate of world output. In U.S. dollars, world foreign exchange transactions expanded from $15 billion per day at the beginning of the 1970s to $900 billion per day two decades later (Government of Denmark 1997, 14).

Apart from invoking additional empirical indicators to counter the ones used by analysts who deny globalization, what bears emphasis is that surely something is new. There is no denying quantum changes. Crucially, a component of neoliberal restructuring is the relaxing of the regulatory framework. Along with major technological breakthroughs in production systems, communications, and transportation—including commercial jet aircraft, enlarged superfreighters, containerization, and telematics—the reduction of barriers has markedly accelerated the movement of goods, services, capital, labor, and knowledge. Not only is there a major rise in the velocity of transactions, but also the cost of various types of transport, telephone calls, and computers has plummeted. For example, owing to satellite technology, the price of a three-minute call from New York to London dropped from $244.65 in 1930 to $31.58 in 1970, and to $3.32 in 1990 (International Monetary Fund [IMF] 1997, 45). Furthermore, in the early 1980s, only a few international companies had invested in fax machines, because they were too expensive. By the early 1990s, the cost of these machines had declined to one-quarter of the 1980 price. Today, what major organization is not equipped with fax machines to communicate around the world?

Similarly, in 1980, there were only two million computers—the epitome of a global product—throughout the world, virtually all of them mainframes. At present, more than 150 million computers are in use, 90 percent being personal computers, which have greater power than the earlier mainframes, bringing private citizens in one part of the globe into direct contact with others in another area of the world (Lopez, Smith, and Pagnucco 1995, 35).

In view of such evidence for technological innovations accompanied by a dramatic rise in cross-border flows, it is sometimes argued that globalization is based on a single global market. Ohmae, for example, holds: "On a political map, the boundaries between countries are as clear as ever. But on a competitive map, a map showing the real flows of financial and industrial activity, those borders have largely disappeared" (1990, 18). Some specialists on development add that the globalization of macroeconomic policy converts countries into open economic zones in which industries for the domestic market are not competitive and that individual developing countries can no longer build national economies (Chossudovsky 1998). The opposing position is that borders, even the one between the United States and Canada (supposedly two highly integrated economies), act as significant barriers to the creation of a single market. According to this view, borders are not being dissolved, and there remain distinctive national markets (McCallum 1995; Engel and Rogers 1996). Various contributors to Suzanne Berger and Ronald Dore's *National Diversity and Global Capitalism* (1996) contend that the world economy is indeed less integrated than globalization authors such as Ohmae claim, and that there is considerable latitude for national and sectoral maneuver. Similarly, Dani Rodrik maintains: "We have never truly had a global capitalist system and are unlikely to have one anytime soon. Capitalism is, and will remain, a national phenomenon" (1998, 17; also see Rodrik 1997).

But does it really make sense to dichotomize a full-fledged global economy and a national sphere? Are there only two options? With globalization, surely big is beautiful, but big may not mean global; it also entails regional processes at various levels, and with the advent of a European passport and provisions for the free movement of persons within Europe, national labor markets have changed dramatically. Moreover, although globalization contains a powerful centralizing dynamic and concentrates wealth, it also decentralizes activities and fragments identities. The dominant identities of the twentieth century, labor and the nation, have been split into, or are supplanted by, a complex set of identities—including race and ethnicity, religion, and gender—subjectively relating people to the polity and economy in very different ways. Insofar as observers posit a territorially bounded "U.S." or "Canadian" economy, they are making implicit assumptions about the meaning of borders and neglecting evolving global structures, which transcend borders and are interacting directly with—not through national policy channels or international agencies—individuals, households, and communities formerly far removed from meaningful participation in cross-border flows.

Indeed, for hundreds of millions of persons today, even in remote areas of developing countries, the dreams of modernization are coming true, but, ironically, not as social scientists had envisaged and certainly not through the national, bilateral, and multilateral institutions that some of them had helped to build. A massive transformation is being compressed into a short time—a few years, rather than many generations—and despite officially managed processes. The speed and direction of change in Pakistan's rural economy and social relations exemplify this transformation. Like many labor-exporting countries, Pakistan has in some years received more capital in migrants' remittances than the state has allocated for national development at the federal and local levels. From 1971 to 1988, Pakistani workers in the Middle East generated $20 billion in foreign exchange through official channels—a sum that exceeded the country's entire gross national product (GNP) in a single year. In the peak year (1982), official remittances outstripped export earnings and represented more than half the foreign exchange costs of imports (Addleton 1992, 117, 120).

Reported remittances do not include remittances in kind (commodities purchased overseas and sold in the informal economy) or black market remittances, a category of funds that may be regarded as a form of resistance to the state's efforts to capture income flowing into rural areas. Unlike foreign aid, these flows come without strings attached and are not directed by the dominant classes. By strengthening the underground economy, remittances may undermine authoritative preferred modes of development and contribute to the state's loss of control within what had been portrayed as the national or domestic unit (Addleton 1992). For individual families drawn into transnational flows, there are vast changes in consumption patterns, exposure to a more diversified economy when sectors such as construction and retailing services expand, and new stresses on transformed social structures, especially marked in Pakistan by an overall decline in poverty and increased measures of inequality. This chain of far-reaching events is but one aspect of evolving global structures.

## EVOLVING GLOBAL STRUCTURES

Not an all-encompassing phenomenon, globalization excludes behavior that does not involve linkages to global structures, although one could debate the indirect effects. Indeed, one can conceptualize the implications of evolving global structures as a series of relationships: economic globalization and the state, pressures on the state, globalization and democratization, and democratization and civil society. In introducing these themes, I will briefly clarify key concepts, if only as a point of departure for further development in the ensuing chapters.

### Economic Globalization and the State

In recent decades, several states sought to protect the domestic economy against external forces and to limit the net outflow of surplus by adopting acts of economic nationalism: the nationalization of key industries, indigenization decrees, requirements for local incorporation of a portion of foreign capital, and so on. Some states (e.g., China under Mao, Myanmar, and Tanzania) also professed a more radical course of self-reliance as a means of insulation from the world system. Today, however, there is little to commend strategies of economic nationalism or delinking, for transborder flows (migration, communications, knowledge, technology, and the like) have circumvented the globe and, as discussed, permeate the state.

The scope for state autonomy—a concept that drew considerable attention from scholars in the 1970s and 1980s—is constrained by economic globalization. Additionally, the drive to bring the state back in to the forefront of social theory (Evans, Rueschemeyer, and Skocpol 1985) requires fresh analysis in light of globalization. In a globalized division of labor and power, some states may initiate action in, but mostly react to, worldwide economic forces. To realize material gain from globalization, the state increasingly facilitates this process, acting as its agent (Cox 1987, 253–65; cf. Palan and Abbott 1996). Surrounded by impersonal and unaccountable forces often beyond their control, leaders' capacity to lead is diminished (Hughes 1990). Faced with the power of globalized production and international finance, including debt structures, leaders are constrained to concentrate on enhancing national conditions for competing forms of capitalism. Statecraft, tested as it is by nonstate actors, is reduced in efficacy relative to transnational forces. Among the public in different zones of the world economy, the politics of disillusionment is rife.

The state is restructuring partly because of challenges to sovereignty in the aftermath of the Cold War. With the disintegration of socialist regimes came the eruption of subsurface tensions formerly stifled by the state. Now, state borders are subject to revision (Halliday 1990). East Germany has disappeared, Czechoslovakia split in two, the fifteen republics comprising the former Soviet Union have achieved independence, and Yugoslavia, now dismembered, is riven with ethnic conflict. Predating the end of the Cold War, separatist movements in Quebec, Northern Ireland, the Basque country, and Corsica are challenging the status quo. While North Korea could be absorbed by South Korea, Balkanization is always a danger in Africa, where colonizers arbitrarily drew borders without regard to ethnic distribution and natural frontiers such as rivers and mountains. A number of countries are dubious propositions as unified entities.

Whereas no state is untouched by globalization, the majority of them play a courtesan role. By definition, a courtesan services clients, especially wealthy or upper-class ones. Some countries are cast literally in this role, offering or promoting a sex industry, now organized transnationally in Eastern Asia, where the state does not provide social protection for its young women and men (or children) but rather tacitly forsakes safeguarding the local culture in favor of global market forces. For other countries, the courtesan stance is less blatant and more figurative, but nonetheless emblematic of the state's role serving dominant interests embodied in the neoliberal global political economy. In all cases, the courtesan is not a distinctive form of state, as is, say, a "welfare" or "developmental" state, but a policy orientation characteristic of very different forms of state.

Broadly, a state in its capacity as a courtesan is beholden to more powerful interests in the global political economy, submissive in its policies, if not in rhetorical flourishes, because choice is constrained, and engaged in illicit relationships (although the line between licit and illicit is increasingly blurred). More specifically, the courtesan is a syncretic configuration, an amalgam of different traits. To varying degrees in diverse settings, it reflects a subordinate position in the geopolitics of globalization. In addition, a characteristic of the courtesan is loss of control in the geoeconomy, which is evident from the least developed countries in Southern Africa to the Newly Industrializing Countries (NICs) in Eastern Asia. Notwithstanding ministrations to unregulated economies, the courtesans countenance heavy bureaucracies, partly a vestige of colonialism in states that have graduated to political independence in recent decades, partially a relic of national development plans from the 1960s and 1970s, and surely collusive in the sense that political power is a route—sometimes the only one—to wealth.

So, too, are some states in the guise of courtesans strengthening their coercive quotient in a mix with electoral and democratic procedures. Police powers have broadened; in many cases, police budgets have expanded despite overall governmental reductions; and imprisonment represents a major growth industry. Finally, in certain countries where there is no apparent external enemy, especially after the Cold War, the state qua courtesan is providing security for the holders of state power and its beneficiaries, not the citizenry at large. Subscribing to the ideology of globalization, the courtesan is not solely a national phenomenon, but is rapidly becoming a trans-state structure in its own right: a multidimensional entity rooted in a multiclass coalition of its sponsors and sustained by those who are carried along in a process of consensual participation, a hub of cross-border flows spurred by the lowering of barriers, and a central element in the global policy framework of neoliberalism.

### Pressures on the State

Trans-state structures, some of them incipient, are integral to the dialectic of supranationalism and subnationalism. The state is being re-formed from above by the tugs of economic globalization and from below by the pull of subnationalism. On the one hand, many polities seek advantage in global competition through regionalism; despite the past failings of regional groupings, regional cooperation is widely regarded as a way to achieve mobility in the changing GDLP. On the other hand, states are often disrupted by substate actors.

With globalization, an explosion of pluralism involves a renewal of historical forces—a maze of religious loyalties, ethnic identities, linguistic differences, and other forms of cultural expression. While globalization constrains state power, there is a reassertion of historical forces. Just as globalization gives impetus to cultural homogenization (e.g., the diffusion of standard consumer goods throughout the world), so too does a global thrust undermine community structures and unleash subterranean cultural pluralism.

Culture is an elusive concept that resists definition, especially because under different conditions, it is represented in diverse ways, including as fixed stereotypes (e.g., "Asian values"), as a factor that shapes and is shaped by resistance, and as orientations that have a transformative basis. An emphasis on the ways that culture is constructed may be contrasted with primordial notions of culture, which ascribe inherent traits, such as obedience and loyalty to societies, thereby denying the historical and changing role of cultural forces. From the social constructionist point of view, culture is neither static nor homogeneous. In fact, Eastern Asian cultures are mixed, being medleys of ethnic groups, languages, and religions—Confucianism, Buddhism, Taoism, Hinduism, Islam, Christianity, and others. Southern African cultures are also multifarious, comprising different races and ethnic groups, many languages, and diverse religions. The more plausible use of culture as one component of an explanation is the appreciation of subjective and selective orientations in contingent terms, including the capacity of both the state and resistance movements to mobilize these resources under given conditions.

Although the study of culture has been through different phases which, one after another, have come under attack, the so-called soft questions, as opposed to the muscular structural issues, persist. The former include, How do people portray their lives, what do they imagine life to be about, and what are their representations of pain, reward, and aspirations (Geertz 1995, 43–44)? Rather than propose a hard-and-fast concept, it is better to jab at this issue, coming at it in a roundabout way by suggesting a point of departure. Culture may then be approached in terms of interest-based social processes that fashion or undermine the sum total of ways of life, of which material life is a part (Williams 1977). In the analysis that follows, culture is seen as a vehicle in the search for new themes and ordering propositions

## Globalization and Democratization

Pressured by nonstate actors, the state seeks to fortify itself by adopting such measures as computerized surveillance in finance and establishing transnational police forces (e.g., Europol). Nonetheless, the state must accommodate the new pluralism and allow for demands for political reforms. With the revolution in Eastern Europe, the release of Nelson Mandela from prison, and the assertiveness of the human rights movement, the drive toward democratization won legitimacy. Equally important, pro-democracy forces have gained confidence. But what type of democracy is appropriate for the twenty-first century? While democracy is a universal concept, there are very different versions of democratic theory.

From a liberal perspective, democracy centers on the principle that the right to rule should be based on the consent of the governed. Liberal democracy calls for public influence on government through such institutions as political parties, regular elections, and an alternation in power. Beginning with the work of Robert Dahl (1971), U.S. academics developed an institutionalist concept of democracy known as polyarchy: a system of mass participation in decision making that focuses on choosing leaders in periodic elections, a process managed by competing elites. It is assumed that the elites will be sensitive to the interests of the majority, but critics point out that this definition is limited to the political sphere. The institutionalist definition of democracy does not address the question of access to wealth and social equality (Moreira Alves 1988, 9–13). While tolerating vast inequalities of material and cultural resources, polyarchy is now promoted by U.S. policy makers in the international realm, and it is seen as being complementary to promoting neoliberalism. Consolidating polyarchic, or liberal democratic, political systems and building market-oriented, or neoliberal, economies are meant to go hand in hand (Robinson 1996, 55, 319).

Another concept of democracy is rooted in the classical Greek theory of rule by the people, and has also been known as direct democracy. Recalling this legacy, contemporary popular movements have put forward a model of populist democracy, understood as government by popular majorities, not dominant minorities or competition among the elites. In this model, there are various channels that permit the popular sectors to use the state for their own ends, with the mobilization of civil society as an important spur in the process (Robinson 1996, 58–60). In practice, this ideal has often been overtaken by neoliberalism such that it is superseded by authoritarian forms of governance. Some Latin American countries, notably Brazil and Argentina, have experienced phases of "authoritarian democracy"—other qualifying adjectives, including "limited," "guided," and "protected," are sometimes attached to the term "democracy"—which is justified as a more flexible system of political representation and a route to gradual liberalization. Armed with the power to enforce order, however, the state, while attempting to elicit consent, can wield the means of coercion to safeguard the nation against "chaos." This domination and its social ramifications often engender mounting conflict: protests against abuses of human rights and demands for the pursuit of substantive justice (Mittelman 1990, 67; Moreira Alves 1988, 9–13).

A challenge to democracy as an ideology of domination is emerging from the mobilization of social movements, which are pursuing a third model, "participatory democracy." The self-aggrandizing individualism characteristic of polyarchic and authoritarian democracy, coincident to economic globalization, is rejected in favor of a belief that the individual depends on society for development. The liberal-economic conceptualization of globalization allows for tolerance of social inequality, which purveyors of participatory democracy find intolerable. Currently more a potential than a reality, "participatory democracy" is not only a national structure, but also implies continuing pressure from social forces at the base of society in keeping with the transformative mode of regionalism and globalization from below, discussed in subsequent chapters (especially chapters 6, 10, and 12). The participatory democratic alternative is then linked to a supreme challenge: how both to manage the socially disruptive costs of economic reform and to democratize. Put differently, the major problem is how to make economic revitalization compatible with democratization. The question of democratization also centers on contradictory forms of accountability. To whom are elected officials responsible? Whereas in theory, democracy means accountability to the governed, in practice, leaders are held accountable to such market forces as debt structures, structural adjustment programs, and credit rating agencies. Hence the search for an alternative. Although no one can argue convincingly that participatory democracy has been realized anywhere, there is no doubt that such mobilizing ideals have been powerful historical forces.

## Democratization and Civil Society

With globalization, politics is being redefined. Electoral politics is the conventional arena, but, of course, not the only one. Politics beyond the parameters of the state is more fluid than it is within the state. Civil society transcending the state, if only in an incipient manner, is emerging as a major site of contestation where diverse groups seek to recast politics, including its time-space dimensions (Lipschutz 1992). In a Braudelian sense of time, shared mental frameworks, including paradigms, are shifting, and borders are being redrawn not only in a formal manner, but also in terms of real flows of capital, population, information, knowledge, technology, and consumer products.

The concept of civil society has its roots in the European intellectual tradition, especially the Scottish Enlightenment of the seventeenth and eighteenth centuries, and Western political culture. As the idea is most often used in the West, civil society has Hegelian overtones. In this manner, it is regarded as that realm of associational life above the individual—or, some would say, the family—and below the state (Wapner 1996). For many activists who seek to build an alternative order, however, this interpretation is challenged and qualified. Their concept is perhaps more in line with Gramsci's notion that "[b]etween the economic structure and the State with its legislation and its coercion stands civil society" (1971, 208). It was Gramsci's insight that hegemony is exercised not only through the state but also in civil society, whose institutions—various voluntary associations, religious institutions, and the like—are vital in forging consent. In other words, for Gramsci, civil society—the ways in which groups represent themselves—is both inside and outside the state. The state itself, especially in its interactions with civil society, becomes a terrain of struggle. Indeed today, some of the leaders of civil society occupy important positions in state agencies. This poses an ethical dilemma for the "independent" organs of civil society.

Whereas its boundaries are blurred and must be negotiated, surely civil society has its own character. I understand civil society to be a contested political space, established and extended by collective action, and composed of voluntary associations distinct from economy and, while not completely separate from, nonetheless outside the direct control of the state.

The idea of civil society has been imported into the politics of globalization partly because of neoliberalism's lack of a philosophical dimension and also partly because of multiple signs of the disintegration of social order. Emblematic of this degeneration are the environmental scars that mark the late twentieth century. In response to the state's unwillingness or inability to respond effectively to these signals, civil society may act as a watchdog, a switchboard of information, a testing ground of ideas, and a voice for citizens. In counterbalancing the state, civil society may also reinvent and recast itself; it is riddled with tensions as well, but thrives on diversity (Serrano 1994, 309). Although civil society pressures the state and is a potential spur for democratization, as we shall see (chapters 5, 10, and 11), the idea and practice of civil society may also become corrupt, either tainted by or tainting the state with illicit activities.

Finally, the state-civil society complex varies dramatically from one context to another, and there are several different kinds of civil society. In some cases, the state monopolizes resources, but there are other permutations. In many parts of the non-Western world, claims emerging from civil society were not a feature of political life before recent decades; the idea itself was transported from the West, and now is a key feature of—indeed, a critical venue—in resistance politics. Let us wend our way to resistance, the counterpoint to globalization, by exploring the context in which it arises: the global division of labor and power as it is refracted through regional processes, viewed here in Eastern Asia and Southern Africa.

# Part One

THE GLOBAL DIVISION OF LABOR
AND POWER

# CHAPTER 2

# Rethinking the International Division of Labor

TODAY, the familiar imagery of a core, semiperiphery, and periphery no longer applies to a new structure that envelops both vertically integrated regional divisions of labor, based on the distinctive comparative advantages of different locations, and horizontally diversified networks that extend their activities into neighboring countries as part of corporate strategies of diversification and globalization. The old categories do not capture the intricacy of the integration of the world economy as well as the ways in which it constrains all regions and states to adjust to transnational capital. The global transformation now under way not only slices across former divisions of labor and geographically reorganizes economic activities, but also limits state autonomy and infringes on sovereignty.

While escalating at a world level, globalization must be regarded as problematic, incomplete, and contradictory—issues to be taken up below. A hybrid system, globalization is not only an intensification of interactions among nation-states, but also, in certain respects, undermines them. Although globalization is frequently characterized as a homogenizing force, it also fuses with local conditions in diverse ways, thereby generating, not eroding, striking differences among social formations. Fundamentally an outgrowth of the bedrock of capital accumulation, this structure embraces and yet differs in important ways from trends posited by theorists of the international division of labor (IDL) and the new international division of labor (NIDL), two theses that provide both a point of entry for analyzing global restructuring and an opportunity for developing an alternative formulation. To examine major facets of global restructuring, inquiry must revisit (even if only sketchily) previous attempts to come to grips with novel systems of production, the distribution of rewards, and the political and social consequences. Briefly reviewing classical theories of the IDL offers a fruitful way of posing relevant theoretical questions for later discussion. Plainly, it will be important to understand why and how classical authors understood and defined the IDL. Even from a short synopsis, it should be apparent that there are serious disagreements not only about what engenders the division of labor, but even about what constitutes its essential characteristics. The IDL interpretation must be supplemented by the idea of a NIDL, which seeks to explain the shift of manufacturing from advanced capitalist to developing countries—a spatial reorganization of production in the second half of the twentieth century. After subjecting the NIDL thesis to critical scrutiny, I will propose another perspective, which I have called the global division of labor and power.

My main argument is that the GDLP introduces more complexity into the "division of labor" and adds structural depth to the classical and contemporary theories. In brief, the GDLP involves a restructuring among world regions, including their constituent units, notably states, cities, and the networks that link them. Another element of reordering is massive transfers of population from the developing countries, Eastern Europe, and the former Soviet Union to the West, though there are also significant migratory flows internal to these regions and within the South. Acting as magnets attracting imports of labor, global commodity chains form networks that interlink multiple production processes, as well as buyers and sellers. Mediating among these macro political and economic structures are micropatterns rooted in culture—family, communal, and ethnic ties. Culture becomes a switch on the tracks of regulation and segmentation of the labor market.

Since prior meanings assigned to the term "division of labor" underpin my argument about the GDLP, the first section of this chapter examines the concept of IDL in classical political economy, while the second turns to the NIDL hypothesis. Next, by focusing on the interactions among levels of analysis—regionalism, migration, commodity chains, and cultural forces—in a globalizing division of labor, I will attempt to offer an alternative explanation of restructuring. A central purpose of this chapter is thus to introduce these levels of analysis, and subsequent chapters will detail them as well as further explore the synergy between them. Finally, on the basis of a juxtaposition of the three formulations—IDL, NIDL, and GDLP—the conclusion identifies trends and notes major aspects of a hierarchical—yet rapidly changing—world order, today marked both by the persistence of the interstate system and a challenge from different types of nonstate actors.

## THE OLD DIVISION OF LABOR

### *Classical Political Economy*

As first studied by Adam Smith, David Ricardo, and Karl Marx, the division of labor refers to novel forms of specialization separating the production process into compartments, each one performing different tasks, with varying rates of profit and implications for comparative advantages in trade. Smith's 1776 treatise on the division of labor concerned the wealth of all nations and became the seedbed of modern theories. Positing a "propensity to truck and barter" innate in humankind, Smith (1970) provided the first major attempt to examine the potential for the emergence of a complex division of labor that later developed during the industrial revolution and on the Continent.

The emerging industrial form of production, Smith argued, entailed the erosion of artisan skills and their replacement not by collaboration among several craftsmen, but by coordination among a large number of people carrying out specific, assigned activities, enabling any one person to do the work of many. The combined labor of a workforce in a single establishment outstripped the total effort of individual workers in the old system. Productivity gains were attributable to increases in dexterity because of the reduction of tasks to discrete operations, savings in time lost passing from one activity to another, and inventiveness stemming from intimate familiarity with and attentiveness to a single function. This specialization was paralleled by differentiation in other spheres as well—politics and society—as outlined in Smith's first book, *The Theory of Moral Sentiments*, originally published in 1759 (Smith 1976). Although classical political economists are frequently portrayed as positing that society is, in large part, driven by self-interest, Smith in fact also stressed that in civil society, social propensities constrain egoism and help to avert discord. *The Theory* contains ample discussion of "fellow feeling," personal conduct, rules of justice, and morality.

Smith remained optimistic that the evolving division of labor would be a propellant for higher standards of living and thus offer enormous benefits, but was not unaware of the disruptive and deleterious consequences of repetition and overspecialization. Notwithstanding the dehumanization of work in factories, he was sanguine about economic society insofar as the state provides public goods (notably in the realm of culture and education) to facilitate commerce, sufficient justice to protect from oppression and to secure property rights, and security from invasion. While market society necessitates a relatively autonomous state to sustain laissez-faire and the division of labor, the scope of the domestic market is an inherent limitation. Whereas in inland, scattered, or scarcely populated areas, individuals retain the need to be able to do many kinds of work, it is trade that increases the reach of the market.

Entering the debate at this juncture, Ricardo argued that commodities are valued according to the quantity of labor required for their production and can be enhanced through foreign trade, for the rules that govern the relative value of commodities in one country do not regulate the relative value of commodities exchanged among countries. Through the efficacious use of "the peculiar powers bestowed by nature," each country "distributes labour most effectively and most economically: while by increasing the general mass of productions, it diffuses general benefit, and binds together by one common tie of interest and intercourse, the universal society of nations throughout the civilized world" (Ricardo 1932, 114). Hence, Ricardo's basic law of comparative advantage, which undergirds a good deal of contemporary theory, may be summarized as follows: The pattern of international trade is dependent on the principle of comparative labor costs, which holds that if two countries engage in trade relations, each one producing the same commodities, one country would sell the commodity in which its relative (rather than absolute) cost was lower and, similarly, the other country would sell the commodity in which its own cost was low. Like Smith's concept of division of labor, Ricardo's theory of comparative advantage presupposes the separation of politics and economics, and the notion of civil society—a term used by classical political economists to cover bourgeois society, not in the contemporary sense of autonomous organizations, some of them grassroots movements.

Viewing the division of labor as the "prevalent characteristic of capitalism," Marx did not share Smith's and Ricardo's faith in the beneficial consequences of the division of labor in manufacturing, where tasks are partitioned and repartitioned, and of the division of labor in society as a whole. Marx maintained that the division of labor in manufacturing brings the laborer face to face with the material power of the production process, cutting down the worker to a detail laborer. Knowledge, judgment, and will are formally exercised only for the factory as a whole, often crippling the worker's body and mind as well. The detailed division of labor—subdivisions of tasks within industries—is thus distinguished from the social division of labor, which sets off whole groups from one another in society. Both criticizing and building on the theoretical foundations laid by Smith and Ricardo, Marx thus sought to recast their arguments and to make explicit a political dimension of the theory of division of labor.

### Sociological Theory

Notwithstanding the attempt by classical political economists to interweave economic theory and what is now regarded as industrial sociology, there were only minor advances in the theory of division of labor between the nineteenth century and the second half of the twentieth century, except for the interventions of Max Weber and Emile Durkheim. Raising quite different questions from the debate over the costs and benefits of increases in productivity surrounding the IDL, sociologists have given specific meaning to the notion of division of labor. Emphasizing "specialization of function" as a motor force in history, Weber held that "functions may be differentiated according to the type of work, so that the product is brought to completion only by combining, simultaneously or successively, the work of a large number of persons" (Weber 1947, 225). To develop this basic proposition, he focused on aspects of the social relations engendered by the division of labor, and established a sociological typology applying to historical cases, though not to the division of labor or the economy in general. Weber nonetheless envisaged the advance of the division of labor in tandem with the centralization of the means of administration—an overall trend toward bureaucratic specialization in all spheres of social life.

For Durkheim, the major issue was the structurally disruptive and cohesive tendencies in the division of labor, which ultimately furthers social integration or what he called "organic solidarity." Unlike mechanical social orders held together by common beliefs and values, modern organic societies rest on the complementarity of different specialized functions. In transitions where the division of labor replaces mechanical solidarity without yet developing the morality (i.e., social solidarity) to mitigate societal tensions, an increased volume and density of interactions entail a prevalence of crime, economic crises, conflicts between labor and capital, and emigration. However, these forms of anomie would lessen, while flexibility and individual freedom would accompany an increasing specialization in the division of labor, which in turn promotes an integration of society (Durkheim 1984, 291–341).

## Old Theories, New Realities

From this brief overview of the classical writers, it is clear that IDL theory provides a springboard for understanding modern capital accumulation, the expansion of the market currently manifest in economic globalization, and the social consequences of these processes. What is lacking in the theory, however, reflects the general limits of the classical tradition and has important implications for the contemporary period. Although the classical school allowed for the state to be the guarantor of the division of labor in a laissez-faire economy, democratic or liberal forms of state were not deemed necessary. (Utilitarians like Jeremy Bentham and, later, liberals such as John Stuart Mill were concerned with forms of state. Conservative reformers like Bismarck and mercantilists, most notably Friedrich List, regarded the state as central to capital accumulation.)

The risk in highlighting the logic of capital and labor costs while underrating the role of the state lies in invoking economism linked to the rising power of capitalism, a tendency somewhat corrected by the followers of Weber, who emphasize divisions of labor by age, race, ethnicity, and gender (Cohen 1987, 231–32). Though not silent about the role of culture, classical authors said relatively little about the attitudes, beliefs, and habits of different strata in the international division of labor. Nowhere did they analyze, say, the constraints that some cultures place on the mobility of labor (e.g., as do contemporary Islamic communities in rural areas in certain developing countries). In fact, classical political economy is not explicit about the spatial dimensions of the division of labor—a curious deficiency addressed in the NIDL thesis.

## THE NEW INTERNATIONAL DIVISION OF LABOR

Apart from contributions by Weber and Durkheim, the concept of division of labor remained largely dormant until the beginning of a spatial reorganization of production involving the formation and expansion of a world market for labor and production sites in the 1960s. Varying in emphasis from a neo-Smithian focus on changes in the world market to a neo-Ricardian one on capital exports, NIDL theorists sought to explain the shift of manufacturing from advanced capitalist to developing countries, with the fragmentation of production and the transfer of low-skill jobs while the bulk of research and development (R&D) activities was retained in the heartlands of world capitalism. Fröbel, Heinrichs, and Kreye hold that the traditional international division of labor, in which the developing world was relegated to the production of raw materials, has markedly changed (Fröbel, Heinrichs, and Kreye 1980; Lipietz 1985). TNCs have established a global manufacturing system based on labor-intensive export platforms in low-wage areas. This move toward industrialization in the developing countries and a decline in manufacturing relative to GDP in the West and Japan are driven by the structural capitalist imperative to maximize profits under conditions of heightened global competition.

With new technologies, especially space-shrinking systems of transport and communications, the sites for manufacturing are increasingly independent of geographical distance. Capital now not only searches for fresh markets, but also seeks to incorporate new groups into the labor force. Initially through the "global assembly line" of textiles, many women from developing countries have become part of the international working class. It was the electronics industry that developed the first truly integrated world assembly line.

Contributing importantly to understanding dramatic changes in the division of labor, Fröbelians clearly identified the growing power and sophistication of transnational capital and its ability to optimize differing opportunities for profit by decentralizing production across the globe (see

Gordon 1988 for qualifications to the NIDL argument). This approach also provides an important angle for studying North-South relations, especially large-scale migrations of capital to the developing world and specific linkages that increasingly differentiate countries at various levels of development.

The NIDL thesis, however, overstates the significance of cheap labor as the propellant of capital around the globe. Surely, low wages do not explain decisions of TNCs to touch down where labor is relatively costly (Fernández Kelly 1989, 150–51). Locational decisions represent a mix of considerations and often favor countries where labor costs exceed those in neighboring countries. Hence, a 1998 rating of fifty-three countries by the World Economic Forum (WEF), a private, not-for-profit foundation with headquarters in Geneva, Switzerland, and supported by more than one thousand member companies, uses a weighted composite index. The measures are open markets, lean government spending, low tax rates, flexible labor markets, a stable political system, and an effective judiciary. On this basis for 1998, Singapore ranked best in the world in competitiveness—ahead of its counterparts in runners-up Hong Kong, the United States, the United Kingdom, and Canada. Table 2.1 presents weighted averages of competitiveness by country, according to the indices noted above.

Clearly, the cost of labor is but one among the factors in the matrix of competitiveness and in the calculations of global firms that bear directly on job gains and losses. Another difficulty with the NIDL thesis is that the old international division of labor (for example, in agriculture) has not disappeared but coexists with the new division, forming what might be regarded as an articulation of the old and the new or a redivision of labor. If, indeed, the issue is to identify continuities and discontinuities, it is appropriate to ask, Exactly what is new about the new international division of labor? The claim that industrialization in the developing world is new neglects the establishment of import-substituting industries in Argentina, Brazil, and Mexico in the 1930s and 1940s. Actually, industrial growth in some parts of Latin America dates to the interwar period (Gereffi 1990, 3). The structuralist logic embraced in the NIDL perspective leads analysts to glide over historically specific conditions prevailing in individual countries, regions, industries, and sectors that form a pattern of incorporation into a global mosaic.

Moving beyond economism, the key questions are: What conditions in respective zones of the world economy are propitious for entry into this division of labor, and *on what and whose terms?* In other words, what are the political dynamics that both join and separate global linkages in production, exchange, and consumption?

**TABLE 2.1**
Global Competitiveness Index, 1998

| Country | Competitiveness Index 98 | Rank 98 | (Rank 97) | (Rank 96) |
|---|---|---|---|---|
| Singapore | 2.16 | 1 | (1) | (1) |
| Hong Kong | 1.91 | 2 | (2) | (2) |
| United States | 1.41 | 3 | (3) | (4) |
| United Kingdom | 1.29 | 4 | (7) | (15) |
| Canada | 1.27 | 5 | (4) | (8) |
| Taiwan | 1.19 | 6 | (8) | (9) |
| Netherlands | 1.13 | 7 | (12) | (17) |
| Switzerland | 1.10 | 8 | (6) | (6) |
| Norway | 1.09 | 9 | (10) | (7) |
| Luxembourg | 1.05 | 10 | (11) | (5) |
| Ireland | 1.05 | 11 | (16) | (26) |
| Japan | 0.97 | 12 | (14) | (13) |
| New Zealand | 0.84 | 13 | (5) | (3) |
| Australia | 0.79 | 14 | (17) | (12) |
| Finland | 0.70 | 15 | (19) | (16) |
| Denmark | 0.61 | 16 | (20) | (11) |
| Malaysia | 0.59 | 17 | (9) | (10) |
| Chile | 0.57 | 18 | (13) | (18) |
| Korea | 0.39 | 19 | (21) | (20) |
| Austria | 0.37 | 20 | (27) | (19) |
| Thailand | 0.27 | 21 | (18) | (14) |
| France | 0.25 | 22 | (23) | (23) |
| Sweden | 0.25 | 23 | (22) | (21) |
| Germany | 0.15 | 24 | (25) | (22) |
| Spain | 0.02 | 25 | (26) | (32) |
| Portugal | −0.02 | 26 | (30) | (34) |
| Belgium | −0.03 | 27 | (31) | (25) |
| China | −0.15 | 28 | (29) | (36) |
| Israel | −0.17 | 29 | (24) | (24) |
| Iceland | −0.18 | 30 | (38) | (27) |
| Indonesia | −0.19 | 31 | (15) | (30) |
| Mexico | −0.23 | 32 | (33) | (33) |
| Philippines | −0.31 | 33 | (34) | (31) |
| Jordan | −0.42 | 34 | (43) | (28) |
| Czech Republic | −0.47 | 35 | (32) | (35) |
| Argentina | −0.48 | 36 | (37) | (37) |
| Peru | −0.50 | 37 | (40) | (38) |
| Egypt | −0.52 | 38 | (28) | (29) |
| Vietnam | −0.53 | 39 | (49) | (n/a) |
| Turkey | −0.57 | 40 | (36) | (42) |
| Italy | −0.69 | 41 | (39) | (41) |

| Country | Competitiveness Index 98 | Rank 98 | (Rank 97) | (Rank 96) |
|---------|--------------------------|---------|-----------|-----------|
| South Africa | -0.84 | 42 | (44) | (43) |
| Hungary | -0.85 | 43 | (46) | (46) |
| Greece | -0.87 | 44 | (48) | (39) |
| Venezuela | -0.98 | 45 | (47) | (47) |
| Brazil | -1.10 | 46 | (42) | (48) |
| Colombia | -1.12 | 47 | (41) | (40) |
| Slovakia | -1.17 | 48 | (35) | (n/a) |
| Poland | -1.18 | 49 | (50) | (44) |
| India | -1.61 | 50 | (45) | (45) |
| Zimbabwe | -1.70 | 51 | (51) | (n/a) |
| Russia | -2.02 | 52 | (53) | (49) |
| Ukraine | -2.51 | 53 | (52) | (n/a) |

*Source:* World Economic Forum, *Global Competitiveness Report* (Geneva: WEF, 1998), http://www.weforum.org/publications/gcr/98rankings.asp

## THE GLOBAL DIVISION OF LABOR AND POWER

### *Regionalism and Globalization*

What is new about the contemporary period is the manner of and extent to which domestic political economies are penetrated by global phenomena. There is no single wave of globalization washing over or flattening diverse divisions of labor both in regions and in industrial branches (Henderson 1989). Varied regional divisions of labor are emerging, tethered in different ways to global structures, each one engaged in unequal transactions with world centers of production and finance and presented with distinctive development possibilities. Within each region, subglobal hierarchies have formed, with poles of economic growth, managerial and technological centers, and security systems.

It would be fruitless to seek to define a single pattern of regional integration, especially a Eurocentric model emphasizing legal principles, formal declarations, routinized bureaucracies, and institutionalized exchange. This would be an inadequate guide for infrastructural and production-based orientations—to some extent a reality, and certainly a goal among the members of ASEAN and the Southern African Development Community (SADC). Regional divisions of labor are, of course, not static but change rapidly, reflecting expansion and contraction in production in different locales, the instantaneous movement of finance, the coalescence of production and trade networks, as well as the consolidation of production and distribution systems.

A changed actor relative to global forces, the state facilitates the reorganization of production, and the interstate system remains an important point of reference in an increasingly integrated world society. With proper timing during a period when the world economy was robust, state interventions promoted remarkable economic growth in Eastern Asia's NICs, marked to varying degrees by fragmented and weak indigenous classes that allowed ruling coalitions in which the military and bureaucracy often controlled state apparatuses. By such activities as coaxing foreign investors, ensuring ample quantities of scientific and engineering labor power, and offering a generous tax policy, the state in Singapore has played a key role in the country's "free market" economy. To industrialize and attain upward mobility beginning with the IDL and during the NIDL, as well as to manage the GDLP, the state in Eastern Asia has deliberately gotten the prices "wrong" through incentives and subsidies to local businesses (Amsden 1989; Gereffi and Fonda 1992).

To adjust to globalization, some states have adopted an EPZ or a *maquiladora* (assembly plants as subsidiaries or subcontracting firms for the manufacture of exports) strategy for gaining access to external capital and creating jobs. An important aspect of neoliberal regionalism, this globalizing trend is on the rise. Data collected by Jeffrey Hart (1995) indicate that by 1984, seventy-nine EPZs were functioning in thirty-five countries; by 1989, the number of zones reached 200, employing more than 1.5 million workers, with another one hundred EPZs being built. In 1990, Mexico alone operated 1,938 *maquiladora* factories; 68 percent of the labor force was women—a reversal of the male/female ratio in nationwide manufacturing. As a consequence of the rapid and unregulated growth of these industries, environmental problems include congestion in border towns, unmet demand for services such as the supply of clean water, and the pollution of rivers. Nonetheless, zone-based strategies of managing globalization are expanding, albeit differently in various regions.

The state has also taken a hand in reconfiguring labor processes, sometimes through repression, partly to keep down the cost of labor, and also, as in Japan, by encouragement of experimentation with the "just-in-time" manufacturing system. Calling for synchronized and continual supplies to reduce storage and overhead costs, this method can reduce the size of the labor force otherwise required to maintain production levels. The leading economic power in the Asia-Pacific region, Japan has exported its "just-in-time" system to neighboring countries, demonstrating that regional hierarchies can contour patterns of labor supply within various zones of the global economy and exercise transnational influence over the bargaining power of workers.

Regional hierarchies form patterns of *inner globalization* and *outer globalization*. The formula in establishing the zones of inner globalization is to use small-scale, decentralized negotiations among fewer parties committed to locally based and relatively informal arrangements, rather than to involve the cumbersome and time-consuming bureaucracies of macroregional groupings (Lim 1995). In Asia, there are attempts to employ both the inner and outer strategies and, also, to combine them. Whereas globalization constrains choice, to a large extent circumscribing the state's policy options and responses from labor, the inner variant is inward-looking and places greater emphasis on the regional market; the other configuration's outward focus seeks to reap maximum benefit from the world market. Inner globalization enhances interactions within a region and may divert transactions from without, but an open globalizing policy may, in fact, limit regionalism.

The Asian regional division of labor (ARDL) varies by industry and sector within a highly stratified hierarchy: Japan; China, together with the other areas comprising the "Greater China Economic Zone" (built on extensive kinship networks linking the southern provinces of Guangdong and Fujian to investors in Hong Kong, Macao, and Taiwan, with their ties to the other powerful Chinese business communities overseas); the rest of ASEAN; and South Korea. The economic growth associated with the Japanese-led "flying geese" mode of regional integration, involving countries at quite different levels of development, suggests a hierarchy and tiers of production systems variously penetrating global markets in diverse branches of industry (see Henderson 1989 for a study of the semiconductor industry; Doner 1991 on automobiles; Dixon 1991; and Machado 1997).[1] While the ARDL developed partly in response to different labor costs, today subregions play an important role as intermediaries between transnational corporations and the supply of cheap labor. Two "global cities" in the ARDL, Singapore and Hong Kong, are regional hubs for concentrations of direct foreign investment. In an attempt to overcome limitations stemming from economies of scale, before Hong Kong became part of China in 1997, these regional centers, both city-states, adopted a strategy of "twinning," a type of coordination that is

[1] The term "flying geese" was introduced and employed as a model by Kaname Akamatsu (1962 in the English translation) to explain the product cycles of industries in economic development, say, from textiles to chemical industries and then to steel and automobiles. This metaphor is used to describe a V-shaped curve, with a leader in front and others following in an orderly fashion, as with the shifting of electronics production from Japan to the four tigers (Hong Kong, Singapore, South Korea, and Taiwan) and, then, besides Singapore, to the other ASEAN countries and China. Notwithstanding the appeal of this image, the notion that countries advance sequentially through stages with specific product and technological characteristics does not fully capture the changing dynamics within Eastern Asia. Spatially and organizationally, this formation is, in fact, marked not by a sequential mode but a shifting hierarchy of production, with different linkages to Japanese markets and American innovation (see Bernard and Ravenhill 1995). I owe this point to Rajah Rasiah.

but one form of linkage. Another blend of state initiative and private entrepreneurship, mentioned earlier, is the concept of a growth triangle, or a growth polygon, composed of nodes in different countries in Eastern Asia (mapped in chapter 8).

In terms of outer globalization, today there is considerable hostility to the formation of exclusionary trading blocs. Out of a commitment to *liberal multilateralism*, Japan is reluctant to support measures that bolster regional economic alliances, and favors a policy of de facto economic integration with limited formalization (as for example, with the East Asian Economic Caucus, or EAEC). From a liberal perspective, multilateralism may be defined as an "institutionalized form which coordinates relations among three or more states on the basis of 'generalized' principles of conduct" (Ruggie 1992, 571, building on Keohane 1990). Even including scholars like Ruggie (1993), who reject an orthodox realist interpretation and give credence to an "extranational realm," the prevailing paradigm in academic journals on international relations acknowledges, yet fails to theorize, the role of civil societies and social movements in multilateralism and, therefore, is of limited use in explaining the extent to which economic globalization reinforces or undermines the neoliberal order. Quite clearly, globalization suggests the need for global economic management, but existing international institutions were designed to coordinate a system of nation-states in which each state was meant to be sovereign over its own domestic economy (Emmerij 1992, 8). There is thus an inherent disjuncture between economic globalization and international institutions, establishing the potential for a transformation of global governance.

An alternative concept of multilateralism stems from both the notion that as the process of globalization is now unfolding, no one can be held accountable for the direction of events in the world economy, and a normative preference for inclusiveness, or empowerment, of less privileged groups in the restructuring of global institutions. *Transformative multilateralism* therefore implies the articulation of nonstate forces in the process of international organization. In this sense, Robert Cox views multilateralism as "a commitment to maximum participation in a dialogue among political, social, economic, and cultural forces as a means of resolving conflicts and designing institutional processes" (Cox 1991, 4). An emancipatory project, this approach calls for a significant opening to popular movements during a period of global restructuring. As yet, however, there is insufficient evidence to suggest that participatory channels are becoming both accessible to and genuinely representative of different elements in the GDLP.

What appears to be emerging in the near term is *truncated multilateralism*: not a world of competitive trading blocs, but of states locked into global regions in very different ways, trying to optimize their positions, and encountering resistance from social groups and movements adversely affected by globalization. Three regions—North America, Europe, and Eastern Asia—form "megamarkets," as well as dominate global production and trade. In 1994, they produced 87 percent of total world manufacturing output and generated 80 percent of world merchandise exports, up from the 1980 figures of 76 percent and 71 percent, respectively (Dicken 1998, 60). One of the principal challenges to this form of multilateralism in recent years is massive displacement of labor, an aspect of global restructuring that accentuates differences between sending and receiving countries.

## Interregional and Intraregional Migration

With the simultaneous restructuring of global production and global power relations, the growth poles of competitive participation in the GDLP are drawing large-scale and increasingly diverse imports of labor from their points of origin. Seeking to escape a marginalized existence and repression, population transfers within a stratified division of labor reflect a hierarchy among regions, countries, and different rates of industrialization.

While migratory flows are as old as history itself, the dimensions of the contemporary upsurge are staggering. The United Nations Population Fund (1993) estimates that there are at least 100 million international migrants living outside the countries in which they were born. Their annual remittances to families at home amount to $66 billion, more than all foreign development assistance from governments. By 1987, New York City alone had 2.6 million foreign-born residents, representing 35 percent of the city's total population. A 1991 projection predicted that by the year 2000, the immigrant population (foreign-born and second generation) would account for more than 50 percent of the city's population (Sassen 1991, 316). Europe is also one of the areas particularly vexed by numerous new streams of migration, as well as countless asylum-seekers. According to the United Nations Economic Commission for Africa, 30 percent of Africa's skilled workforce was living in Europe in 1987. It is estimated that today, one out of eighteen Africans resides outside his or her country of origin (Keller 1993). Among European countries, Germany is host to the largest number of foreigners—5.2 million. Next is France with 3.6 million, followed by Britain with 1.8 million, and Switzerland with 1.1 million, or 16.3 percent of that country's population (Kamm 1993). As will be detailed in the next chapter, but important to point out in this context, what is new about this influx of migrants is the direction of flows from sending to receiving countries, as well as the spatial dispersion of growth poles, forming a *distinctive territorial division of labor*.

Although market power is the galvanizing force in the extensive movement of peoples from their homelands to other areas of work and settlement, this propellant is not merely a by-product of a structural tension between capital and labor. To be sure, capital is forming large unregulated markets, and labor is less capable of transnational reorganization. Capital is increasingly globalized, but trade unions still imagine their identities primarily in national terms. With calls for "borderless solidarity" and for the eventual establishment of regional trade union structures (Lambert 1992), international solidarity is an ever important motif, but the nation-state remains a key point of reference.

One effect of a global restructuring of the division of labor and power, however, is to fragment labor into different identities. The salience of class thus lies in its integration with nonclass categories. At issue are the interactions of production and the formation of multiple identities. Insofar as employers exercise vast control over the conditions of labor, identities are very largely constructed in the realm of leisure—i.e, in the community or household—where work experiences are given meaning. Often, activities such as sports, neighborhood associations, or festivals provide the milieu for the formation of identities. In this sense, a changing GDLP is situated at the crossroads of class and cultural differences. The regulation of migrant labor is performed not only by the state and formal multilateral processes, but also by informal monocultural and multicultural mechanisms.

The presence of distinct immigrant cultures has posed problems for the identity of a number of host countries. In France, the immigration issue became highly politicized in the 1960s and 1970s, when it became evident that waves of laborers were of decidedly different origins from those of their predecessors. Not only did the duration of stay increase, but workers also brought their families, settled, and produced second-generation immigrants, many of whom do not conform to a national identity imagined as a unitary French culture impervious to race and ethnicity. In fact, new elements of the French population who maintain their own languages, religious traditions, dress codes, and dietary practices encounter employment opportunities restricted to persons of indigenous culture or to those who have assimilated local culture (Zinniker 1993).

So, too, immigration is central to the question of identity in Germany. After 1945, Germans invented a myth of "cultural cohesiveness" to replace "racial cohesiveness" as a defining identity. This imagery was not problematic as long as the original guestworker system brought in a modest number of foreigners from southern Europe to provide cheap manual labor for the German economic miracle. The idea of "Germanness"—ethnic and cultural homogeneity—is a myth that is still widely embraced, though contested, and one that cannot measure up to the test of history. In fact, German culture is an accretion of polyglot European influences. For instance, many residents of the Ruhr area are thoroughly assimilated but directly descended from Poles who came to work in the mines in the nineteenth century (Wettern 1993).

Setting aside the question of the veracity of identity, a series of wildcat strikes among foreign workers in 1973 made it clear that Germany would have to invest substantially in housing and education for migrant workers and their families. A supposedly disposable labor reserve emerged as long-term residents. As the Swiss author and playwright Max Frisch said of the receiving countries, "We asked for workers, but human beings came" (as quoted in George 1992, 123).

A naturalization program would require a redefinition of German citizenship, which is inherited from one's parents (*jus sanguinis*) and is not based on a person's place of birth (*jus soli*). Hence, only children of at least one German parent are legally entitled to German citizenship. Excluded from this rule are the descendants of "ethnic Germans" who settled in Eastern Europe in the eighteenth century, a group persecuted after World War II, and since 1980, some members of the second generation (sons and daughters of migrants). Many new arrivals from the east have few or no ties to Germany, but are thus able to circumvent the stringent regulations applied to other immigrants, including guestworkers' children born in Germany. The maxim that "Germany is not a country of immigration" means that some Germans even consider naturalized immigrants still to be Italians, Greeks, or Turks. They may have resided in Germany for all of their lives, may speak only German, but they are nonetheless viewed as outsiders (Wettern 1993).

Notwithstanding a multicultural workforce, monoculturalism remains the dominant identity among Germans. To be sure, there have been public debates about multiculturalism, particularly during the 1980s, and the new government (a coalition of Social Democrats and the Greens) installed in 1998 has prepared a far-reaching proposal on migration reform. Despite this emphasis on broadening access to citizenship, thoroughgoing assimilation is a possible route to employment but still does not guarantee equal access to a job, because multiculturalism would require a reinvention of German identity.

What directly impinges on the lives of migrants is the informalization of labor supply and the emergence of new linkages between North and South. Smuggling networks and international gangs have become important conduits largely outside the reach of multilateral regimes. In the chains connecting the United States and Mexico, a "coyote" escorts clandestine entrants across the border. Highly sophisticated, illegal systems of labor supply actively recruit potential migrants, some of whom slip into the United States while others remain in servitude in Mexico, often in brothels where Central American women are forced to pay off the coyotes.

Working underground, especially if they do not speak the language of the receiving country or lack specialized skills, illegal immigrants typically subsist in the informal economy—e.g., sweatshops, peddling, gypsy taxicabs, and industrial homework. A burgeoning illegal market for low-cost labor provides entry-level jobs through family and communal networks. Meanwhile, in the smaller towns and villages of the sending countries, migration has had a profound impact. In a Polanyian sense, the extension of the labor market tears the social fabric and inserts new polarities between those who receive remittances and can now purchase a variety of consumer goods and those who do not have such largess. In countries with a large portion of the male population holding jobs overseas, a nationwide shortage of workers boosts salaries but also makes the lives of countless people more desperate and deprived. The separation of families, a generation of orphans, and the introduction of AIDS into rural areas by returning emigrants are but some of the tangible consequences of a changing division of labor. Enmeshed in a complex structure of dependence, migrant workers and their families are commodities like other commodities bought and sold on a global market, and are thus one part of a chain of commodification in modern capitalism.

### Global Commodity Chains

Labor flows are integral links in global commodity chains, serving as rough locators of position in geoeconomic structures. As originally defined by Terence Hopkins and Immanuel Wallerstein (1986, 159), a commodity chain is "a network of labor and production processes, whose end result is a finished commodity." By tracing these chains, one can delimit a division of labor and the transformation of production systems. For each commodity, one focuses on different nodes from distribution to marketing, production, and the supply of raw material. These chains not only join multiple production processes, but also reflect the totality of production relations in an extended social division of labor.

About commodity chains, a theme that bears on subsequent chapters, I have little to say at this juncture, not because this level is less important than the others, but because it has been usefully explored elsewhere. Other authors have provided detailed studies of the organization and geography of commodity chains in a variety of industries (shipbuilding, garments and apparel, footwear, automobiles, and so on), and I will not rehearse their work here (see, most notably, Gereffi and Korzeniewicz, 1990, 1994; searching questions raised by Whitley 1996; and for a critical evaluation, Dicken, Kelly, Olds, and Yeung 1999). There is no need to belabor the point that from production to consumption, the interlinking of commodities is an increasingly important aspect of globalization. Empirical research shows the diverse ways in which the evolution of networks of complex industrial, commercial, and financial ties has created distinctive nodes that link raw material supply, manufacturing operations, and trade flows into commodity chains in an increasingly integrated global economy. These chains cut across the geographic and political boundaries of nation-states, and are explained in part by social and cultural patterns.

### Cultural Networks

Transnational linkages are essentially stateless and held together not only by flows of commodities but also by marriage, clans, and dialects—in short, a common culture. Indeed, the impact of culture is perhaps the most neglected factor in division of labor theory (Munck 1988, 101). What is often overlooked is that class ties are formed by both impersonal economic forces and shared beliefs and values; lives are shaped and meanings are formed in distinctive cultural contexts. Hence, class is overlaid by racial, ethnic, and sexual divisions of labor. With the impetus toward globalization, cultural responses to the expansion of the market provide intersubjective meanings and intermediate inequalities arising from a changing division of labor, as illustrated below.

There are varied manifestations of regional and global networks in which culture and the division of labor are intertwined. A notable example is the Chinese transnational division of labor, a vitalizing force in the remarkable rates of growth experienced by Eastern Asian economies in recent decades. A powerful regional network—an informal, though pervasive, grouping—comprises the combined wealth of forty million overseas Chinese in Southeast Asia, estimated at $200 billion, the worth of Hong Kong's seven million residents (another $50 billion), Taiwan, and the People's Republic of China (PRC) (Sender 1991). It is estimated that Sino-capitalists, who constitute only 6 percent of ASEAN's population (excluding Brunei), own an estimated 70 percent of the equity of listed companies not controlled by government and foreigners (Heng 1994, 24). Taiwan now represents the world's fourteenth largest economy and commands one of the biggest accumulations of cash reserves—at present, more than $80 billion—of any country in the world. What the World

**TABLE 2.2**
GDP Comparisons for Four Economies:
Market Price and Standard International Price Estimates
(trillions of U.S. dollars)

| Country | At market price | | At standard international prices | | |
|---|---|---|---|---|---|
| | 1991 | 2002 | 1990[a] | 2002[b] | Per capita income (US$) |
| Chinese Economic Area | 0.6 | 2.5 | 2.5 | 9.8 | 7,300 |
| United States | 5.5 | 9.9 | 5.4 | 9.7 | 36,000 |
| Japan | 3.4 | 7.0 | 2.1 | 4.9 | 37,900 |
| Germany | 1.7 | 3.4 | 1.3 | 3.1 | 39,100 |

*Source:* World Bank, *Global Economic Prospects and the Developing World* (New York: Oxford University Press, 1993), p. 67.

[a] The source of these estimates is World Bank, *World Development Report 1992* (except Taiwan, China). Estimates vary widely, however. The International Comparison Program's (ICP's) estimate for China in 1990 may be conservative. For instance, the ICP estimate for 1985 was $2.6 trillion for China alone.

[b] Per capita figures are in parentheses, expressed in thousands of U.S. dollars. In making the ICP projections, it is simply assumed that GDP at ICP will increase at a similar percentage rate as GDP at market prices. This growth rate is an upper bound for the CEA because ICPs tend to rise more slowly than market prices at official exchange rates as relative income per capita increases (reflecting the higher relative price of services in high-income economies).

Bank refers to as the Chinese Economic Area (CEA or China, including Hong Kong, and Taiwan) has had an average growth rate of more than 7 percent a year since 1962, and by the year 2002, will have a GDP ranking ahead of that of France, Italy, and Britain and approaching the United States' output (World Bank 1993, 66–67). With PRC growth in GNP exceeding 15 percent in some six-month periods, there have even been fears that market reforms have generated a runaway train—an overheated economy that the state cannot cool without considerable political ferment (Walker 1993). Table 2.2 compares the CEA's economic size—the "fourth growth pole" of the global economy—to that of other leading economies.

This structure, fueled by a Chinese transnational division of labor, originated with various waves of migration from the mainland to neighboring territories and Southeast Asia. One of the important functions served by Hong Kong was to assemble Chinese emigrants for shipment to other areas as contract laborers. Singapore provided a transshipment point for most workers destined for Southeast Asia's plantations and tin mines. When the Chinese settlers had established themselves in receiving countries, they filled a vacuum in trade, marketing, commerce, and service occupations. The indigenous populations had access to land, but not to capital and growing international markets. Despite perceptions identifying ethnicity with particular types of economic activity (namely, stereotypes of middlemen), the Chinese minority established superior access to capital and credit through family associations, dialect groups, clans, and places of origin in China. Throughout Southeast Asia, Chinese big businesses have dominated the national economies, notwithstanding state assistance for indigenous entrepreneurs, and have constituted family firms traditionally controlled by one man or one family. Their formation and economic role reflect Chinese immigrant and minority status in receiving countries, for these groups and associations in China exist mainly for rural-urban migrants in commercial centers (Lim 1983, 2–3).

Once settled, "ethnic Chinese" in Southeast Asia sent funds home through remittance brokers. Typically, brokers aggregated these monies and transferred them through Singapore and Hong Kong, which had the sole free-exchange market for remittances after World War II. Those in the remittance business diversified their holdings, using the funds they collected to purchase goods for export to China and channeling the proceeds from sales to pay off the remittances (Wu and Wu 1980, 91–92). Clan, and especially linguistic, ties provided the channels for funneling the funds, with capital moving through the network in circuitous ways.

Major changes in the circuits of capital reflect structural shifts in the economies of Asia related to the relative decline of entrepôt trade and the rise of domestic manufacturing. The drop in entrepôt trade led to a reduction in the activities of import-export agents acting as middlemen between the mainland and Southeast Asia. There followed the development of international financial centers in Hong Kong and Singapore, which became conduits of funds for foreign investment as well as sources of capital for other developing countries. In Southeast Asia and Hong Kong, "ethnic Chinese" own and manage many banks, as well as their foreign subsidiaries in Japan, the United States, and elsewhere. Flush with refugee capital and short-term funds parked for placement, these banks are able to perform vital services for their Chinese customers and have made them attractive partners for financial and trading institutions in the United States, Japan, and Europe (Wu and Wu 1980, 90–107; Redding 1990; Hamilton 1991).

Faced with the political challenge of economic nationalism by local ruling classes, large-scale Chinese traders dispersed control of their firms among relatives, trusts, and shelf companies in such locales as Panama, Vanuatu, and Liberia. There emerged a labyrinthine complexity of family interests and numerous cross-shareholdings (for a detailed mapping of the extensive holdings of the Kuok family, for instance, see Cottrell 1986;

Heng 1997; and Tanzer 1997). Chinese tycoons, as they are known, have also established myriad joint ventures with foreign interests, many of them "ethnic Chinese" in other countries. The business ties of the Kuok family, for example, emanate from the group's offices incorporated in Singapore and Hong Kong to all of Southeast Asia, Fiji, China, and Australia (Heng 1992, 131). Another strategy for repelling the challenge of economic nationalism has been to form alliances with non-Chinese capital in ways acceptable to local power brokers. Thus, a new generation of Chinese business leaders has sought political patronage in countries such as Malaysia while maintaining communal business ties at home. The new breed identifies closely with the interests and needs of the Malay capitalist class and the imperatives of a Malay-dominated state. The two-pronged strategy of building ties to Malaysian and non-Malaysian capital is based on a realization not only that political alliances are crucial to capital accumulation, but also that the patrons of Chinese clients can be submerged by changing political currents (Heng 1992, 142).

Similarly, in Indonesia, following a number of anti-Sinitic riots, Chinese businessmen have sought protection by the authorities and have aligned their economic fortunes with those of the local ruling class (Robison 1986, 317). To reduce their risks as a politically vulnerable minority at home, many overseas Chinese families are also remitting investment capital to their provinces of origin in the "motherland" not only for sentimental reasons, but also because of economic performance there.

With a combined GDP of almost $400 billion, greater China emerged during the 1980s when Hong Kong and Taiwan, bolstered by investment from "ethnic Chinese" around the Pacific Rim, moved their manufacturing bases to the People's Republic in order take advantage of cheap labor, low rent, and an enormous potential market. Opening to external capital, Guangdong Province integrated its economy with that of Hong Kong, many of whose residents or forebears emigrated from there and speak the regional dialect, Cantonese. In the provincial capital of Guangzhou, efforts are under way to establish contacts among the twenty million overseas Cantonese all over the world (almost 40 percent of an estimated fifty-five million Chinese outside the mainland). With sixty-three million people, Guangdong itself is more populous than any European country except Germany, and has increasingly operated as a single entity with the six million people of Hong Kong, even before the latter officially became part of China in 1997. Guangdong also draws on the neighboring provinces of Guangxi, Hunan, and Sichuan for much of its labor supply, raw materials, and markets. Urban areas in Guangdong attract large numbers of Chinese laborers looking for work and wages, which are low in comparison to the pay in Hong Kong and Taiwan but exceed those on state farms and state-run factories (Sun 1992).

In one of Guangdong's consumer electronics factories, for example, the average take-home pay of its four thousand workers is 4,000 yuan per month (about $72) or twice the average pay of a worker in a state-run factory. Producing remote-control toy cars for Hasbro, telephones for Radio Shack, and hair dryers for Conair, this factory is one of the 30,000 enterprises in Guangdong managed by Hong Kong businessmen; together, these firms employ nearly four million workers. The factory noted above is part of the Grande Group—a microcosm of greater China. Most of the production is on the mainland, R&D is carried out in Taiwan, and the group's managers and corporate headquarters are based in Hong Kong (Sun 1992).

In a classic Polanyian pattern, the expansion of the market is a disruptive and polarizing force in China—a country of 1.5 billion people with the world's largest surplus labor pool and without an effective framework for regulating mass migration to booming microregions along the coast. With FDI concentrated in the coastal region, socioeconomic differences with the vast interior are widening. From 1981 to 1988, the gap between gross industrial output in the coastal provinces and the nine western provinces grew by 2.7 times. Young women from all over China flock to the south to work in female-intensive industries such as prostitution; some become mistresses to foreign entrepreneurs or local millionaires, easily identified by their fancy luxury cars and associations with thugs crossing the border into Hong Kong. Income inequality, criminal activities, environmental degradation, the incidence of venereal disease, and fear of AIDS are on the rise. In southern China, there is nonetheless a long tradition of redressing grievances, peasant unrest, and rebellion when disparities grow too far out of line with what is politically tolerable. Perhaps approaching the second phase of a Polanyian double movement, an evolving and countervailing source of power represents a potential challenge to Beijing.

While Guangdong attracts migrants, Taiwan faces serious labor shortages and greater worker militancy, which prompts national capital to invest more rapidly in the People's Republic, and following Singapore, to import foreign workers. Transcending the microregion and subregion, further extension of Chinese-owned or -controlled corporations includes syndication and cooperation in joint ventures with Western and Japanese capital. While clan and especially linguistic ties continue to reinforce business interests among "ethnic Chinese," traditional family linkages are increasingly integrated with professional management practices. Generational divergence within the Chinese networks has challenged the customary, intuitive style of the aging patriarchs. Modern English-speaking, MBA-toting managers, many of them financial technocrats, reflect the tenets of liberal-economic globalization transmitted by business and law schools not in their ancestral villages, but in Western countries where they now invest, trade, and borrow.

Clearly, Chinese culture mediates the institutional arrangements in the regional and global divisions of labor. Broadly speaking, it is an adaptive, flexible, and dynamic culture. It is responsive to market forces, the requirements for business success, necessary interactions with the local population, and transnational opportunities. It is also employed selectively as a business strategy where it is advantageous to demonstrate minority characteristics to mobilize an investable surplus and engage in trade. But the use of cultural identity is not limited to the minority community. For the general population, intersubjective meanings attached to the interactions between culture and economic activities supersede or mask their objective significance, promoting conflicts within the ethnic and racial divisions of labor—to a large extent, a transnational phenomenon in Eastern Asia—and leading to state policies that only contradict stated government goals and accentuate societal tensions (Lim 1983, 20–23).

## CONCLUSION

The theoretical framework established here is a three-stage historical sequence in theory and practice: the classical Smithian/Ricardian IDL, identifying the importance of the specialization of function and the comparative advantage of trading products for which costs are relatively low; the NIDL, accounting for the spread of manufacturing to developing countries; and the GDLP, showing the intricacy of distinctive regional processes in their institutional and informal aspects, interregional and intraregional migratory flows, the complex web of commodity chains among global producers and buyers and sellers across a number of territorial jurisdictions, and the ways in which cultural networks lubricate these chains to facilitate flows of capital and labor and ease (or sometimes heighten) tensions.

These division-of-labor theories are a valuable tool for examining global restructuring, especially because they delimit major trends that constitute the changing social geography of capitalism. However, classical theory (notwithstanding Marx's concern for the division of labor) and its neo variant are economistic, underrate the role of culture, and fail to allow for the possible reversal or interruption of contemporary restructuring. The IDL and NIDL interpretations do not offer a theory of transformation. The future is not best understood as more of the present—straight-line projections—for change in a post-Cold War world is a spasmodic process. Neither the economism of the IDL and NIDL theories nor the political primacy argument ingrained in realist and neorealist approaches to liberal multilateralism are an accurate guide to an emerging world order. The problem with primacy arguments is that they presuppose a separation between an interstate system grounded in a territorial division among sovereign powers and an economic arena in which divisions are mediated by the market. By demarcating politics and economics as separate spheres, the dominant conceptualization of globalization rooted in liberal economic theory serves the interests of the beneficiaries of an expanded market. In the conventional manner of thinking, the disruptive and socially polarizing effects of globalization are obscured. The challenge is to provide an alternative to the terms of reference employed by the torchbearers of economic globalization.

In the search for alternatives, and beyond the other theories, the GDLP incorporates the concept of power. Although power is a multifaceted construct assigned a large variety of meanings, the power element in the global division of labor and power involves both physical components, such as aggregates of resources, which are measurable (e.g., GNP), and more subtle dimensions, including legitimacy, trust, and community. In other words, as a feature of the GDLP, power is a combination of objective and subjective factors, and one should not underestimate the efficacy and potential of the latter, especially when the ideology of globalization has become an ascendant force in world order. The GDLP thus joins a concept of structural power—but not the sort of structuralism that may prompt the thought that power is everywhere in social life and beyond escape (the promiscuous use of the concept sometimes found, for example, in Foucault 1980)—and an agential view of power relations, displayed here in the downside risks of globalization for those who get hurt by it and by the voices of actors engaged in resistance politics.

Politically, globalization does not sideline the state but, rather, conduces it to accommodate domestic policies to the pressures generated by transnational capital. State initiatives represent attempts to maneuver and achieve *national* mobility within the GDLP, often by seeking to build productive capacity and to gain a technological edge. In the fastest-growing subregional economy of the 1980s and well into the 1990s—Eastern Asia—state policies were fashioned to establish an enabling environment (including R&D centers, industrial parks, nodes for information technology, and the like) so as to move toward higher value-added activities. Nevertheless, there is a disjuncture between the state and transnational economic forces, for the former aggregates the energies and synergies of human activity at a political and territorial level that does not correspond to evolving flows of labor, capital, and technology. Links are increasingly developing between subregions promoted by states and the global economy. Formed by parts of states, as in "the third Italy" (the dynamic prov-

inces in the country's northeast spurred by their flexible enterprises, innovative capacity, and primarily local government involvement) and in
Baden-Württemberg, or by economic patterns that overlap state boundaries, such as in the cross-border zone radiating across the Straits of Ma-
lacca, subregions fostered by states hook into and seek to derive advantage from market expansion in the GDLP. In this configuration, however,
the seeds of conflict are sometimes sown by leaders who contest the reality of globalization and either try to fan the flames of economic nationalism or build competitive trading blocs (Mittelman 1994). Another response is to accept the brute fact that no country or region can escape the
effects of globalization, and different strategies are adopted to manage
these processes and adjust to a multilevel system in which the state is not
necessarily declining but has become one of several actors (as suggested in
the section on the ontology of globalization, pp. 8–11). Accordingly, it is
necessary to define interests in terms other than the imagined "nation"
and avoid primarily defensive responses. *Global regions* may then seek to
navigate the currents and ride the tide of market expansion in a GDLP
(Sadler 1992).

As the GDLP itself changes, the role of each region and state varies.
Quite clearly, globalization is an uneven process, forming what
Durkheim might have termed *supra-organic solidarity.* At the world
level, there are multiple structures of specialization binding and yet acting
as *spacers* among zones of the global economy. Given the disparities between global regions and marginalized regions, there are different globalization scenarios. While the former are riding the waves of globalization,
the latter are driven by its currents and have lost or are losing control. No
longer socially embedded in a national political economy, market forces
are increasingly unaccountable and disembedded, less dependent on the
social structures that gave rise to them.

Although Polanyi (1945) conceived market expansion as a global phenomenon, he also believed that regionalism offers an alternative to the
universalist attempt "to make the world safe for the gold standard." Contrary to a universalist conception of capitalism based on the principles of
liberal economy, the regional characteristics of globalization suggest another strategy for market societies. Not a panacea, regionalism may be a
remedy for the by-products of the utopian conception of the market.
Within the megastructure of globalization, the adoption of new regional
instruments for managing large-scale flows of labor, economic noncoop-
eration, and intolerant nationalism may be a way toward achieving social
justice. Moving beyond market-driven, private-sector-led forms of integration, advocates of the social market argue that regionalizing programs
can be developed to curb the antisocial tendencies of transnational capital. They conjecture that regionalism has the potential to provide space

for fresh forces to spring up, align, and look more to a future of post-globalization.

At the end of the day, does this emancipatory possibility constitute anything other than a utopian vision? Unlike the world economy of the 1930s, the raw material of Polanyi's analysis, the contemporary form of disembedded globalization clearly defies his ideal—though the future remains open-ended—of re-embedding the economy in society. To the extent that economic globalization congeals the material power of capitalism on a world scale, the re-embedding of society today implies a thoroughgoing reordering of the world economy (major dimensions of which are examined in subsequent chapters). In the present-day GDLP, the asymmetry between capital and labor will not be resolved by the imminent unity of a global working class. Not only is the bourgeoisie of the world uniting more rapidly and more effectively than is the proletariat, but also labor is predominantly particularistic and local. Working-class identity is not primordial, but one of several mobile identities deriving from the racial, ethnic, religious, and sexual divisions of labor. Forging a political culture of resistance—a counterhegemony—and organizing a countermovement draw on the salience of class and aim toward a reinvention of the interactions between production and identity.

Thus far, I have suggested that the region provides the starting point for analyzing a changing GDLP, for it is the site of distinctive divisions of labor and a major arena for large-scale transfers of population. Although in another context, the discussion will detail the new regionalism, let us first turn to the relationship between globalization and migration, which permits a focus on regional flows.

# CHAPTER 3

# Globalization and Migration

LARGE-SCALE transfers of population are a long historical process common to all regions of the world, but in recent decades the global restructuring of production has accentuated differences between receiving and sending countries, drawing massive imports of labor primarily from Africa, Asia, and Latin America to the advanced capitalist areas. Migratory flows from the South are increasingly diverse, for they include new "birds of passage," such as elements of North Africa's middle strata fearing Islamic resurgence and environmental refugees propelled by natural disasters. Meanwhile, the global restructuring of power has brought an influx of migrants from Eastern Europe and the former Soviet Union to Western Europe, North America, Israel, Australia, and elsewhere. Competition between immigrants from the South and the East reflects the interrelationship of the restructuring of global production and global power relations.

The changes in migration patterns are not merely matters of individual choice, but rather reveal structural factors beyond the control of individuals. The displacement of labor is best understood as a movement that both shapes and is constitutive of a restructuring of the global political economy.

Flows of human capital are linked to a hierarchical system of production and power. Increasing specialization and spatial dispersion are part of a shift toward a globalizing economy, a consequence of which is the redistribution of human capital. An area's position in the GDLP and its forms of specialization establish terms for the exit and entry of migrant labor. Powered by technological change, the more dynamic economies act as magnets, attracting mobile resources from their points of origin (Griffin and Khan 1992, 43, 47). These interactions, of course, have profound implications for distribution, inequality, and social justice on a world scale.

The objectives of this chapter are to examine the link between global restructuring and migration, as well as to propose a framework for explaining it. To apply the concept of the GDLP to global migration, I will suggest relationships among structural factors and note major trends. Next is a discussion of whether international regimes regulate migration, and the conclusion points the way toward a reformulation of liberal economic theory.

## DIVISIONS AND REDIVISIONS OF LABOR

Although the extensive movement of peoples from their homelands to other areas of work and settlement has been an enduring feature of world history since the 1500s, the patterns and scope of migration have changed dramatically. With the expansion of European capital from 1500 to 1815, peoples from the developed zones of Northern and Western Europe emigrated to the Americas and parts of Africa and Asia. Concurrent to colonizing migration was the expulsion of slaves, indentured workers, convicts, and dissidents. These flows disrupted indigenous communities, fostered new multiracial and multicultural societies, and formed a basis for tethering different societies to the international division of labor.

The Industrial Revolution extended capital overseas, altering the supply of and demand for resources, including labor. The primary movements of population between 1815 and 1914 included 60 million Europeans leaving for the Americas, Oceania, East and South Africa; about 10 million Russians settling in Siberia and Central Asia; 1 million Southern Europeans going to North Africa; 12 million Chinese moving to East and Southern Asia; and 1.5 million Indians finding homes in Southeast Asia, East Africa, and South Africa. In the interwar period, the depression and restrictive immigration policies substantially reduced transfers of population. After 1945, however, the number of international migrants rapidly increased. From 50 million immigrants in 1989, the world total doubled in 1992, representing 2 percent of the world population.

Migrants are unevenly spread across the globe, with the largest numbers, some thirty-five million, in sub-Saharan Africa, and another fifteen million in Asia and the Middle East. Strikingly, a substantial portion of these people remain within their region of origin. An estimated twenty-three million represent "internally displaced" persons, and the bulk of the world's seventeen million officially registered refugees and asylum seekers stay in the region where they were born (United Nations Population Fund 1993, 7, 8, 15). Taking into account other migration streams, most international migration today is within—not between—regions (Keely 1992, 1).

Of the interregional flows, the transfers are especially from the South to the North, although movements within the South and within the North have remained significant (Segal and Marston 1989, 36–41). Also, a large portion of South-to-South migration becomes South-to-North flows. Given both political and economic pressures, migrants (e.g., Salvadorans) leave home because of fear of violence and in search of economic well-being, reach a second country (say, Mexico) where short-term jobs are available, and perceive better opportunities elsewhere (the United States).

For migrants from countries such as Guyana or the Leeward Islands, locales in the South (e.g., the Virgin Islands) are merely stopovers as the
newly arrived leapfrog from island to island along the Caribbean archi-
pelago on the way north.[1] There are also countries in the North (Italy and
Austria) that serve as way stations for migrants from the South and the
East. With the development of Southern Europe, Italy, Spain, and Greece
have become both transit areas and receiving countries.

Moreover, the levels of the intraregional flows are exceptional.[2] Although the large number of illegals makes it difficult to come up with
reliable data, studies by demographers and economists in the mid-1990s
put the figure for international migrants in East Asia at 2.6 million (Silverman 1996, 61). This figure, however, is dwarfed if one adds internal
migration, especially in the PRC since the breakup of the commune system in the late 1970s and the launching of the special economic zones
(SEZs) in the 1980s. Excluding movement within home districts, a 1996
projection of trends indicated that the number of internal migrants in
China would swell to 110 million in the year 2000 (Gilley 1996, 18). Not
only is the scale unparalleled in the region, but what is novel is the
speed of the movement of investment and the need for a flexible labor
force.

## PRODUCTION AND IDENTITY

This need can be seen globally and partly explained by the shift toward
post-Fordism, which, as noted, entails a more flexible, fragmented, and
decentralized system of production making use of a segmented and often
geographically dispersed labor force. The new model is based on greater
specialization—batch production in small firms linked through dense networks and niche marketing. Accompanying the movement from Fordism
to post-Fordism is a shift from vertical integration of production to vertical disintegration, especially as enterprises seek to establish distinct

[1] In addition to the classic elements of economic promise and proximity, long-established
West Indian and Hispanic communities in North American cities serve as magnets and
facilitators, furnishing family ties, legal aid, and places to hide. With its depressed economies, and subject to the influence of tourism and satellite television from the United States,
the Caribbean exports more of its people in percentage terms than does any other region.
Such ministates as St. Kitts and Nevis, Grenada, and Belize send 1 percent or 2 percent of
their nationals to the United States each year, transferring all of their population growth to
North American cities (Sassen 1991; French 1992).

[2] Whereas it is sometimes argued that contemporary levels of international migration do
not exceed the *percentages* of population in earlier years—notably, at the beginning of the
twentieth century in the United States—one must bear in mind that the 1989 world total of
50 million international migrants had doubled by 1992, the directions have changed, and
internal displacement must also be taken into account.

niches. Fordism is not defunct but based in different sectors of production, namely in low-skill services, such as fast food, and in various types of labor-intensive processes, sometimes in the peripheral (or export) zones of industrial systems. Although there is vast organizational diversity and no single post-Fordist model, these two emphases draw varied groups of migrants, primarily unskilled and semiskilled workers in the sectors dominated by Fordism and more defined skills in the post-Fordist sectors.

Closely related is technological innovation: a social process linking knowledge and production. Technology is inextricably connected to all phases of movement up the value chain, from labor-intensive to capital- and energy-intensive to technology-intensive processes in advanced countries; it is also integral to the devolution of labor-intensive, energy-intensive, and polluting operations to underdeveloped areas. Each phase of innovation entails job creation and loss, requiring diverse skills, incorporating new workers in the labor force, and driving others to search for different sources of employment.

An integral part of this restructuring process is the weakening of trade unions based in the old Fordist industries. The strength of organized labor has clearly declined in the West, and workers are docile in some other regions, notably so in some countries in Eastern Asia; however, this trend is not a universal phenomenon, as demonstrated by the militancy of trade unions in South Africa. While capital is forming large unregulated markets, labor is less capable of transnational reorganization. Capital is increasingly globalized, but labor unions and the collective rights of workers still primarily delimit their identity in terms of the nation-state. Alternative sources of identity—e.g., gender, race, ethnicity, and religion—are more prominent among new and the more segmented elements of the labor force. Moreover, low-paid, segmented employment has developed in zones formerly considered as core economies. Inasmuch as the core is where core activities—high-value-added operations—are spatially concentrated, the "peripheralization of the core" is evident in "putting out" in Manhattan and elsewhere. Migrant labor is prevalent in the Fordist sectors of the new production systems. The core-periphery concept, formerly used in a geographic sense, now requires rethinking in terms of social relations among groups engaged in the production process.

## INTERACTIONS

In this analytical framework, there are exchanges among the different elements—exchanges that reflect a hierarchical ranking of power. Some forms of technology flows take place within corporate, not geographical, space; technologies may be transferred within a corporation and are not the property of a "recipient" country. Capital flows to capital-abundant zones of the global economy, and labor follows the flow of capital. What effect does this labor flow have?

The World Bank and some liberal economists contend that labor mobility is a means of reducing income inequality worldwide. The bank argues that emigration helps to relieve population pressure, alleviates unemployment, funnels remittances to the country of origin, and may contribute to the diffusion of new ideas and technologies, either when skilled workers return home or through an exchange of information (World Bank 1990b, 93–94). However, the benefits of migration have been distributed unequally, to the advantage of the already more fortunate receivers. The emigration of skilled personnel to countries where skilled labor is abundant and where incomes are high increases international inequality. The negative flow of human capital from sending countries saves receiving countries the cost of reproducing a sector of their labor force (Griffin and Khan 1992, 57, 65–67).

Although the World Bank renders a valuable service by providing data on "net workers' remittances" by migrants' countries of origin (World Bank 1990b, 212–13), remittances are not a substitute for development. With the most vulnerable groups—the young and the elderly—at home, and a sizable portion of the productive labor force overseas, the system of remitting payments deepens the dependence of some societies (Segal 1992, 11–12). The question of utilization of remittances turns not only on balance of payments, as the World Bank would have it, but also on whether these funds are invested in directly productive activities. Research on the actual use of remittances in various regions shows substantial savings and investment in housing, land purchase, consumer goods, and repayment of personal debts. Data indicate that the bulk of the spending is on consumer items and luxury imports, causing inflationary pressures. Only a small fraction goes toward productive activities (Papademetriou 1988, 249–50).

Quite clearly, a continuing brain drain from capital-poor zones deprives these zones of a large share of their investment in the social reproduction of labor. This implies the extraction of educational services, as in the movement of Jamaican and Filipina nurses to U.S. and Canadian hospitals. The educated strata of disadvantaged zones can most easily migrate, but often these workers find only menial jobs in the more advanced zones. These strata can also prove to be better qualified by education and attitude for skilled employment in modern industry than are some of the semiskilled indigenous workers, a tension that may erupt in zones of immigration. However, when receiving countries shift their policies from favoring particular ethnic groups to emphasizing highly skilled immigrants, as did the United States and Canada, the result is not only a marked increase in the brain drain, but also a corresponding upsurge of illegal migration, drawing semiskilled along with unskilled workers. In this respect, a class analysis of migrants and the immigration policies of different states helps to explain the direction of flows of population. Typically, immigration policies include a system for recognizing professional qualifications, easing entry for groups such as physicians and engineers, and erecting barriers to the free flow of unskilled labor.

Apart from the loss of skilled and semiskilled labor, sending countries have long gained sustenance from the cheap labor of their citizens who are sojourners in receiving countries. Yet migration can detract from a healthy workforce, an essential ingredient of development, by producing changes in sexual behavior, often first encountered in the big cities and labor camps. Away from their family and lacking female companionship, young men are exposed to homosexual practices, as well as easy access to prostitutes and drugs. Migrants who have contracted AIDS return to rural communities and small towns at home and contribute to high infection rates in areas where, until recently, the virus had been unknown. The link between migration and AIDS, while evident, is clouded by stigma and denial.

All told, emigration accentuates the marginalization of zones primarily in the South: sub-Saharan Africa, much of the Caribbean, and enclaves in other regions. With a population of more than four hundred million people and a GDP the size of that of Belgium (a country of eight million people), sub-Saharan Africa is hampered by costs of production that are too high in comparison to those of other regions. Sub-Saharan Africa's transportation costs are exorbitant, and its skilled and educated middle-level labor force is relatively scarce. Although the continent is integrated into global financial markets through debt structures, and notwithstanding the heavy involvement of aid agencies, Africa has not participated fully in the global manufacturing system that has emerged in the last few decades and in the related expansion of export activities. Seeking to escape a marginalized existence, migrants are attracted by the growth poles of competitive participation in the GDLP. Paid jobs in manufacturing or service industries in other parts of the world are preferred to the battle for survival, civil strife, or wars at home.

Added to this, flows of military aid, arms sales, and lending from international financial institutions and transnational banks to the poor countries tie the latter more closely into the economic mechanisms and structures of control of the global financial and production systems. The obligations of debt service require these countries to impose austerity measures that fall most heavily on the socially vulnerable strata. Export-oriented development and structural adjustment policies deepen this pattern. The implementation of these policies often entails repression, which in turn produces a flow of political refugees. The distinction between political and economic refugees, used by receiving countries as a screening mechanism, obscures the fact that both categories of migrants have as their origin the same *globalizing of production relations.*

Although there are many types of voluntary and involuntary migrants (political refugees and asylum seekers, environmental refugees, professionals, legal workers, undocumented workers, and so forth), the lines of demarcation are increasingly blurred. The proximate causes of migration—civil unrest, ethnic and racial strife, and economic conflicts accompanied by marked inequality—are often combined. Determining causality requires a long view of history and of a zone's political and economic role in the GDLP. The key question is, How do local dynamics and globalized production merge and interpenetrate to shape migration patterns?

Whereas the answer to this question is historically contingent, a pertinent example of the interactions between local dynamics and globalized production is the expulsion of foreign workers from Nigeria in 1983. The history of Africa is replete with movements of population propelled by trade, conquest, slaving, natural disasters, and evangelization. The dispersion of Fulani-speaking peoples throughout the northern rim of West Africa is amply documented, as are the seasonal wanderings of herders (Arthur 1991, 65). In the postcolonial period, centers of industrial production attracted large-scale in-migration, with a substantial flow into Nigeria's oil fields and construction sites in the 1970s. Flush with foreign exchange earnings derived from the worldwide boom in oil prices, Nigeria sought to join the global manufacturing system by converting its new-found surpluses into export-oriented industrialization. Added to employment opportunities in manufacturing and petroleum industries, construction of the capital city of Abuja and the Kainji Dam served as magnets for both skilled and unskilled workers. Moreover, the establishment of universities and polytechnics in each state within Nigeria precipitated a brain drain of Ghanaian teachers eager to partake in Nigeria's prosperity.

When oil production dropped to 400,000 barrels in 1982, down from 2.3 million barrels in 1979, Nigerians felt the pinch of unemployment. Lagos came to regard noncitizens as competitors for jobs as well as a strain on the economy, and decided to retaliate for the 1969 expulsion of Nigerians from Ghana. In 1983, Nigeria ordered an estimated two million West Africans to leave the country within fourteen days. The repatriation of foreign workers to Ghana, Togo, Burkina Faso, and Chad entailed a massive displacement of labor, enforced by inspections of households in search of defaulting aliens, and emergency reception centers to help ease the human suffering (Arthur 1991, 72–77).

As evident in West Africa and other parts of the world, regionalism today signifies aggregations of political and economic power competing in the global political economy, with numerous interregional and intraregional flows of population. Heightened competition among and within regions, mediated by such micropatterns as ethnic and family networks, accelerates cross-flows of migrants, as again seen in the case of West Africa.

Not only do West African professionals, traders, and unskilled workers seek employment in Europe and North America, but population transfers within a stratified regional division of labor reflect a hierarchy among countries and different rates of industrialization. Major migrant-sending countries in West Africa are Mali, Niger, Chad, and Burkina Faso, all located in the Sahel and characterized by low levels of industrial production, high rates of illiteracy, and weak infrastructure. These countries have experienced deforestation, recurrent drought, substantial population pressure on cultivated land, and agricultural stagnation aggravated by unequal land tenure systems and lack of employment opportunities in the industrial sector.

The main stream of intraregional labor migration is from Sahel West Africa to coastal West Africa, especially to the more prosperous countries of Ivory Coast, Ghana, and Nigeria. Another stream of migration is taking place within coastal West Africa, where farm workers and industrial wage earners originate in the war-torn countries of Liberia and Sierra Leone, as well as in Ghana, and head for centers of export-oriented production, predominantly Ivory Coast and Nigeria (Arthur 1991, 75–77). The case of Ghana shows that some countries serve as areas of both origination and destination, making the distinction between sending and receiving countries an artificial one in the context of globalized production.

On the one hand, both globalization and regionalism weaken the state's ability to regulate the flow of labor across borders. The movement of undocumented workers between the United States and Mexico, for example, is almost unimpeded. On the other hand, the variation in migration policies and their consequences should not be underestimated. The state's exclusive power to grant citizenship, order repatriation, and delimit the social and political rights of noncitizens in their territories can cause (or prevent) an international crisis. There is marked variation in states' policies on asylum seekers, family reunification, and access to nationality. The interactions between immigration policies and migration flows demonstrate both the diminution and the continuing importance of state capacity.

The various spin-off effects of globalization in the context of migration and the restructuring of production include changing social structures and patterns of conflict, political instability, human rights achievements or abuses, and environmental impact. A marked consequence of globalized production is the feminization of labor in both old and new zones of economic development. From Asia's EPZs and Mexico's *maquiladora* program to U.S. factories, jobs increasingly take on characteristics traditionally used to define and justify female employment: finely tuned, light operations performed by docile laborers. Regardless of their levels of skill, women in the workforce encounter lower wages than those of their male counterparts and limited possibilities for promotion. The growth of precarious employment means repetitive tasks, temporary work, substandard safety, and inadequate health protection. Especially in the newer zones, the feminization of labor entails social dislocation that may be regarded in one sense as liberating for women in a strongly patriarchal context, but that invites exploitation and may leave them marginalized in their own community.

Regarded as important sources of flexible labor, women are becoming international migrants as often as men. The migration experience, while offering potential for mobility, does not necessarily provide women with an escape from subordination. Research shows that migrant enclaves reproduce social controls. It is the successor generation of migrant women—frequently treated as "second-generation foreigners," though many of them are born as citizens of their parents' countries of destination—that has the difficult task of coping with the interaction of different cultural values and attitudes. The offspring group also encounters barriers in securing education and training. Of second-generation Turkish women in Germany, for example, only 21 percent have sufficient education and training necessary for skilled work. Most of them follow their mothers into the lower strata of the labor force (Wilpert 1988, 168–86).

Other women are left behind in the homeland. Many of them are placed in a situation of dependence on in-laws or a male relative, leading to seclusion to guard against improper behavior and adding to a rash of psychological problems, in India known as the "Dubai syndrome": headaches, sleeplessness, loss of appetite, chest pains, fainting, or mock seizures (Kurien 1992, 43–61). In Eastern Asia, women, many of them Thai and Filipina, have been recruited to work in the sex industry, often in other countries and against their will. Primary clients are international businessmen and military personnel. States have taken an active part in promoting the sex industry through tourism, licensing, and international advertising.

The role of states is critical in mediating these processes, either hastening or retarding them. States respond to the pressures of internal social forces. They must also take account of the policies of other states that regulate migratory flows. Given that state boundaries are porous, many "illegal" immigrants may be present and tolerated within a state's political jurisdiction, performing work that some nationals will no longer do. These "illegal" immigrants are subject to rigorous control by internal police procedures and the ever-present threat of expulsion. Hence, EU countries have established a computer information center in Strasbourg, France, to check if a foreign visitor is "wanted" or has been declared "undesirable" elsewhere. European Union members have approved setting up a law enforcement agency, Europol, to coordinate action among their police forces. The mechanisms of political control and surveillance of vulnerable segments of the labor force are a matter of increasing concern in terms of human rights.

The disposable labor force comprises workers employed on a transitory basis in one country, who can be repatriated when they are no longer required, thereby maintaining a high level of employment for national labor, beneficiaries of the expandable-contractible character of a disposable labor reserve. Switzerland and the Persian Gulf states have practiced a disposable labor policy. In the Gulf region, the ratio of foreign to total population has been the highest in the world, ranging from 23 percent in Saudi Arabia to 76 percent in the United Arab Emirates in 1980. As a percentage of the total labor force rather than of population, the proportion of foreign (i.e., temporary) workers has been even greater, reaching around 90 percent in Qatar and the United Arab Emirates in the same year (Tabbarah 1988, 256ff.). Countries in various regions are increasingly opting for "turnkey" projects: A contractor, sometimes the state (as in the PRC), recruits workers, sends them to enclaves in locales such as Botswana, and repatriates them on termination. A different type of example is South Africa, where both external and internal migrants are a disposable labor resource. The apartheid state used migration to promote racial and ethnic segregation as well as labor segmentation. These flows continue and are reshaped—some have even accelerated, while others have declined—in the post-apartheid period.

## REGULATORY "REGIMES" VERSUS BRAUDELIAN STRUCTURES

The role of the state includes the formal and informal regulation of migrant labor within national borders, as well as international and macroregional regulation. Posing the question of regulation focuses attention on vital but understudied questions about "regimes": Are there manifest or latent regional and interregional "regimes" for migration? If so, what kinds of norms or regulatory rules do such regimes embrace?

If international regimes are understood as a set of interactions, it is useful to identify them. However, there is no reason to assume that they exist in every domain. Moreover, principles, norms, expectations, and operative rules are frequently more subtle than or differ from what is publicly recorded. Public pronouncements, of course, do not reveal how regimes were first established, tacit understandings, whether transbureaucratic meanings are shared, and whose interpretations of these meanings really count. Most important is to determine whose interests are served by a regime, the extent to which it deepens or alleviates global inequalities, and how it may be transformed (Puchala 1992).

One explanatory vehicle for examining regulatory regimes is to study migration-driven conflicts. These include conflicts over refugees (Vietnam and Hong Kong), expulsion of nationals (Senegal and Mauritania), and undocumented workers (Mexico and the United States) (Segal 1992, 11–12). In all these categories, migration preferences substantially reflect the globalization trend, whereas barriers to entry, including forced repatriation and financial inducements offered by the host state to go home, are expressions of the Westphalian territorial principle. By condensing the time-space aspects of social relations, the globalization process transcends territorial states and redistributes the world's labor force. Yet the varied immigration policies of states represent attempts by sovereign units to control flows of population, thus affirming the logic of the interstate system.

A starting point for discerning interstate standards is the ideological impetus for the founding of the International Labor Organization (ILO) and the elaboration of its conventions. The mandate for the ILO is contained in the Treaty of Versailles, and reflects pressures from workers' organizations as well as the impact of the October Revolution, pushing postwar governments to establish an international body for the regulation of labor conditions. At the first session of the International Labor Conference, held in Washington, D.C., in 1919, the French delegate, Arthur Fontaine, was the major proponent of placing regulations concerning the migration of workers—equal wages and conditions of employment for immigrant and national workers—on the agenda. France faced a domestic labor shortage, and a number of sending countries sought to protect their workers abroad. Countries favoring restrictive immigration policies (e.g., Canada and Great Britain) feared the adoption and elaboration of international labor standards, and argued that such standards would undermine state sovereignty. This impasse portended common ground limited to vague principles without concrete meaning.

In 1934, the entry of the United States into the ILO, and its status as a major receiving country, promised to give impetus to standard setting. However, when David A. Morse, soon after his election as director-general in 1948, proposed a project for the ILO to manage the transfer of European migrants to Latin America, the United States opposed the initiative and sponsored the creation of another organization, the International Committee for European Migration (ICEM) to do the job. The United States was unwilling to confide this task to the ILO because the ILO had Poland and Czechoslovakia as members, both then part of the Soviet sphere, whereas ICEM was under the influence of U.S. agencies (Cox 1998, 4–5; Hasenau 1991, 687–97). Subsequent decades witnessed an increase in imports of foreign labor, especially on a temporary basis; clandestine migration; international trafficking in labor, sometimes conducted by organized crime; and discrimination and xenophobia targeted at migrants, leading to the adoption of the United Nations Convention on the Protection of the Rights of All Migrant Workers and Members of Their Families in 1990.

Such conventions are buttressed by the activities of the United Nations High Commissioner for Refugees (UNHCR), national groups like the U.S. Committee for Refugees, and a host of research centers that collect data and analyze national and multilateral policies (Segal 1992, 9). On balance, however, an international regime for migration has not been consolidated, its pronouncements largely hortatory and lacking in enforcement mechanisms.

Two macroregions—North America and Europe—emphasize regional solutions and coordinate their efforts, but neither one has adopted common policies. After a number of violent clashes in the Tijuana-San Diego area, the border patrols of the United States and Mexico began to work together in 1990. Law enforcement agencies on both sides are jointly trying to manage problems along a two-thousand-mile border where undocumented migrants are routinely robbed, assaulted, and raped by their escorts, bandits, and smugglers, sometimes with the complicity of police paid as part of the extortion racket. Under the eye of human rights groups, officials of the two governments are now making information available to legal and illegal migrants, advising them of their rights, and aggressively prosecuting abusive patrol agents.

In Europe, pressure is mounting for a common policy on immigration, but the EU lacks judicial authority in this area, and member states guard their prerogatives owing to the sensitivity of the issue and the deeply rooted tradition of dealing bilaterally with immigrants' countries of origin. The Treaty of European Union treats immigration policy as a "matter of common interest." Although the EU subscribes to the principle of free movement of persons, permanent immigration and the right of asylum have been left to national governments. Some countries retain border patrols, but thirteen—and not all of the EU members, notably the United Kingdom and Ireland—have signed the Schengen agreements, which end intra-EU passport checks between them. In 1995, it was decided that two non-Schengen states—Norway and Iceland, joined in a forty-year-old Nordic passport union—should be allowed to participate in the Schengen arrangement as "parties to the Convention." Anyone legally in a Schengen country may travel to the others, but only citizens of one of those countries have the right to work and settle there. Presently, there are provisions that allow non-EU nationals within the EU to enjoy Schengen privileges for up to three months, but only under certain conditions, subject to ongoing treaty ratification. Thus, as the accord stands, a German or an Italian, but not an Angolan citizen residing in Portugal or an Algerian in France, could migrate to Belgium to live and work.

An overarching paradox characterizes immigration in Europe: After relying heavily on workforce immigration in the 1950s and 1960s, the majority of European Community member states sought to halt permanent legal migration beginning in the 1970s; it continues, however, even though unemployment rates in the Community (today, the Union) have been over 8 percent for a decade (to depress wages, some observers would add). Not only does a persistent influx of workers contradict policy statements, but there also appears to be a loss of control in the area of immigration. Having closed their gates, the northerners, for example, are wary that illegal migrants might slip into, say Spain or Portugal, and, given the permeability of borders, could travel unchecked all the way to the North Sea, where they would find ways to stay ("Europe's Immigrants: Strangers inside the Gates" 1992, 154). While the EU's initiatives are concerted through its authority to regulate the labor market, illegal immigration demonstrates the limits of the current approach.

A major limitation is that current regulatory regimes are conceived in terms of exclusivity. In some receiving countries, access to a job is contingent on assimilation to the local, or national, culture, whether through formal or informal mechanisms. The concept of the nation is often based on more than command of a predominant language or the adoption of certain cultural practices, but may be designated in terms of ancestry, or a shared myth about blood lines. Hence the link between nation and race. A stark example of a racialized concept of national identity, touched on in chapter 2, is the automatic right to German citizenship conferred on "ethnic Germans," many of whom do not speak German and whose forebears had migrated to Eastern Europe several generations ago (Glick Schiller forthcoming). Citizenship, however, is a prerogative that has been denied to many Turks and other immigrants born in Germany and who speak German as their first language. In short, culture is one of the instruments in the regulation of international migration, perforce an encounter of people who speak different languages, practice different religions, and have very different habits. It may be hypothesized that regulatory regimes are evolving in the direction of multiculturalism in the workforce, with culture playing a major role in labor market segmentation.

International migration is building multiracial societies beset with severe socioeconomic problems. Many immigrants and their offspring maintain residential and cultural enclaves in Europe, and are not integrated into the welfare system (which is subject to neoliberal pressures for reduction). A particularly nettlesome issue stems from the de facto conversion of workforce migration into settlement migration, which is strikingly evident in the plight of youth. Now there is a successor generation of young people born in the receiving country, some of whom are citizens of that country and who are less compliant than are their parents. Many of these people are marginalized in the educational system and in access to employment. Thus, Britain's young blacks and France's young Arabs feel they are treated like outsiders, even if they are nationals of the countries in which they reside. (A very different situation with multiethnic populations has developed in the Middle East, where governments fear "reverse acculturation": a gradual loss of Arab national identity. Yet a large number of Arab migrants is perceived as a political risk.)

Muslims represent one-third of all immigrants in Western Europe, and, allowing for intraregional flows, two-thirds of non-EU nationals. In fact, the prospect of Islamic resurgence in the southern countries causes serious concern. A perplexing problem is structuring political participation among Muslims in these countries, because the Islamic tradition differs from a secular democratic society with its representative bodies. Furthermore, the EU's five million Muslims include different strands of Islam (Shiite, Sunni, and others) and several nationalities (e.g., Algerians, Bangladeshis, Moroccans, Pakistanis, Tunisians, and Turks) (Commission of the European Communities 1990, 34; 1991, 25).

Attacks on immigrants in EU countries are increasingly frequent and accompanied by a swell of xenophobia. Politicians on the far right, such as the leader of France's National Front, Jean-Marie Le Pen, and his counterparts, appeal to nativist sentiment, economic insecurities, and apprehension of Brussels as a threat to national identity. Indeed, when France won soccer's World Cup in 1998, its star player, Zinedine Zidane, from the Algerian slums of Marseilles, became the national hero, but after the National Front had criticized the composition of the team for including players who were not "real Frenchmen." Those who are alarmed about an "invasion" of immigrants argue that the EU is amid two areas of poverty: the needy ex-socialist countries to the east and less developed countries across the Mediterranean. In this juncture, the interactions of culture, economic patterns, and demographic pressures are stark. It is estimated that North Africa's population will double over the next thirty to thirty-five years, with forty percent of Maghrebians currently being under fifteen years of age. With income levels no more than a sixth of those in Europe, they may seek to relocate north of the Mediterranean ("Europe's Immigrants: Strangers inside the Gates" 1992, 153). Immigration policies in Europe clearly reflect concern that the ascent to power of an Islamist regime in Algeria or other North African countries could spark massive trans-Mediterranean flows of population.

## TOWARD AN ALTERNATIVE CONCEPTUALIZATION

These interactions all bear upon the manner in which multilateralism can confront the issues of restructuring production and migration. Formulating the problem in this way directs attention to access to multilateral processes. Are regulatory regimes the exclusive prerogative of states and interstate organizations, or will they become more open to groups most affected by these processes? Do migrants act as agents who challenge multilateral structures, and, if so, what forms of resistance do they adopt, and under what conditions?

With the creation of a single European market, a key challenge to the EU's multilateral project are the political and cultural patterns of Western Europe's thirteen million immigrants, both workers and their families. As mentioned, Islam is one vector of mobilization among immigrants, although some of the brotherhoods, strident organizations, and religious institutions represent the interests of non-EU homeland states rather than autonomous groups participating cross-nationally in host societies. In other instances, identities are no longer state-based but, in the context of globalized production processes, become reimagined as transnational constructions that include diasporic populations. Hence, government officials in immigrant-sending countries, such as the Dominican Republic, work closely with political leaders in Washington Heights, New York and other locales overseas. In light of the importance of remittances, modern communications technology that provides frequent contact, and in some cases migrants' right to vote at home, these officials actually perceive their diasporic communities as part of their home constituencies. An important aspect of global restructuring, the transnational state (or the deterritorialized state, as it is also called), denies the exclusivity of membership in a single state, which has important implications for changing conceptions of citizenship (Glick Schiller 1999; forthcoming).

The identities and political ties not only are formed along ancestral lines to the homeland, but another pattern of identity formation is also evident. Various immigrant associations sometimes temper their competitive interests and join together in host countries to forge an incipient transnational counterforce. In 1984, immigrant groups formed the Council of Immigrant Associations in France and agreed to a set of common demands addressed to Western European receiving nations. Following the adoption of the Single European Act in 1985, more than 2,500 immigrant associations in fourteen host countries established the Council of Immigrant Associations in Europe. Based in Brussels, it is primarily concerned with the role of non-Union nationals in European integration and the political rights of immigrants. Not surprisingly, the surge of racism and nativist sentiment has been at issue (Ireland 1991).

Subject to the contradictory pressures of immigrant and anti-immigrant movements, multilateralism has thus come to embody certain fundamental human dilemmas that globalized production and migration have thrust into sharp relief. As indicated, international standards, however desirable, are largely unenforced, and receiving countries have no common immigration policy. It is tacit agreements, cultural patterns, and neoliberal economic ideology that underpin a weak regulatory regime in the area of international migration—a potentially explosive issue because of growing inequalities. International conventions cannot eradicate global inequalities that fuel migration, nor can they circumvent the norms and structures of sovereign statehood. Whereas economic globalization advances worldwide labor mobility at turn of the millennium, political units cling to the seventeenth-century doctrine of sovereignty, thus far relinquishing few prerogatives to interstate organizations, which, in any event, preserve the state.

An alternative to the dominant conceptualization is to focus on the interpenetration of the internal dynamics of societies and transnational and global processes. Restructuring must be joined to agency by incorporating the views of migrants themselves and challenging prevalent perspectives of economic globalization so that both efficiency and equity are enhanced. The aim of this new conceptualization is not to return to pre-globalization conditions, but rather to transcend the current globalization syndrome, to re-embed in global society the unparalleled productive capacities of economic globalization in order to help achieve social justice. To take this heterodox conceptualization one step further, the next chapter looks at another facet of the GDLP: poverty and gender.

# CHAPTER 4

# Global Poverty and Gender

## (COAUTHORED WITH ASHWINI TAMBE)

IN THE POST-Cold War era, a major normative commitment in world politics is encapsulated in neoliberal globalization. On the altar of a benevolent market rests the promise that economic gain can benefit all who are faithful to its principles. Neoliberal globalization's normative appeal lies in the vision it offers of the opportunity to ascend the global hierarchy of power and production. This model of world order is not only a set of policies about economic well-being, but also an ethical claim with real implications for distributive justice. Implicit in this value system is the express assurance that neoliberalism will lift millions of people out of poverty, embracing them in a win-win situation, rather than a winner-take-all dynamic.

From a neoliberal perspective, it is argued that as a percentage of world population, poverty is decreasing; hence, the existing pattern of poverty alleviation conforms to the neoliberal promise. This claim, however, invites debates over the most appropriate measures of poverty—minefields that we do not wish to enter. Suffice it to say that among analysts, there is no consensus in this regard.[1] Acknowledging that social scientists do not endorse a widely shared definition of poverty, Mary Durfee and James Rosenau (1996, 523), for example, settle on the formulation "realities and fears of substandard living conditions," including inadequate disposable income, housing, clothing, and employment. This formulation is especially useful in its coupling of both the objective and subjective dimensions of poverty. Even without engaging the methodological issue, it follows that a wide range of empirical indicators may then be employed to gauge the changing incidence of poverty.

There exists evidence to counter the claims of neoliberalism, to argue instead that higher levels of globalization mean more poverty. While average incomes have increased worldwide, the total number of poor people (defined as those who earn less than $1 per day) grew from 1.23 billion in 1987 to 1.31 billion in 1993. This occurred with large inter- and intra-

---

[1] For citations on the extensive literature on poverty and a broader discussion of the different scholarly traditions, see Mittelman and Pasha (1997).

regional variance: The rate of poverty has declined in Eastern Asia (a pattern now changing as the impact of the market turbulence of the late 1990s is becoming fully felt) but is remaining steady at 39 percent in sub-Saharan Africa, where there is a rise in the total number of poor people (World Bank 1996, 7–9). How can this be? How is it that globalization, which helps alleviate poverty in some parts of the world, is antithetical to poverty reduction on a world scale? It appears antithetical to poverty reduction because there is a shifting incidence of poverty, growing polarization among and within regions, and a reconcentration of wealth. In other words, global poverty comprises a downward spiral of economic conditions in some countries, and elsewhere, a sense of the disjuncture between macroeconomic growth and persistent material deprivation for the many.

Against this backdrop, the central questions that frame this chapter are: What are the evolving linkages between globalization and poverty? In light of changing global structures, what is the analytical key to understanding poverty?

The purpose of this chapter, then, is to confront neoliberal claims about poverty and to offer, if only in a preliminary manner, an alternative conceptualization. The focus is on the *production* of poverty, but not on political and cultural resistance to the globalizing structures that underpin it, the subject of Part III of this book. Our core hypothesis is that although poverty is an age-old phenomenon, today it may be best understood as an outcome of the *interactions among globalization, marginalization, and gender*. We attempt to delineate the linkages in this multifaceted process. Central to the chain of relationships are the varied ways in which economic globalization marginalizes large numbers of people by reducing public spending on social services, and delinks economic reform from social policy. This type of marginalization manifests a gendered dimension inasmuch as women constitute those principally affected by it.

With economic restructuring, it is women who take on most responsibilities jettisoned by the state, in its response to globalization, and still carry out traditionally defined work in the household. Notwithstanding new sources of income for some women, traditional tasks become more arduous because globalizing processes, such as the incorporation of women into the formal labor force through the spatial reorganization of production, have an uneven and disruptive impact on ways of life. By delimiting the ways in which everyday life is transformed by the concomitant processes of neoliberal globalization and marginalization, and the ways in which gender is implicated in marginalization, this chapter not only questions the basic promise of neoliberalism but also shows its limits.

Without grounding, however, structural explanations of this genre would also have their shortcomings. It is therefore advantageous to explore gendered marginalization through the use of case studies, which provide fine-grained evidence of increasing poverty amid neoliberal globalization. A central theoretical argument here is that the rise in the number of people living under poverty is attributable to the delinking of society and economy—a *disembedding* of economy from society.

In terms of the dynamics we seek to explain, higher levels of globalization further marginalization, both within and between territorial units. In order to comprehend *marginalization*, one may combine the visual sense of the term "margin"—an outer edge viewed from a center—with the economic usage of the word "margin," that is, the point at which the returns from an activity barely cover its cost. Especially important to our argument is the *gendered* division of labor: a key social stratification system that places most women in subordinate positions. Gender is fundamentally a relationship of power.

Gender ideology consists of ingrained beliefs that order power relations between men and women. As with other kinds of ideologies, structures of domination are preserved in an often unconscious manner through commonsense assumptions. In the case of gender ideology, some common assumptions are that household work is the natural domain of women and that women are nonproductive social actors. A proposition to be advanced here is that gender ideology not only structures power within social relations, but also articulates with—connects in distinctive ways to—the ideology of globalization. The *ideology of globalization* lends legitimacy to shifting functions in the realm of social services from the state to women, as well as to prying open markets, liberalizing trade, and reducing state intervention in the economy. In economies that structurally restrict women's economic participation to subsistence activities, the paring down of the state, which is sometimes theorized as the institutionalization of patriarchal power, in fact works against augmenting this participation. Even in economies where women's economic participation has increased, under pressures arising out of the liberalization of trade and industry, the terms of this participation are often highly exploitative. Thus, although there may seem to be nothing patently masculinist about the ideology of globalization, its specific articulation with gender ideology sustains the marginalization of women. The gendered division of labor is actually one of the factors that make globalization possible.

Our case studies will illustrate the above features of this articulation in two contexts—the informal farming sector and export-processing zones. This chapter offers a cross-regional analysis of countries where these sectors represent important components of the national economy. The poverty-generating implications of the deepening of a market economy for women are explored in both cases. We focus on women in the informal farming sector in Mozambique, often cited as the world's poorest country (World Bank 1990b to 1997b),[2] where women's work in the fields provides much of the sustenance for families (Marshall 1990, 33). For export-processing industries, we anchor our concepts in the case of the Philippines, where export-oriented and female-led industrialization (i.e., with low-paid female labor being a prime component) has been the engine of economic growth in the 1990s. Notwithstanding many dissimilarities, both countries were economic laggards in their respective regions, until the 1990s' growth spurt in the Philippines and Mozambique (chapter 5). Although it is not central to our argument, both countries are also former colonies sharing the imprint of an Iberian and Catholic heritage. Importantly, both countries are undergoing structural adjustment programs. These globalizing programs are aimed at alleviating poverty, but are not gender-neutral in conception or effect.

In both cases, structural adjustment is but one aspect of neoliberal policies aimed at denationalizing economies as well as spreading and deepening the market. Not only does evidence challenge the neoliberal promise, but Polanyi's theoretical insights into market economies may also be enlisted to help explain this disjuncture. Whereas Polanyi focused on the growth of markets in nineteenth-century England (as well as on premarket societies), his notion of "the great transformation" may be extended to understand the dynamics of global poverty at the turn of the millennium. Before the rise of market societies, production, as Aristotle maintained, was for use—a principle the Greeks called *householding*—not primarily for gain. Men and women, bound together in families, treated markets and money as "mere accessories to an otherwise self-sufficient household" (Polanyi 1968, 16–17). In other words, Polanyi's concept of the embeddedness of economic systems in—and subsequent disembeddedness from—society anticipates one form of gender analysis and even offers a mode of inquiry for examining the ways that globalization has disrupted and redirected existing socioeconomic arrangements. To develop this conceptualization, we first offer a critique of the neoliberal framework for poverty eradication and then from an alternative entry point, extend our own formulation.

---

[2] According to World Bank reports (1990 to 1995), Mozambique had the lowest per capita GNP in the late 1980s and early 1990s. Although Rwanda's 1994 average per capita income of $80 was below that of Mozambique's $90 (World Bank 1996b, 188), Mozambique with $80 replaced Rwanda, which rose to seventh from the bottom at $180 in the 1995 rankings (World Bank 1997b, 214). Similarly, the most recent figures, for 1997, place Mozambique, with $90 per capita, at the very bottom (World Bank 1999b, 191).

## RECONCEPTUALIZING POVERTY

### *The Neoliberal Perspective*

Neoliberalism provides the rationale for measures that propel globalization, such as structural adjustment policies. From this perspective, a commitment to reducing poverty can only be displayed by integration into the international capitalist economy. Neoliberal globalization is thus presented as the antidote to the problem of poverty, instead of also being implicated in generating it. Furthermore, neoliberal ideology promotes the expansion of markets as natural and inevitable, while existing social arrangements within which economies are still partially embedded are treated as chains that need to be unshackled. Polanyi would regard such a view as ahistorical, as suggested in the following passage:

> Economic history reveals that the emergence of national markets was in no way the result of the gradual and spontaneous emancipation of the economic sphere from governmental control. On the contrary, the market has been the outcome of a conscious and often violent intervention on the part of governments which imposed the market organization on society for non-economic ends. And the self-regulating market of the nineteenth century turns out upon closer inspection to be radically different from even its immediate predecessor in that it relied for its regulation upon economic self-interest. (Polanyi 1957, 250)

The notion of a self-regulating market is most fundamentally misapplied to labor, when labor is assumed to be a commodity in abundant and variable supply that responds primarily to market signals. Poverty is then explained as a preponderance of underutilized labor, the solution to which is increased employment through macroeconomic growth. The poor are asked to take heart, for they have an asset in the global economy, their labor potential. Nonetheless, the actual erosion of much secure employment in the context of structural adjustment programs brings forth a new contradictory demand. Labor must now "diversify" and "adjust." The speed and the flexibility of capital in the context of globalization are thus projected onto labor: Labor, too, is expected to be flexible and mobile. The result is new winners and new losers, with some segments of the labor force adjusting speedily into poverty.

### *Poverty and Social Relations of Production*

A common pitfall is treating poverty as a static category, fixed in its preponderance in specific regions or in particular social strata. While it is true that various processes ingrain it in certain regions, countries, and enclaves, this should be understood as part of a global problem of poverty generation. In much social scientific analysis, the poor are contained in identifiable and fixed units of society through the drawing of poverty lines. Such lines, although useful in a preliminary way, represent poverty with a false clarity, obfuscating the relationships that generate it. The basis on which these lines are mapped reflect reigning intellectual frameworks. The dominant paradigm in poverty analysis, encompassing at first the modernization school and neoclassical economics, and now extended by neoliberalism, tends to explain poverty on the basis of consumption levels. Emphasis is one-sidedly accorded to underconsumption, not overconsumption. Focusing on the realm of consumption begets policies primarily aimed at raising consumption levels. Typically, these policies are instruments meant to achieve greater market integration, which may actually accentuate marginalization, worsen inequalities, and heighten political conflict.

An example of this manner of approaching poverty is the World Bank's analysis. The World Bank defines poverty as the inability to attain a minimum standard of living, with poverty gauged in terms of the expenditure necessary to procure nutrition and basic necessities, and at a more country-specific level, the cost of participating in everyday life. How the poor derive and spend their income is the stated topic of the World Bank *World Development Report* subtitled *Poverty* (1990b, 6). The follow-up report on poverty reduction (World Bank 1996, 2) also centers on income and consumption. In both documents, the use of expenditure as a starting point in measuring poverty betrays the bank's own interest in international market integration, and the generation of "effective" demand for products in global commodity markets.

Entertaining a different entry point, one based on production relations, may invite easy accusations of economic reductionism in a post-Cold War intellectual climate. However, we hold that the mainstream treatment of poverty within the analytical realm of consumption fixes it as a statistical or gradational measure; the social relations that maintain and, in some cases, extend it are thereby neglected. Poverty needs to be recast as an outcome of the interactions among globalization, marginalization in the production process, and gendered social relations.

In the context of globalization, to be marginalized is to be pushed to the edges of the economy beyond which returns from work are lower than the effort expended. Poverty, then, is the experience and perception of marginalization that have been locked in through structural pressure. When people live in poverty, their work consistently incurs a higher cost than its return. Implied here is all work, whether wage-earning or not, and all costs, especially those of health and the ability to survive. Both formally and informally employed workers, as well as the unemployed, may well be living in varied degrees of poverty.

This conceptualization of poverty departs from mainstream writing on the subject in two ways. First, it focuses on production in order to portray poverty as arising within work relations, however constrained, and not simply occurring simultaneously with unemployment and underemployment. Second, it links poverty to the process of marginalization, rather than limiting it to a category of people. It takes the preliminary step of dissociating poverty from static geographic and cultural categories, to conceive it in relational terms. Such a departure is necessary in order to place poverty within the same framework as that used to understand globalization, and the language of changed spatio-temporal relations. Poverty, too, is transnational; its margins cut across states and regions of the world.

The powerlessness of the poor may then be partly explained by the disembedding of markets from society. They are excluded from the processes that determine what will be produced. The rigidity of the structures of authority in work relations are important, because these sustain marginalization. Referring back to the earlier conceptualization of marginalization, the poor may be identified as those for whom the rewards from work are lower than the effort expended. What distinguishes the relations of poverty from other kinds of top-down relations of production is precisely the high degree of social constraints against escaping those structures. For the poor, individual resources are insufficient for surmounting social forces that maintain their marginalized relations of production.

Gender ideologies pervade social relations of production. Women generally have less access to and control over means of production than do men. The undervaluation of socially productive work by women keeps them working harder for longer hours. The marginalization of women arises from social forces that organize and segment production. Women's economic impoverishment is accentuated by the modalities of supposedly self-regulating markets. This articulation of gender ideology with globalization ideology creates and sustains persistent poverty, as the following brief case studies show.


### POVERTY IN MOZAMBIQUE

Although Mozambique exemplifies "involuntary delinkage" from the global manufacturing system, it is all but delinked from the global financial system. Mozambique's debt amounted to $5.4 billion in 1994, which is four-and-a-half times its GNP (World Bank 1996b, 220). Much of its foreign aid is drained back into donor pockets through debt payments (chapter 5).

Two events from Mozambique's recent history demonstrate the conditions that reinforce poverty there. In March 1993, 12,000 tons of food aid that had been stockpiled for sale were sold as animal feed because they had rotted while waiting in a port warehouse in Maputo. The reasons given by trade minister Daniel Gabriel for this occurrence was "market saturation" in southern Mozambique and the inability of companies to sell existing stocks of maize (Mozambiquefile 1993a, 21). The food aid was part of a donation that designated 200,000 tons for free distribution and 100,000 tons for sale. While the 200,000 tons of free maize had been easily disbursed, the remaining amount was left to deteriorate. The so-called saturation in the market was clearly at odds with prevailing hunger caused by drought and the ongoing civil war between the governing Mozambique Liberation Front (FRELIMO) and a contra group known as the Mozambique National Resistance Movement (RENAMO). The theft of other food aid in the following month attested to this problem (Mozambiquefile 1993b, 21).

In another incident, in October 1995, food riots rocked the capital city, Maputo. Hundreds of people blocked roads, stoned vehicles, and rampaged through marketplaces, in response to an escalation in food prices. In a sudden increase driven by the need to align domestic prices with international ones, the cost of a 50-kilogram bag of rice had gone up from $15 to $50 ("Disquieting Signs in Mozambique One Year On" 1995, 11). The annual purchasing power per person being barely $90 at the time, a price hike of this magnitude spelled massive hunger. Both of these events illustrate the harmful dissonance between the workings of the market and actual conditions of hardship; they signal the disembedding of the market from social control.

That women farmers are found to be among the poorest people in Africa at large is well known. Currently, this poverty is becoming entrenched as a structural relationship through globalizing forces. Mozambique's proportion of women in the labor force is among the highest in Africa, 49 percent in 1990 (United Nations Development Program [UNDP] 1996, 169). Owing to male migration to cities and to neighboring states, women head 60 percent of Mozambican households, which is well over the average of 43 percent for the rest of sub-Saharan Africa (James 1995, 6–7). Nevertheless, women's access to land and credit is limited, and much of their labor cannot be diverted from subsistence. Let us turn to how structural adjustment works in regard to these social relations.

## Pricing Mechanisms and the Persistence of
## Food Insecurity

Hunger is a most urgent social problem in Mozambique. Not only is there restricted access to arable land for food production, but existing methods of cultivation also have low yields. This creates the need for a market to obtain food from other sources. In modern economic terms, the existence of a food market depends on cash income being available to create effective demand. Cash income can be generated by cash crop sales or off-farm work, but each of these activities takes away from the subsistence base of households. Off-farm work decreases food production and the possibility of surpluses becoming available for sale on the market.

Pressure on rural land has been increased by two facets of structural adjustment: the promotion of cash crops and exportables such as cashew nuts and cotton, and the drive to privatize landholding. The problem is rooted in the colonial political economy, because the metropole, Portugal, designated areas for exclusive commercial cultivation and provided incentives for growing cash crops. Although most of these commercial lands were placed under state farm control after Mozambique graduated to political independence in 1975, many of them have been privatized (chapter 5). Land intended for redistribution is being sold, often to large-scale commercial producers. Most recently, schemes to sell land to groups of white South African farmers in the northern provinces have been negotiated (Economist Intelligence Unit [EIU] 1996, 10). In irrigated areas, some poor peasant families, particularly those headed by women, have lost or sublet their holdings (O'Laughlin 1995, 105).

Owing to low wages and high food prices, even urban households depend on farming by wives to bring in substantial provisions of food. In many urban families, women work on the "machamba" (small farms) adjacent to Maputo. Such labor is regarded as obligatory for women. In fact, Marshall's interviews with male workers in Maputo reveal that wives who farm are considered as not working and "doing nothing" (1990, 33). The pressure on peri-urban land is increasing markedly as a result of both high food prices as well as the incentives for cash crop cultivation. Only an estimated 30 percent of families have access to an agricultural plot in Maputo (O'Laughlin 1995, 105).

On the question of higher food production, Diane Elson points out that there are two contrasting ways in which poverty can be tackled: "[O]ne seeks to reduce the power of money through extending social provision; the other seeks to extend the power of money by introducing financial criteria into the operation of all public services, and by deregulating labor markets" (Elson 1994, 517). Under a neoliberal reform program in Mozambique, it is clearly the latter that has been followed. In 1988, under the IMF/World Bank-sponsored Economic and Rehabilitation Program (PRE)-2, the removal of subsidies for food prices was an attack on a vital social provision for urban dwellers. The logic of raising food prices in order to stimulate agricultural production was controversial, since the bulk of farming is for subsistence. Because food markets do not play a preponderant role in assuring food security in rural households, the hike in prices precipitated more hardship in both rural and urban areas (Tschirley and Weber 1994, 159–73).

### Gender and Food Security

As in many parts of the world, women in Mozambique have access to land only through their husbands or male relatives. Food crops are customarily the domain of women; gender ideology militates against food cultivation by men, for whom the call to grow cash crops is compelling. In recent times, land used by women for food growing has been appropriated by men for cultivating cash crops. This increases the pressure on women's labor on marginal food-growing land. The privatization of land often means closing doors to women who head households; the drive to commercialize land frequently forces rural women off the land. Price signals in the food market do not evoke the response presumed by macroeconomic monetarist policy, since they do not reach subsistence farming by women. Thus, the dual pressure of privatizing land and raising cash crops works against the interests of women farmers. Inasmuch as resources to produce food are taken away from women while the need to provide sustenance remains, one may expect continued food insecurity.

### Poverty and the Paring Down of State Spending

Within the household, there is no decline in the time spent by women on child rearing, food preparation, and care of the elderly. Even women's claims on food are subordinated to those of other family members, in the hierarchy of the household. Current social provisions in Mozambique do not redress the high toll on women's health taken by this combination of increased labor and food scarcity. Instead, under PRE-2, privatization of health care drove up the cost of medical services, which in turn resulted in an immediate 50-perent to 80-percent drop in attendance at local clinics and hospitals, particularly by women (Marshall 1990, 36). A downward spiral of inadequate nutrition and lack of health care for women has been accelerated by structural adjustment.

Rural infrastructure recovery after the end of the seventeen-year civil war is urgently required, but structural adjustment has meant that spending by provincial governments is highly constrained. Reductions in expenditure on rural transport have serious consequences for women, whose chores include gathering fuel and water. According to the Ministry of Agriculture, women spend an average of 4.5 hours daily just on transport (Berman 1996, 9). But it is not all expenditure on transport that has been curtailed. For its landlocked neighbors, Mozambique's location is strategic in providing railroads to the sea. Recent development efforts have concentrated on rebuilding regional railways, but not on new spurs connecting outlying areas to major cities and ports. The creation of wage-labor employment through rural rebuilding, including transport, is necessary for improving the conditions for demobilized soldiers. Increased spending on regional infrastructure to facilitate trade, however, means decreased spending on domestic transportation, which women need. Yet the priorities of structural adjustment work actively against aspects of such social provisions.

The impact of reductions in the face of social need is also evident in the realm of education. There is currently a shortage of teachers, and this will undoubtedly get worse, because programs for in-service training of teachers have largely been terminated since the late 1980s (Marshall 1990, 36). Decreased expenditure on education entrenches women's marginal economic position. This occurs in two ways: Women have to take on child-rearing responsibilities for longer periods, and their own access to education as a means of opening new productive opportunities is limited.

The argument here is that global structures—notably, deregulation, liberalization, and privatization—are gendered in conceptualization and effect. In conceptualization, they assume women's ability to bear increasing demands on their labor, in household obligations of food provision, child-rearing and education, and caregiving for the elderly. They are also gendered in their effect inasmuch as "self-regulating" markets and privatization of land restrain women's access to productive resources. In an already impoverished country such as Mozambique, these tendencies consign most women to relations of poverty within a highly hierarchical society.

In a Polanyian sense, women are experiencing the instituting of a market in ways that disembed their claims to well-being in terms of health, land, and education. Women farmers have been marginalized, pushed to labor in conditions where the returns barely cover, or fail to meet, the costs to their well-being. According to the ideology of women's domestic duty, food provision and care-giving for the family are activities whose "rewards" are intersubjectively produced through love and the gratitude of family members. However, no amount of love or gratefulness can substitute for adequate food and medication to counter women's hunger and ill health, a proposition that applies across regions.

## POVERTY IN THE PHILIPPINES

Prescriptions for a globalized economy have long been followed in the Philippines, a country that has been through twenty adjustment programs. Forty percent of its annual budget is spent on repayment of foreign debt, which amounted to $39 billion in 1994 (World Bank 1996b, 220). During the mid-1990s, annual economic growth figures in the range of 5 percent would lead one to think that the Philippines was experiencing a boom. Persistent poverty, however, was and is the actual experience of large portions of its population. Only 9 percent of respondents to a nationwide survey in 1994 felt that they were "not poor," even fewer than in 1992, when 19 percent made the same claim (Social Weather Station 1994). What explains this contradiction between macroeconomic gains and deepening poverty is scant spending on social policy and the predominantly enclave-based growth in the country. Gauged in terms of a "social allocation ratio" (public expenditure on health and education as a share of total central government spending), the Philippines, at 20 percent, trails such countries as Mauritius's nearly 60 percent, Zimbabwe's 40 percent, Pakistan's more than 50 percent, and Trinidad and Tobago's 33 percent (UNDP 1996, 71). Furthermore, the notion that growth channeled by international financial institutions filters down is a premise embraced by successive Philippine regimes, whose support has been directed to specific sectors such as electronics, garments, and finance, with few domestic linkages, most often located in geographically distinct export-based enclaves.

The first EPZ in the Philippines was established in the early 1970s, in Bataan province. Incentives offered to foreign firms by the Philippine state included 100 percent ownership backed by the right to borrow within the country, with government guarantees for foreign loans. No taxes were placed on imports or exports, and there was no minimum investment requirement. EPZs attracted "quota refugees"—investors from countries with restrictions on exports to the United States, such as Japan, South Korea, Hong Kong, and Taiwan. By basing themselves in the Philippines, foreign firms were able to secure U.S. markets through Philippine export quotas. Light manufacturing, electronics, garments, and heavy fabrication form the bulk of the activities of the firms, with electronics on the rise and garments on the decline. The Bataan EPZ is the most export-oriented, world market-dependent of the country's economic ventures. It represents the classic disembedded enclave, where the neoliberal economic logic that sustains the zone lifts it away from the context surrounding it.

## Female-Led Growth and Female Poverty

The economic growth experienced by the Philippines is fueled by women workers. Eighty-five percent to 90 percent of the workforce employed in EPZs are women, and much of the economy is buoyed by remittances from overseas contract workers, over half of whom are women. The workforce in EPZs is usually drawn from neighboring rural areas, most of the laborers being between the ages of seventeen and twenty-nine. In the case of the Bataan zone, high unemployment marks the adjacent areas. Supporting families is therefore an important reason for taking up employment there (Rosa 1994, 77).

One would think that because EPZs offer jobs, they help to eradicate poverty. However, wages are low in the EPZs relative to other industrial areas—for example, around the capital, Manila. In addition, gender differentiation segments the workforce such that 40 percent of the women employed in EPZs receive less than the legal minimum wage, compared with 17 percent of the men. As one manager in the Bataan zone put it, women were recruited because they "endure poverty well" (Eviota 1992, 121). If the criteria for their recruitment are poverty and "low skill," what results is a downward pressure on women to remain poor and low-skilled. Living conditions in the zones are also reported to be spartan, food prices are higher than in nearby areas, and boarding houses for the women are often overcrowded and costly. Moreover, unsafe working conditions threaten the women's future. In the microelectronics industry, for instance, blurred vision is a common ailment among workers. These pressures, combined with the fact that they often have to remit a portion of their wages to their families, means that the women, despite being wage earners, live in persistent poverty.

Gender relations merit careful consideration because they are a major means by which male managers and supervisors subject labor to authority. A regime of patriarchal discipline is reproduced in the factories, with managers presented as father figures to the young women employed there. Strict control of the workers' time is attempted, down to rules regarding the use of the bathroom. In some cases, looming over this disciplinary pattern is the threat of sexual coercion—job security often depends on the exchange of sexual services (Eviota 1992, 123). Recreational activities initiated by the company preserve or inculcate sexual stereotypes (e.g., cosmetic product promotions and company-sponsored beauty contests). Such contests are especially common in the microelectronics industry, where an explicit effort has been made to construct the assembling of semiconductors as "women's work" (Eviota 1992, 120).

It is gender ideology, and not the intrinsic quality of the labor, that structures hiring policies. It is who does the work, not the work itself, that leads to its identification as "high" or "low" skilled labor. Maintaining the category of low-wage work as women's work is the dynamic. The treatment of women as secondary workers originates in the concept of women as temporary workers, for whom waged work is a source of income in addition to an already assured dependent livelihood. Although it is sometimes argued that EPZs enable the women workers to escape patriarchical rural life, they do come under wage discipline. As a result of the high cost of living under structural adjustment, it is not supplemental income, but basic sustenance, that women are trying to assure. Marriage is not necessarily a way out, for many women continue to have to earn wages, often working harder after marriage.

Although the justification for hiring women by naturalizing—i.e., referring to the supposed natural qualities of—women's labor is common, slippage occurs when this assumption is also accepted by observers of globalization. The same ideology that threatens women in the workplace keeps up demands on their labor in the household. The expectation that women perform multiple duties, along with the rising cost of food and health care, drive women to seek waged jobs. Single women seek jobs as a means to gain some measure of independence from restrictive conditions at home. Whereas the experience of women in EPZs is often an alienating one, with workers' connections to society forcibly changed, it is improved relations of production that they struggle for, not a return to their former conditions of dependence. Hence, any escape from their marginalized social relations of production, and any re-embedding of the local economy within the society, which implies a reordering of the world economy, necessarily involve challenging the prevailing norms inculcated by gender ideology.

## THE MATRIX OF GLOBALIZATION, MARGINALIZATION, AND GENDER

We have argued that neoliberalism concentrates on categorizing poverty according to aggregate growth, individual expenditure, and other symptomatic indicators rather than the relational and more fundamentally structural factors, thus failing to tug at the deepest roots of poverty. Whereas globalization offers unparalleled economic opportunities for some, it also reconfigures the incidence of poverty within and between countries. That is, globalization and marginalization are interconnected processes, the former driving the latter. Propelled by hypercompetitiveness, globalization pushes some groups, typically women, to the margins, which further entrenches poverty. Inasmuch as gender ideology helps to segment women in particular positions in the production process, it is important for analysts to overcome the separation between structures of class and gender, and examine the varied ways in which they are interrelated. Our thesis, then, is that the interactions among these processes—globalization, marginalization, and social forces—shape patterns of poverty as well as other distributional outcomes. In this context, it is important to conceptualize poverty in terms of social relations of production.

Moving to the question of remedies, it would be wrong to trivialize the pain of poverty, but there is a danger in some attempts to suppress it. The supposed suppressant of neoliberalism only perpetuates poverty, by reconcentrating it. While neoliberal policies pull many people out of poverty in some regions, they also lodge women into its mechanisms. Not only does neoliberalism worsen inequality, but it also breeds consumerism. The neoliberal strategy conflates a would-be solution to poverty and an underlying cause of it. But is there an alternative poverty suppressant? If our approach to the structuring of poverty is correct, the problem of poverty suppression is transposed into the question of how to challenge underlying structures. To answer, it is instructive to draw on the case studies. Mozambique, the poorest country on the poorest continent, and the Philippines, for long the most poverty-stricken and until recently, the most marginalized country in a subregion that experienced explosive economic growth, appear dissimilar in terms of their resource endowments, historical trajectories, social structures, and cultural mosaics. Yet, when taken together, these countries embody dynamics that are similar and telling about the structuring of poverty: While an economic condition, poverty is also integrated with other forms of social discrimination, frequently but not exclusively gender; the rigid hierarchies of patriarchy work to impoverish women. In other words, the structures of poverty comprise parallel and mutually reinforcing processes.

With neoliberal globalization, it is ever more difficult to dislodge this structure because the technical caliber of production—organized not primarily on a national, but now on a worldwide, scale—seems to exceed the capacity for social control. In this sense, neoliberal globalization is a development anticipated (but of course not delimited) in Polanyi's seminal analysis of the disembedding of unfettered market forces from society. In an age of globalization, poverty is not only set in a rather different constellation of market forces from those examined in Polanyi's studies, but also must be construed as a political condition. In more graphic terms, poverty becomes a crucible in which social discrimination, including the degradation of institutions such as health care and education, and the arbitrariness of power, fester and become self-sustaining. "Growth," often presented as a cure-all in dominant policies of poverty alleviation, appears a faint solution to this deeper political condition.

If the challenge is to alleviate poverty, the first step is to create new knowledge and norms about the problem in specific contexts, and also locate them within the globalization process. Inasmuch as neoliberal globalization diminishes the state's role in combating structures of gendered marginalization, it entrenches poverty while further opening the market. Markets have ingrained poverty on a gendered basis partly because of a lack of popular control over them. To mitigate poverty, political interventions must pull at the roots of the problem of how to re-embed the economy in society. At present, society still takes the national framework as its main point of reference, and is itself pocked with gendered and other forms of inequality. In the absence of fundamental social change within society, to re-embed globalizing markets would not ipso facto solve the problem of poverty generation. As a precaution about the peril of a Polanyian prescription of re-embedding, it must be emphasized that different societies bear their own forms of patriarchy and distinctive dynamics of poverty. The interplay of neoliberal globalization and local, historical structures produces varied permutations, as our case studies demonstrate. Nonetheless, in the final analysis, the resolution of poverty lies in establishing a social market—resubordinating economies to society but without maintaining the gender ideologies that helped to animate these inegalitarian and hierarchical societal structures in the first place.

To deepen the discussion of marginalization, and to consider other facets of this structure, the next chapter places the Mozambique case in the context of subordination in the global political economy and of a swing from an attempt at autocentric development to a neoliberal strategy. The implications of embracing neoliberal globalization in terms of economic growth, political control, and social welfare are assessed. Admittedly, Mozambique is an extreme example of vulnerability, but the extreme case has the advantage of illuminating the possible effects, which of course vary from case to case, of globalizing structures for a developing country seeking to ascend in the GDLP by toeing a neoliberal path.

# CHAPTER 5

# Marginalization: Opening the Market in Mozambique

MOZAMBIQUE is a country that lends itself to metaphor—of high ideals, of challenge to the world system, and of unfulfilled aspirations. There, questions that elsewhere are raised in academic forums have been articulated as matters of public policy: searching questions about the structures that perpetuate inequality, the ability of a mass movement to erode the basis of worldwide domination, and a striving for democracy amid pervasive poverty. In an extreme form, to be sure, Mozambique has gone the way of the continent—from lofty expectations to an increasingly marginal position in the GDLP. Whereas globalization entails the increasing integration of markets, Africa has not kept pace with the spatial reorganization of the world's manufacturing system and the related upsurge of export activities. Although industrialization is not a magical remedy for the problems of underdevelopment, upgrading the role of manufacturing and technology are key components of productive economic growth. Efforts to promote manufacturing are constrained by market-based reforms, however, insofar as they are anti-egalitarian and may erode the basis of democracy at the very time when forces at home and abroad are pushing for democratization.

Building on the conceptualization already developed in this book, this chapter examines the varied interactions among the components of the GDLP: regional processes, migration, commodity networks, and culture. By demonstrating that older division-of-labor constructs must be stretched to account more fully for the regionalization of problems and solutions, this discussion provides a bridge to Part II on globalization and regionalism. Empirically, the analysis will indicate the varied links between globalization and marginalization, using Mozambique as a case study, subject, of course, to the usual caveat concerning the difficulty of generalizing from a single instance.

The discussion that follows will first identify the historical structures that constitute the GDLP in Africa. The empirical sections of this chapter consider the ways in which Mozambique is tethered to the global division of labor and power, review the country's market-based reform program and its loss of control, and evaluate various adjustment policies in transnational relations. The conclusion focuses on the dilemma of reconciling democratization and economic revitalization, a problem endemic to Africa and some other regions as well.

## AFRICA IN THE GDLP

By the late 1970s, the developing countries had become an extremely heterogeneous group. A handful enjoyed remarkable upward mobility in the GDLP; some experienced downward mobility; and others remained on the bottom of the heap, though not in a static position. Notwithstanding spurts of economic growth and signs of democratization, the cases of rapid upward mobility have hardly included Africa, where industrialization has, in many cases, accentuated dualism in the economies. Insertion into the lower reaches of the global manufacturing system may even further marginalization by reinforcing dependence on selective imports, especially of capital goods, and requiring acceptance of the limits of participation in highly competitive global markets. With transnational corporations vying with one another, this competition sets wages and working conditions in the higher tiers of the GDLP against those on the lower end. The result is the continuing fragmentation of the global labor force, with pockets of poverty alongside an expanding service sector in the advanced economies and growing labor reserves in Africa.

Growth rates of many national economies in Africa hovered around zero in the 1980s, while several countries in Asia experienced an annual increase in GNP of around 10 percent. With a population expanding faster than that of any other region, sub-Saharan Africa's real income stagnated. Sub-Saharan Africa also has the world's highest long-term debt as a percentage of GNP: 81.3 percent in 1995, compared to 41 percent for Latin America and the Caribbean in the same year (World Bank 1997b, 246–47). It is noteworthy that in 1980, sub-Saharan Africa's level of debt relative to GNP, 30.6 percent, was lower than Latin America and the Caribbean's 36 percent (World Bank 1989b, 2, 6, 15, 18).

Perhaps the most revealing indicator of participation in the GDLP is the changing structure of production, seen in terms of sector growth rates from 1990 to 1995: Industry in sub-Saharan Africa reflected a bare 0.2 percent increase versus a 15 percent increase in East Asia (World Bank 1997b, 238–39). Manufactured goods as a percent of export volume in sub-Saharan Africa edged up from 13 percent in 1970 to 16 percent in 1993, whereas the figure in East Asia and the Pacific climbed from 24 percent to 30 percent in the same period (World Bank 1995b, 167). Equally telling are consumption, investment, and saving as a percent of

GDP in the two subregions. In 1995, the most recent year for which figures are available, private consumption in sub-Saharan Africa represented 67 percent of GDP compared to East Asia and Pacific's 51 percent; gross domestic investment, 19 percent versus 39 percent; and gross domestic saving, 16 percent against 38 percent (World Bank 1997b, 238–39). These few statistics illustrate the sharp contrast between the two zones of the global political economy.

Just as cross-regional comparisons are useful for analysis, so too are intraregional differences. In 1995, Mozambique's external debt as a percentage of GDP was 443.6 percent, more than five times higher than that of sub-Saharan Africa's as a whole, 81.3 percent (World Bank 1997b, 246–47). From 1990 to 1995, Mozambique's average annual industry growth rate was minus 2.4 percent, compared to 0.15 percent for sub-Saharan Africa. In 1995, Mozambique's private consumption as a percent of GDP came to 75, while sub-Saharan Africa's was 67; gross domestic investment, a vigorous 60 versus 19; and gross domestic saving, 5 versus 16 (World Bank 1997b, 234–35, 238–39).

Quite clearly, Mozambique, fashioned as it was by colonialism as a service economy linked to the interior, occupies a bottom rung on the global ladder. The experience of this poverty-stricken and war-torn country helps to invalidate excessively voluntarist and optimistic thinking about mobility in the global political economy derived from the special conditions under which the Eastern Asian NICs first experienced rapid economic growth (see Mittelman and Pasha 1997, 130–53), some of which suddenly dissipated in the late 1990s.

Mozambique is an important case to consider because of the combination of its economic potential and strategic location in Southern Africa. Citing the significance of Mozambique's ports, harbors, and railway lines for its landlocked neighbors, Olusegun Obasanjo, Nigeria's head of state, noted: "Literally and metaphorically, all routes in independent Southern Africa lead to Mozambique" (Obasanjo 1988, 14). Adding that the strategic vulnerability of these neighboring countries goes hand in hand with their economic vulnerability, Obasanjo concluded his report to the Commonwealth by emphasizing: "I was told by all the [SADCC, today SADC] leaders consulted that they saw in Mozambique the key to the security of the region in the prevailing geopolitical context. Mozambique was regarded as both the most vital and the weakest link in the chain" (1988, 20). As these observations suggest, Mozambique is crucial to any mobility that the countries of Southern Africa might enjoy. To grasp Mozambique's alternatives—and by extension, Southern Africa's—within the GDLP, let us first see how present-day patterns came to be.

## THE GENESIS OF MARGINALIZATION

Mozambique has been joined to the GDLP in a variety of ways. Long before colonial rule, Mozambique's ports provided the transit routes to the interior of Africa for merchants from as far as China. In the colonial era, Portugal developed economic infrastructure in Mozambique, but did little to augment productive capacity. Colonialism cast Mozambique as a subordinate economy to serve the settler-dominated hinterland of Southern Rhodesia (today, Zimbabwe) and South Africa.

During the colonial period, Mozambique produced basic raw materials (mainly from intensive and forced labor schemes in agriculture) for the metropolitan power. Colonial Mozambique also operated as a market for Portugal's manufactured goods. Mozambique's economy depended on the revenue from its ports, east-west railways (in a long, narrow country that stretches from north to south), and workers' remittances. Essentially, Portugal sold black African labor for South African gold. Mozambique acted as a labor reserve for the mines and farms in South Africa, with a portion of the wages paid in gold to Lisbon's Banco Nacional Ultramarino.

Whereas the colonial economy entered a steep recession in the early 1970s, settler tourism and power from the Cabora Bassa dam helped to sustain a faltering structure. In the waning years of colonialism, Mozambique derived 42 percent of its GDP and between 50 percent and 60 percent of foreign-exchange earnings from the rand zone (Mittelman 1981, 23–63). Recalling this legacy, the World Bank aptly noted: "These structural distortions meant that Mozambique was highly vulnerable to a series of exogenous shocks from which the economy has suffered in the post-independence period" (World Bank 1989a, 306).

At independence in 1975, Mozambique inherited a nonviable economy in which exports covered less than half of imports. Five hundred years of Portuguese colonialism left an illiteracy rate of 93 percent and fewer than fifty Mozambicans with a university education. The exodus of 90 percent of the Portuguese settlers caused major disruptions throughout the economy. The shortage of trained personnel impaired key economic activities. To make matters worse, Pretoria sharply reduced the number of Mozambican migrants working in South African mines, ended gold payments for miners' salaries, eliminated tourism to Mozambique, and rerouted freight. Maputo's 1976 decision to implement United Nations-sponsored sanctions against Southern Rhodesia, at an estimated cost to Mozambique of $150 million per year, added to the economic burden. Despite a rich resource endowment, Mozambique's economy was in a chronic foreign exchange crisis.

Against this backdrop, the FRELIMO government sought to gain control over the national economy. The state was obliged to take over abandoned enterprises to ensure the basic functioning of production and distribution. In the agricultural sector, FRELIMO established state farms and parastatals to manage the marketing of produce. Similarly, in industry, state trading companies were formed. With the development of a National Planning Commission in 1978, the role of administrative allocation increased throughout the economy, and FRELIMO initially regarded heavy industry as the driving force of an advanced economy. The immediate priority was to strengthen consumer industries and to build agricultural-processing activities. For the long term, FRELIMO sought to develop transforming industries in order to reduce dependency on foreign imports and to expand exports. Planners envisaged that many industrial projects would be placed in northern Mozambique, close to most of the country's raw materials and away from the axis in the south designed by colonialism and overshadowed by Johannesburg, the submetropole.

In international economic relations, FRELIMO steered a middle course between acquiescing to the situation it inherited from colonialism and rejecting established ties. Having professed a desire to expand dealings with countries of diverse orientations, Mozambique first had to decide how to deal with South Africa. FRELIMO repeatedly expressed its determination to end its dependence on Pretoria, but understood that it would be self-defeating to attempt an overnight divorce. The long-run strategy for disengagement from South Africa was to build an independent home economy and to diversify international economic relationships.

The major constraints on this strategy of escaping from underdevelopment were natural disasters, FRELIMO's own errors, and the intensification of South Africa's policy of destabilization. Beginning in 1977, Mozambique encountered a series of natural calamities, including the worst floods of this century in the country and, later, cyclones and drought. In the face of these difficulties, and under pressure to meet the goals of the Ten-Year Plan, promulgated in 1980, local officials increasingly diverged from FRELIMO's avowed procedures of consultation and discussion and resorted to change by decree. In Nampula province, for example, officials repeatedly justified such actions on the ground of security (Roesch 1989, 10).

Not only did South Africa continue to engage in the economic destabilization of Mozambique, but it also stepped up its low-intensity war against its neighbor. The South African Defence Forces waged a covert campaign through a surrogate. A rebel army, RENAMO, was constituted by the Southern Rhodesian intelligence service after Mozambique's independence in 1975 and transferred to South Africa in 1980 when Zimbabwe became independent. With no professed ideology apart from its staunch opposition to the FRELIMO government, RENAMO engaged in wanton destruction, killing first the few trained personnel and targeting schools, hospitals and clinics, communications stations, power lines, the oil pipeline, and farming areas.[1]

In January 1984, the government assessed its losses since 1975 at $556 million for destruction and sanctions during the Rhodesian war; $3.46 billion for South Africa's reduction in railway and port traffic and mineworker recruitment; and $333 million for direct military aggression by South Africa and RENAMO. Against a GNP of $2.05 billion in 1982, a seven-year loss of $4.02 billion is a staggering amount (Government of Mozambique National Planning Commission 1984, 41). A 1987 study commissioned by SADCC (now SADC) estimated the direct and indirect cost of destabilization in Mozambique at $6 billion. This sum was nearly twice the country's external debt and sixty times the value of Mozambique's exports in the year in which the study was carried out (Government of Mozambique National Executive Commission for the Emergency, and Department for the Prevention and Combat of National Disasters 1988, 5–6). By the time the twelve-year war ended, one million people were dead and the damage to Mozambique's economy came to an estimated $30 billion (Hanlon 1997a).

## MARKET REFORM POLICIES

To arrest the drop in production, the 1983 Fourth Party Congress reassessed FRELIMO's overall strategy. The congress decided to shift priority from state farms and collectives to family farms and private commercial agriculture. Emphasis was no longer placed on new investment, but on the rehabilitation of existing facilities and increased efficiency. The congress pledged to broaden the role of the private sector in the country's economic development. In return for this wide range of reforms, Mozambique gained the support of the IMF and the World Bank, which it joined in 1984.

Buffeted by direct military raids from South Africa and attacks by insurgents, FRELIMO committed as much as 46 percent of the national budget to defense in the mid-1980s (United States Department of Commerce 1989, 6–7). Clearly, resolving the security situation was key to

[1] Dimensions of the human tragedy were monstrous. With the disruption of health services, the infant mortality rate was 173 per 1,000 live births nationwide and the under-five-years-of-age mortality rate reached 297 per 1,000 in 1988 (United Nations Children's Fund 1990, 19). A report by an independent consultant to the U.S. Department of State (Gersony 1988) documents atrocities by RENAMO, including summary executions, mass kidnaping, forced labor, rapes, robbery, murder, mutilation, and torture.

economic revitalization. FRELIMO thus negotiated the Nkomati Accord, a nonaggression pact with South Africa, in 1984. However, in violation of this treaty, the apartheid regime continued to support RENAMO and, also, systematically reduced Mozambique's foreign exchange earnings.

As the economic situation deteriorated, the government adopted an Economic Action Program for the 1984–86 period. This program included an export retention scheme, which allowed export enterprises to use a portion of their foreign exchange earnings for imports of inputs. The program also involved a new code to facilitate FDI. Other measures were enabling legislation for some enterprises to trade directly abroad, and a new labor law permitting enterprise managers to lay off workers and reward increased productivity. Agricultural policies focused on augmenting production in the family sector through the provision of farming tools and production incentives. In industry, rehabilitation centered on the manufacture of textiles, shoes, and other consumer goods.

The Economic Action Program provided the basis for debt rescheduling under the aegis of the Paris Club in 1984. The IMF and the World Bank regarded Mozambique's reform program as an improvement in management but insufficient to engineer an economic turnabout. As the bank put it:

> The fundamental system of centralized management and control continued, and the isolation of the economy from the forces of international and domestic markets only intensified. Fundamental problems were not addressed; notably those concerning the over-valuation of the exchange rate, the allocation of scarce resources including foreign exchange, the provision of incentives to agricultural producers, and the continuing rigid controls over distribution and pricing throughout the economy. (World Bank 1989a, 307)

Doubtless, the fund and the bank conveyed these observations in their discussions with the government of Mozambique in 1985 and 1986, paving the way for agreements with London Club banks and Paris Club creditors in 1987. These agreements afforded debt rescheduling and commitments for new loans, including concessionary interest rates.

To create the structural conditions for economic revitalization, the government introduced the 1987–88 PRE, which focused on reversing the cycle of economic decline and restoring output by 1990 to a level approximately equal to that of 1981. The PRE sought to realize this objective while boosting production and correcting financial imbalances. The idea was to shift the terms of urban/rural trade in favor of rural dwellers and to offer material incentives by rejuvenating industries producing inputs and trade goods for the agricultural sector. Meanwhile, the program aimed to narrow the gap between the official and the parallel market exchange rates. To undercut the parallel market, there were devaluations accompanied by measures to enhance efficiency and incentives for profitable management of productive enterprises. Consequently, in 1987, the metical was devalued from MT40 to the U.S. dollar to MT200 in January and MT400 in June. By October 1988, the metical was MT620 to the dollar; by 1991, MT1,050 to the dollar.

Despite continuing destabilization sponsored by South Africa, the implementation of these neoliberal measures had an unambiguous impact on the economy. In 1987, the economy experienced a recovery of gross domestic output of about 5 percent, as well as a substantial rise in production in the family and private commercial sector. In 1988, GDP again increased—by approximately 4 percent ("Chissano Says Stop" 1989, 45; EIU 1989, 26, 31). It is important to keep in mind the context of this 4 percent hike: growing social stratification and a substantial infusion of foreign aid. It is noteworthy that the economy showed signs of recovery in 1986 even before the PRE was announced. Government figures reflected a 1.5 percent increase in real GDP during that year.

Given the vast scope of the economic distortions, the reform program had been phased over several years, the second phase from 1989 to 1991. The overall objectives of the PRE remained the same as in the first stage and targeted the major policy issues. Priority was accorded to the extension of price decontrols and a wider scope for market forces to guide price formation. Fiscal policy concentrated on instilling financial discipline and restoring profitability to enterprises. Of considerable importance were improved coordination and utilization of external assistance. Monetary policy continued to be restrictive, with controls on bank credit and emphasis on the provision of credit to enterprises. In agriculture, pricing and marketing reforms were aimed at increasing production and boosting the income of rural dwellers.

Along with modest economic growth during the late 1980s, there were serious social dislocations caused by the structural adjustment programs. The devaluations in 1987 sparked massive price hikes. Although wages rose by 70 percent, average prices jumped 200 percent. Budget cuts meant a decline in support for health and education programs. Per capita spending on health fell from $4.70 in 1982 to $1.40 in 1987, then to $0.90 under the PRE in 1989. Education spending in 1988 was only one-third of the amount budgeted for the schools in 1982. While deregulation enlarged the amount of food available in the market and in stores, in 1988 the prices of rice, corn, and sugar increased 300 percent to 500 percent.

The problems accompanying structural adjustment intensified during the 1990s. Mozambique's imports became more expensive relative to the prices of its exports. Exports covered only 15 percent of the country's imports. The external debt in 1993 reached $5.3 billion, almost four times Mozambique's GNP.

The impact of the IMF framework has been evident in the lowering of the quality of education and limiting access to it. There has been a marked shortage of certified teachers and no budget for in-service training. Similarly, services in health care have continued to spiral downward, with per capita expenditure dwindling to as little as an estimated $0.10. The privatization of health care has led to a substantial hike in the price of examinations, hospital fees, and medicine. These high costs result in fewer visits to clinics and hospitals. Women absorb the tasks shed by public institutions, because they bear the burden of caring for family members who are ill and children without school fees (chapter 4).

Faced with sudden increases in food prices in the 1990s, the urban poor rioted in Maputo, blocking roads, stoning vehicles, and storming marketplaces. Similarly, served by only a handful of buses, angry urban residents mounted street barricades and marched in protests over the doubling of fares of private minibuses. Also propelled by dire economic conditions at home, large numbers of Mozambican migrants seeking employment in South Africa have been the target of hostile attacks in townships and mines around Johannesburg, causing them to return and join the throngs of former soldiers searching for jobs.

Within this framework, civil society in Mozambique has not developed according to the Western model of spontaneous organization of voluntary associations. Rather, in the absence of local funding, Mozambican NGOs, which are mostly located in the capital, not in the rural areas where more than 70 percent of the population lives, are closer to the donor agencies than to the social base they are supposed to represent. The partnership being forged is often with international donors, not across Mozambican communities or with civil societies throughout Southern Africa. The top-down vertical ties are largely taking precedence over a bottom-up thrust of civil society (Costy 1995). It is important to bear in mind the context of this "representation deficit": In the early 1990s, official development assistance constituted 98 percent of GNP. This injection of foreign funding was conditional on both economic liberalization *and* political reform.

The government transferred power to elect the president from the party's central committee to the People's Assembly (renamed the Assembly of the People in 1990), in which non-FRELIMO members have seats. At FRELIMO's Fifth Party Congress in 1989, references to Marxism-Leninism were dropped from party statutes and programs. The congress decided to redefine the party as a "vanguard party of the Mozambican people" rather than as a vanguard of a worker-peasant alliance. Mozambique's legislature approved a new constitution in 1990, clearing the way for a multiparty system, with provisions for universal suffrage and secret ballot. The 206-article constitution called for the separation of the executive, legislative, and judicial branches of government.

In 1990, FRELIMO and RENAMO opened talks that culminated in the General Peace Agreement for Mozambique, signed in Rome by President Joaquim Chissano and, for the opposition, Alfonso Dhlakama. The UN Security Council deployed 7,500 troops, police, and civilian observers to oversee the demobilization process and national elections. In 1994, nearly 88 percent of 6.1 million registered voters went to the polls. In a field of twelve candidates for the presidency, Chissano and FRELIMO won more than 53 percent of the ballots, well ahead of second place finisher Dhlakama, with 34 percent. Among 14 parties, FRELIMO gained a narrow majority (129 seats) in a 250-member Assembly, and RENAMO, at 112 seats, came in close behind. Each of the two top parties carried the vote in five of the country's ten provinces.

Protagonists on both sides of the war cooperated with international forces. Although peace could not have been achieved without the political will of Mozambicans, it came at a cost. The country relinquished another slice of sovereignty, this time to a multilateral military presence. Also, UN affiliates—donor agencies—deepened their position within Mozambique's weak economy. Partly to open the spigot of foreign assistance further, in 1995 Mozambique joined the Commonwealth of Nations as well, the first non-English-speaking country to be admitted to that organization.

With its economy coiling in crisis, Mozambique was anything but a free agent. It had little choice but to yield to the demands of more powerful states and international institutions. A *donor-driven response to globalization* means that a country is integrated into the world political economy on someone else's terms. In stark contrast to Mozambique's attempt to secure its autonomy in the 1970s, the locus of decision making shifted outward. With external debt more than one thousand times larger than its exports, Mozambique has lost whatever modicum of control it had over the development process. An ever-tightening web of conditionality constricts Mozambique's economic and political options. This vulnerability severely limits the state's ability to formulate policies appropriate to national needs. (Hence, when IMF and World Bank officials came to Maputo and told Mozambicans to tighten their belts, local authorities were incredulous. Knowing full well that many of their compatriots are so threadbare that they must substitute potato sacks for clothing, the government's negotiating team matter-of-factly responded that the people do not have belts to tighten.)

Evidently, the government of Mozambique and the World Bank have not merely dismantled the country's planning mechanism, but also have implanted a "technical unit" in the Ministry of Finance. According to a Policy Framework Paper for Mozambique jointly prepared by the government and IMF-World Bank staff, this unit's task is "to provide technical assistance for enterprises in the area of management and finance, to ensure the application of economic efficiency criteria in the assessment of the proposals for rehabilitation and new investment, and . . . to provide plans for the restructuring, divesting or closing of specific enterprises" (Government of Mozambique and World Bank 1988, 7).

Thus, with its own survival at stake, and with a populace suffering from war and hunger, the state undertook dramatic measures to change its development strategy. The FRELIMO-led state turned anew to various countries and international agencies in a bid to fulfill its revised plans for adjusting to globalizing processes.

## LOSS OF CONTROL

Although 80 percent of the 16.2 million Mozambicans are employed in the agricultural sector, many of them depend on food aid. These are vulnerable segments of the population who encounter difficulty in getting food, in good part because poor infrastructure, especially rural roads, restricts access to markets. Eighty percent of the food consumed by Mozambicans is imported. Nearly every conceivable aid agency has worked to relieve the situation in Mozambique. Net disbursements of development assistance from all donors to Mozambique climbed from $144 million in 1981 to $649 million in 1987, or to 40.9 percent of GNP (World Bank 1989b, 202). By 1994, this percentage increased two-and-one-half times.

Assistance to Mozambique is widely regarded as aid not to a single country but to the entire subcontinent (Obasanjo 1988, 17). Mozambique's role in SADC as the leader of the Southern African Transport and Communications Commission, based in Maputo, makes it the pivotal point for regional projects in railroad rehabilitation and telecommunication development. SADC projects on all three railroad corridors through Mozambique are well advanced in their ten- and twenty-year plans. Top priority among SADC projects is a U.S.-supported, ten-year plan to rehabilitate the port of Beira and improve transportation links to Zimbabwe, Malawi, and Zambia. This plan is backed by fifteen other countries, with Italy the largest single donor and the Nordics the major regional donor. SADC launched an appeal for several phases of this project, known as the "Beira corridor" program. The Maputo and Nacala corridors are also aimed to give further impetus to enhancing communications and transportation in the subregion. South African firms, sometimes with TNCs as partners, have won most of the tenders for construction and road rehabilitation in the World Bank-promoted Maputo corridor. In this bidding, as well as with privatization, it is difficult for local capital to compete; large state companies are sold to foreign firms, with Mozambicans sometimes involved as junior associates (Hanlon 1997b).

In terms of foreign trade, exports plummeted between 1981 and 1984 and subsequently hovered around the 1984 level. Exports—mainly agricultural products—came to $79 million in 1986. Imports—mostly food and other consumer goods, crude oil and oil products, and machinery and transport equipment—amounted to $543 million in the same year, leaving a sizable trade deficit (EIU 1989, Appendices 4, 5).

Not only did light industry and food processing decline markedly from 1980 to 1986, but industry also accounted for only 12 percent of GDP in 1986. Manufacturing activity is concentrated in Maputo, where 47 percent of industrial production takes place. The important subsectors are food processing, beverages, textiles, chemicals, and bicycle and automotive assembly (Canadian International Development Agency [CIDA] 1989).

To encourage trade and Western investment, Mozambique adopted a flexible policy on repatriation of earnings, allowing some new investors to export up to 80 percent of hard currency profits from the country. Given the historically dire security situation, however, economic incentives have not been enough to attract appreciable amounts of foreign capital. Thus, the government gave foreign enterprises nearly a free hand to set up what are in fact semiprivate militias. Security is part of the cost of investment in Mozambique.

External financing for Mozambique has included a marked increase in foreign loans. In the period from 1982 to 1987, the country's total external debt rose from $1.13 billion to $2.0 billion (Organization for Economic Cooperation and Development [OECD] 1989, 162). It then jumped to $4.3 billion in 1989, and reached $5.8 billion in 1995. As noted above, debt represented 443.6 percent of GNP, prompting donors to mandate that Mozambique reduce investment in human resource development (EIU 1989, 35; *Africa Research Bulletin* 1996, 12557). With a debt service ratio variously reported as between 150 percent and 250 percent (CIDA 1989; "Siege Survival Tactics" 1987, 28), it has been virtually impossible for Mozambique to repay its creditors.

Under these conditions, the hardship imposed on the people most affected by structural adjustment left them with little choice. In fact, those who bear the pain were consulted only after agreement with the IMF had been reached. This tendency toward technocratic and top-down decision making is reflected in a statement by the prime minister of Mozambique:

> We explain the [adjustment] measures after they have been taken. You must understand that given their nature, these matters cannot be announced before taking effect since the people would act in such a way to cancel their effect. We explain frankly to the people why the measures have been taken and they understand that additional sacrifices are necessary and that we are rehabilitating our economy in a time of war. The people also understand that in the first place we must be free. (Machungo 1988, 25–26)

This approach is a radical turn from the early postcolonial period, when FRELIMO formed brigades to go to the countryside to collect opinions and suggestions, not to provide post facto explanations of directives. Partly because of the dynamics of domestic politics and partly because of globalizing pressures, the emphasis has shifted from participatory structures to strict economic growth—and, critics would add, before or without equity.

To Mozambique and other developing countries, globalization of the economy offers greater access to capital, technology, and overseas markets; however, merging domestic and foreign capital also has its drawbacks. As the above quotation makes clear, the free entry of outside institutions can lead to the abandonment of valued aspects of a political culture, in FRELIMO's case extensive grassroots participation in decision making. Globalization also requires sacrificing a large measure of autonomy in policy making. The rise in the share of foreign loans means that external lending agencies, which are supposed to promote competition and efficiency, in fact capture local rents: surpluses that will not be invested in the domestic economy but used to pay for interest on loans from abroad. Some foreign participation in the national economy may indeed be beneficial, but without effective mechanisms of local control, represents a costly way to deal with the deeply rooted problems of underdevelopment.

## ADJUSTMENT OPTIONS

To conclude, we may assess Mozambique's options by fixing our sights on the two crucial starting points of analysis: the country's inherited economic vulnerability and its integration into a regional and global grid. It is important to bear in mind that Mozambique has always been an entrepôt, from the period when the Arabs in Sofala traded for gold with the interior. Mozambique's position as a natural outlet has been enhanced by its role in SADC, which has sought to make use of Mozambique's ports and railway system.

Nonetheless, just as Mozambique has not become an African Singapore, there are no African NICs'. Rather than delinking itself, Africa has been delinked from the global economy. Increasingly marginalized in a rapidly changing GDLP and forced to remain a service economy, Mozambique exemplifies an involuntary form of delinkage.

On the one hand, Mozambique is integrated into global financial markets: International banks and agencies are heavily involved in this Southern African country. On the other hand, Mozambique, like the rest of Africa, has not participated fully in the global manufacturing system that emerged in the last few decades and in the related expansion of export activities by the NICs. Mozambique, like other African countries (except for South Africa, a special case), has failed to capture higher levels of surplus through integrated production and marketing strategies at the global level. Not for a lack of political will or clear thinking, Mozambique has been unable to upgrade its mix of economic activities toward capital- and technology-intensive products (Gereffi 1989, 518).

A critical element in the NICs' ability to generate spectacular economic growth was the priority accorded to manufacturing industries. As stated, industry/GDP ratios for Mozambique, and for sub-Saharan Africa as a whole, do not approach those of the Asian NICs. Export-based industrialization is not without its problems, including the accentuation of income inequality and social tensions. New technologies—e.g., in bottling, milling, and cement operations (Vann 1997)—are reducing the share of labor in total production, but Mozambique is a country with surplus labor. Obviously, industrialization is not tantamount to development. As service sector activities increase in the heartlands of globalization, their industry/GDP ratios diminish to a level below those of the NICs. Similarly, the composition of manufacturing industries shifts, with greater emphasis on new technology (Gereffi 1989).

Today, Mozambique maintains little control over the development process. The IMF and the World Bank not only condition the macroeconomy, but also intervene in all sectors: Project Units—monitors—have been set up in each ministry. Whereas Mozambique's IMF-sponsored reform program has stimulated economic growth, price increases have outstripped wage hikes. Prices for food, housing, and other essentials have skyrocketed, with wages falling behind. The reform program has contributed powerfully to a severe reduction in consumption. In this vein, one gains perspective on reports that Mozambique has attained "higher economic growth rates than any other African country over the past five years, about 8.4 percent, according to a study by the Harvard Institute for International Development" (Duke 1996).

To be sure, there have been real achievements in economic reform—genuine efforts in some parts of Africa to escape underdevelopment and turn the currents of globalization to advantage. But the data must be evaluated in conjunction with purchasing power and dependence, including the practicalities of debt repayment. Since the base figure for growth rates in the 1990s was extremely depressed, owing to the declines in the 1970s and 1980s, percentage increases could be substantial even without approaching the base before political independence in 1975. Additionally, one must bear in mind that macroeconomic growth is fully compatible with no improvement or a decline in the standard of living for the majority. Indeed, an attempt to bring incomes in Mozambique into line with economic growth—including establishing a minimum wage of less than $1 per day, representing less than half the rate of inflation—was termed "excessive" by the IMF, which warned that it might declare the country "off-track" and stop debt negotiations. Faced with this pressure, the Mozambique government spent twice as much as its education budget and four times its health budget on debt payments in 1996, according to Oxfam International (Minter 1998; Hanlon 1998). Meanwhile, one out of four children in Mozambique dies of infectious diseases before reaching the age of five. The international financial community has pledged to reduce the debt burden of "Heavily Indebted Poor Countries," including Mozambique, though not to the level or at the pace desired, but at this writing, the foreign component in the capital expenditure budget rose from 59 percent of the total in 1997 to 77 percent in 1998 (Gumende 1998). Crucially, alongside macroeconomic growth, aid as a percentage of Mozambique's GNP came to 101 in 1994, the most recent year for which statistics are available, up from 8.4 in 1990. The comparable figure for sub-Saharan Africa as a whole was 16.3 percent in 1994 (World Bank 1997b, 218). (Similarly, one should be cautious about optimistic reports that the GDPs of certain other African countries grew substantially in the mid-1990s, for, among other considerations, the question is whether this short-term performance can be sustained. Moreover, aggregate statistics pointing toward the demarginalization of the region hide the pronounced difference between the countries that export oil and those that do not. The decline in oil revenue in the late 1990s nonetheless underlined Africa's vulnerability to shifts in worldwide commodity prices.)

In the meantime, Mozambique's cities are swelled by an influx from the countryside, and the impact of cuts in subsidies is felt most acutely by the urban poor. In the 1993 to 1995 period, three million internally displaced people returned to their home communities. Whereas only 13 percent of Mozambicans lived in urban areas in 1980, the figure soared to 38 percent by 1995, a good portion being external migrants (World Bank 1997b, 230). In the largest repatriation ever undertaken by the UNHCR,

1.7 million Mozambican refugees from neighboring countries were resettled from 1993 to 1995 (UNHCR 1997). Postwar Mozambique is both a receiving country, mostly of its own returnees, and a sending country, whose migrant laborers head for such destinations as Europe and South Africa. What is driving these flows is not only the end of war, but also the uneven impact, the differential effect of market-based reforms on a post-revolutionary society that fought a war of liberation over egalitarian ideals. As we have seen, the reforms are felt most intensely in terms of income levels and distribution of services. Some private-sector entrepreneurs and state and party officials enjoy increasingly different life styles as well as privileged access to services (for example, private schools and health care facilities) previously limited by FRELIMO. Careful observers document rampant corruption—a corruption of both need, when real salaries are driven down, as well as of greed—and the rise of a variety of other social ills: unemployment and domestic and transnational crime, such as drug trafficking, prostitution, orphaned children, and juvenile delinquency (Marshall 1989, 7–8; Egerö 1987, especially 193).

Various FRELIMO Party Congresses have provided an opportunity to debate these issues. Delegates have openly questioned the party and its management of the economy and the war. The debates have covered sensitive matters: the avoidance of military service by privileged groups, the retention of Portuguese as the only national language, incompetence in the handling of the emergency aid, the expropriation of funds and property by party veterans, and the government's failure to protect the poor from austerity programs (*Southern Africa Online* 1989, 2, 6).

To be sure, the government of Mozambique and international monetary institutions are aware of the social consequences of the adjustment program. A World Bank report expressly noted:

> To cushion those sectors of society most affected by the adjustment measures, the government has already introduced a safety net for staples and other essential goods in Maputo and Beira. Other actions to mitigate the impact of the adjustment process on vulnerable groups are being prepared. (World Bank 1989a, 310)

The state has indeed adopted policies to buffer the negative social effects of the reform program. These policies include general wage and salary increases to offset the impact of devaluations; continued subsidies in select areas; and the establishment of special funds for education, health, a social security system, and energy. But are these measures sufficient to assuage the unemployed and their families, pensioners, orphans, drought and war victims, returnees, and urban and rural workers whose wages cannot meet their basic needs?

To reverse course and wrest a measure of control, Mozambicans must first solve the complex puzzle of how to make democratization compatible with economic revitalization. Clearly, there are major obstacles in the path of intertwining democracy and economic rehabilitation. Postrevolutionary Mozambique is heir to both the pluralism of precolonial society and a labyrinthine bureaucracy implanted by the colonial power. A serious problem bequeathed by the colonial state was also the absence of basic technical knowledge. Moreover, in the postcolonial period, the Eastern European model of central planning and state authority contravened FRELIMO's own professed procedures of creativity and debate developed during the liberation struggle (Egerö 1987, 185).

Generally, democracies are not established through democratic means. Rather, democratic procedures, such as voting, are usually adopted after political independence is won, a consensus is reached, and some authoritative body declares that a vote will be taken. Democratic procedures then become an institutional method for arriving at political decisions. In Mozambique, a consensus, however uneasy, with varying degrees of dissent, was reached in the throes of a liberation war, providing the possibility of democratic rudiments. However, adjustments to cope with a deteriorating security situation and a slumping economy furthered marginalization. The market-based reforms have proven to be anti-egalitarian. The social costs of reform impede democratization because the government must inflict harsh pain on millions of already hard-pressed people, some of whom constitute the FRELIMO-led state's very basis of support, thereby undermining consensus. To survive, the state must comply with structural adjustment; however, the implementation of these measures requires increasingly authoritarian actions. To complicate matters, like other countries, one undergoing structural adjustment is subject to pressure to respect fundamental freedoms by international human rights groups. Surely to democratize, adopt the IMF's prescriptions, and promote human rights all at the same time is a tall order.

States are in different structural positions in the GDLP. At the lower end, the state's ability to shape the domestic economy is quite constrained. The old idea of independent, national political economies, as it was known before recent decades, is incompatible with today's range of transnational flows of commodities, labor, capital, technology, finance, and information. To benefit from this transformed order, Maputo must upgrade its output to higher-value-added goods. But Mozambique cannot expand nonexistent manufactured exports and establish its own niche in an increasingly specialized global process of industrialization without maintaining peace and good governance. Democratization, however, is eroded by structural adjustment measures that require the enforcement of unpopular policies. The political clock is ticking so fast that we will soon know whether these two tendencies, democratization and structural adjustment, can coexist. To resolve this tension, Mozambique, with a small domestic market and a manufacturing sector lacking technological capacity, must further coordinate its openings to a transformed world order through the new regionalism.

# Part Two

REGIONALISM AND GLOBALIZATION

# CHAPTER 6

# The "New Regionalism"

THE CENTRAL questions that frame this chapter are: Is regionalism merely a way station toward neoliberal globalization, or a means toward a more pluralistic world order in which distinct patterns of socioeconomic organization coexist and compete for popular support? What forms does this dialectic take? What is the analytical key to understanding the evolving linkages between these multifaceted processes?

Following its decline in theory and practice in the 1970s, regionalism both revived and changed dramatically in the 1980s, gained strength in the 1990s, and today is emerging as a potent force in globalizing processes. Regionalism may be regarded as one component of globalization—a chapter of globalization—and a response or a challenge to it. Moreover, regionalist processes may be best understood as arenas for contestation among rival forces from above and from below, gaining and losing ground in different parts of the world as the intensity increases. In an emerging post-Cold War configuration marked by globalizing tendencies, there are multiple (sometimes overlapping) regional projects, detailed below: the autocentric, development, neoliberal, degenerate, and transformative forms.

The point of entry to the top-down/bottom-up distinction, central to deriving these types, is the "new regionalism" approach, an important advance over the different versions of integration theory (trade or market integration, functionalism and neofunctionalism, institutionalism and neoinstitutionalism, and so on). While this is not the place to rehearse a critique of each variant, all of them are deficient inasmuch as they understate power relations, deal inadequately or not at all with production, and fail to offer an explanation of structural transformation. In some ways a break with this tradition, the new regionalism approach explores contemporary forms of transnational cooperation and cross-border flows through comparative, historical, and multilevel perspectives.

Building on this foundation, I try to provide the conceptual underpinnings for addressing the new regional realities. This chapter stakes out the postulates that constitute the new regionalism approach, critically evaluates the literature, and extends the theoretical framework to include neglected dimensions. The architecture of the new regionalism is incomplete without analysis of the interactions among (1) ideas and their ties to institutions, (2) systems of production, (3) labor supply, and (4) sociocultural institutions, all undergirded by (5) power relations.

Although the discussion here is primarily at a conceptual level, it is supported by illustrations from my fieldwork. By drawing on the experiences of Eastern Asia and Southern Africa in the global political economy, this chapter suggests some of the linkages between different levels of regionalism—i.e., macroregionalism, subregionalism, and microregionalism—and with the Westphalian interstate system.

I first examine the concept of the new regionalism and, subsequently, challenge the Eurocentric scenario. In the third section, I identify key actors and patterns of institutionalization under divergent conditions. Next is a discussion of relationships between the aforementioned elements missing from the extant theoretical framework. Although this chapter cannot provide a fully elaborated alternative conceptualization, it will point toward a reformulation of the new regionalism thesis.

## THE NEW REGIONALISM APPROACH

Regionalism at the turn of the millennium is not to be considered as a movement toward territorially based autarchies as it was during the 1930s. Rather, it represents concentrations of political and economic power competing in the global economy, with multiple interregional and intraregional flows. During the 1930s, a period marked by *autocentric regionalism*, world trade dropped dramatically and protectionism was widely practiced. Moreover, regions of trade and regions of currency were identical. Trading blocs were, in fact, named after major currencies—sterling bloc, yen bloc, and so on. Today, in comparison to the 1930s, there are additional currency blocs, and some of them do not correspond to the zone of trade—for example, the German mark in Eastern Europe, or the U.S. dollar in China and increasingly in the Baltics and other parts of the former Soviet Union. In the developing world, autocentric regionalism has involved calls for delinking and collective self-reliance, the goal of the 1980 Lagos Plan of Action, inscribed in the proposed African Economic Community of the Final Act of Lagos. Today, the prospect of an inward-looking regionalism—the specter of a "fortress Europe"—involves establishing a self-contained entity and closing the door to outside suppliers.

With the spread of deregulation and privatization, however, the outward orientation of *neoliberal regionalism* has meant the diminution of the ability of states and interstate organizations to control aspects of trade and monetary relations (Hessler 1994). Unlike autocentric regionalism, the neoliberal variety is extroverted; it entails an opening to external market forces. In the neoliberal perspective, regional groupings need not be either building blocks or stumbling blocks to world order. Rather, they envelop large regions, their subsets, and smaller economies in a variety of institutional configurations that range from de jure pacts, such as the EU, to a de facto, firm-driven formation in Eastern Asia. The current trend is to establish wider regionalism.

Within this compass, there is an emergent layering of the three levels of regionalism (noted above), all of which interact with other elements of a globalized political economy. For example, within the Asia-Pacific macroregion, there are now attempts under way to join nodes of states. Subregional economic zones, known as SREZs, transcend political boundaries but need not involve entire national economies. Rather, they intersect only the border areas of the national economies (Chia and Lee 1993, 226). One SREZ has been mentioned in another context (chapter 2): the Greater China Economic Zone, which links Hong Kong, Macau, Taiwan, and Guangdong and Fujian provinces of southern China in an informal grouping. And at the microregional level, lead provinces, EPZs, and industrial districts are another dimension of this multilevel process.

These levels intersect in a variety of ways, constituting the new regionalism. Despite their diverse emphases, scholars generally agree that the new regionalism differs from the earlier wave of regional cooperation in several respects. A growth area of scholarship (e.g., Hurrell 1995; Marchand 1994; Morales and Quandt 1992; Robson 1993; Gamble and Payne 1996; Sum 1996; Mansfield and Milner 1997), its characteristics are encapsulated in the following composite.

The most important features of the new regionalism are its truly worldwide reach, extending to more regions, with greater external linkages (De Melo and Panagariya 1992, 37; Palmer 1991, 2). In comparison to the specific objectives of classical regionalism, the new regionalism is multifaceted, more comprehensive than the older paradigm. Unlike the pattern in the Cold War era, the new regionalism is developing in a multipolar context. Superpowers are not driving this movement from outside and above (as with the Australia-New Zealand-United States [ANZUS] Treaty and the Central Treaty Organization [CENTO] or the Southeast Asia Treaty Organization [SEATO], for example), but it is more spontaneous, springing from within and below (Hettne 1994, 2). In this formulation, "constituent states" are deemed the main actors, although the growth of a regional civil society, including social and cultural networks, provides impetus. Unlike Palmer (1991, 185), who maintains that significant breakthroughs, at least in Asia-Pacific regionalism, are primarily in the economic domain, Hettne (1994, 2) argues that the political dimensions of the new regionalism warrant stronger emphasis.

Elaborating on these points, Hettne advances a framework for comparing regions as geographical and ecological units circumscribed by natural and physical barriers; social systems, which implies translocal relations, in some cases including a "security complex" (Buzan 1991); members in organizations; civil societies with shared cultural traditions; and acting subjects with their own identities, capacities, legitimacy, and apparatuses for making policy. Movement toward the higher levels of "regionness"—i.e., the latter criteria—in this multilayered conceptualization are said to delimit the new regionalism (Hettne 1994, 7–8).

The exact form the new regional project might take is unclear. The growth of protectionist pressures and trade conflicts has led to the possibility that industrial production and trade will increasingly be organized in regional blocs. On this issue, one school of thought stems from the neoliberal notion and holds that by helping national economies to become competitive in the world market, regional integration will lead to multilateral cooperation on a global scale and thus reduce conflict. Another school regards the new regionalism as disintegrative, dividing the world economy into trade blocs, and ultimately promoting conflicts among exclusionary groups centered on the leading economies. Perhaps more theoretical than real, this debate has captured public attention, but tension among the macroregions is not the most interesting or potentially consequential aspect of conflict prompted by regionalizing tendencies, a theme to which we will return. Nonetheless, it does identify the contradictory nature of regionalism, which is both an integrative and disintegrative process, partly the result of the interplay among variants of this phenomenon in different zones of the global political economy.

## THE EUROPEAN MODEL VERSUS AFRICAN
## AND ASIAN MODELS

The new regionalism is described as the model for a novel type of political and economic organization. In what is perhaps the most elegant elaboration of this prototype, Hettne indicates:

> The comparative framework has . . . been derived from studying the process of Europeanization, the development of a regional identity in Europe . . . and applied to the case of other regions . . . , under the assumption that despite enormous historical, structural, and contextual differences, there is an underlying logic behind contemporary processes of regionalization. (Hettne 1994, 2)

Claiming that Europe is a "more advanced" regional grouping relative to the arrangements on other continents, he uses this case as a "paradigm for the new regionalism in the sense that its conceptualization eagerly draws on observations of the European process" (Hettne 1994, 12).

The 1958 Treaty of Rome established what is now called the European Union. With six founding members, this unit has undergone three enlargements, and a number of applications are pending. The Treaty of Rome set up an institutionalized system enabling the European Economic Community to enact legislation that is equally binding on all of its members. Hence, the paradigmatic case developed in an institutionalized setting, with declaratory purposes. Its mandate is state-centered, and has expanded according to a legally fixed framework and a series of deadlines.

African and Asian countries do not share the stated aspirations found in the Treaty of Rome and that inspire the EU. Legally binding instruments are not characteristic of SADC or ASEAN, and are unlikely to propel their experience. In fact, European-style integration has never been the objective in Asia-Pacific and African development, because, rhetorical flourishes aside, both regions lack political commitment to deeper integration.

The only initiative to institutionalize political cooperation in the Asia-Pacific region was Malaysian Prime Minister Mahathir Mohamad's idea, put forward in 1990, to form an East Asian Economic Group (EAEG), which would bind Japan, China, South Korea, Taiwan, Hong Kong, and the ASEAN members. He sought to establish an exclusively "Asian" alternative to APEC. The idea was unacceptable to the United States, and the Japanese had reservations. It was therefore transformed into a modest EAEC, or arena for discussion, and in 1993, incorporated within APEC (Stubbs 1994, 374; Mahathir 1989), which had been established at the ministerial level in 1989. (Containing the world's three largest economies—the United States, with 22 percent of world GDP; Japan, with 7.6 percent; and China, with 6 percent [IMF 1993, Annex IV, 116–19], APEC clearly carries more economic weight than do the other macroregions.)

Another difference is that unlike the EU, safeguarded since its precursors' inception by the North Atlantic Treaty Organization (NATO), security was a major reason for the formation of SADC and ASEAN, one seeking disengagement from apartheid South Africa and protection against Pretoria's destabilization campaigns, the other against any designs from revolutionary movements in China and Indochina. In other words, at the inception of these groupings, traditional security issues—concerns over strategic-military threats and, for most of Southern Africa, stagnant or declining economies—formed the regional agenda. Whereas intraregional trade within SADC (except with South Africa today) and ASEAN is slight, Europeans are joined by a high degree of trade among themselves. Further, in terms of economics, intra-APEC trade grew from about 56 percent of the Asia-Pacific total in 1970 to 65 percent in 1990 (Drysdale and Garnaut 1993, 183–86). By 1992, APEC economies accounted for 75 percent of each other's trade and 44 percent of world trade (Garnaut 1993, 17). In comparison, intra-SADC (and before 1992, intra-SADCC) trade never exceeded 5 percent of the total international trade of its members, and intra-ASEAN trade is less than 20 percent of its member states' world trade.

Owing to their dissimilar contexts, the Eurocentric model differs in essential respects from Asian and African regionalism. SADC and ASEAN have rejected a secretariat-led approach, opting instead for lean bureaucratic mechanisms. More important, SADC and ASEAN eschew emphasis on trade and, rather, aim for production-driven and infrastructure-oriented arrangements. Whereas both bodies have had measured success in improving infrastructure (especially transportation in Southern Africa), by all accounts industrial expansion projects in the two subregions have not taken off and have not generated substantial capital formation (Curry 1991; Østergaard 1993, 44).

Clearly, both ASEAN and the macroregion within which it is embedded are market-induced and private-sector-driven constellations. In fact, Drysdale and Garnaut (1993, 186–88, 212) suggest that "the Asia-Pacific model," also termed "the Pacific model of integration," comprises a combination of three elements: Trade liberalization augments economic performance and downplays political perceptions of any disadvantages in income distribution; trade expands without official barriers that discriminate between intraregional and extraregional transactions; and the reduction of nonofficial discrimination (e.g., cultural barriers) to trade contributes powerfully to economic development.

One could refine this model by engaging a discussion of the range of its subsets in the subregions of the Asia-Pacific zone, but that would take us too far afield. Apropos of Southeast Asia, what bears emphasis is that ASEAN's engines of growth have been fueled by Japanese, and later, Korean and Taiwanese, private sector investments. More important, however, is that unlike the portrait of neoliberal regionalism vividly painted by Drysdale and Garnaut, the fourteen members of SADC (which postapartheid South Africa joined in 1994, followed by the Democratic Republic of Congo and the Seychelles in 1997) have sought to respond to the shortcomings of market integration theory, especially its silence about equity and calls for redistribution.

The *development integration* model was introduced as an alternative to a one-sided emphasis on efficiency maximization of existing capacity— not surprisingly, in the context of a low level of productive capacity. This approach stresses the need for close political cooperation at the outset of the integration process. Not only does it assign priority to the coordination of production and the improvement of infrastructure, but it also calls for a higher degree of state intervention than does the market model, as well as redistributive measures such as transfer taxes or compensatory schemes administered by regional funds or specialized banks. Trade integration is to be accompanied by attempts to promote coordinated regional industrial development. A counterweight to economic liberalism, it seeks to redress external dependence, especially through the regulation of foreign investment. Hence, development integration is a multilevel approach engulfing production, infrastructure, finance, and trade.

In practice, the development integration model has fallen short of the professed aims of its architects in Southern Africa. In SADCC's first decade, its professional staff and representatives of member states infrequently consulted the private sector and failed to involve capital in planning regional industrial development. Partly as a result, its regional industrial strategy, while ambitious, is vague and largely unimplemented. Moreover, a distributional crisis besets intraregional trade, with Zimbabwe accounting for large surpluses with all of its SADC partners except South Africa—the type of imbalance that Pretoria's membership magnifies. The more vexing issue, however, is the conflict between the fledgling model of development integration, weakly embraced by social forces in the subcontinent, and the institutionalization of the neoliberal concept, ascendant in the post-Cold War world. This issue is integral to constructing a revised framework for thinking about regionalism.

## ACTORS, INSTITUTIONS, AND GLOBAL GOVERNANCE

To sharpen the focus of this framework, it is useful to revisit the conceptualization of the new regionalism approach, especially the distinction between the "formal region" and the "real region" (Hettne 1994, 7). This point deserves special mention because, increasingly, membership in international institutions imperfectly corresponds to transnational processes, many of them subsurface movements. As indicated, zones of production may arise spontaneously with little or no government intervention and bridge territorial boundaries. Furthermore, culture is constructed and reconstructed at speeds that differ from those of the workings of international institutions, usually at a much slower pace and occasionally forming a regionalized civil society, the Nordic community perhaps being the foremost example.

Clearly, with a multiplicity of interstate and nonstate actors, there is a tendency toward fragmentation of institutions. The Asia-Pacific landscape is marked by a labyrinth of international institutions: APEC,

ASEAN Free Trade Area (AFTA), EAEC, Pacific Trade and Development Conference, Pacific Basin Economic Community, Pacific Economic Cooperation Council, South Asian Association for Regional Cooperation, and so on. So, too, resource-poor Africa is spawning these bureaucratically laden entities, too numerous to enumerate here but including the Commission for East African Cooperation (an effort to relaunch the East African Community), the Economic Commission for Africa (a UN body), the Economic Community of West African States, the Maghreb Union, the Organization of African Unity, the Preferential Trade Area for Eastern and Southern Africa, and the Southern African Customs Union. The list goes on. Not only is there a lack of coherence among these intergovernmental institutions, but they also articulate only sporadically with the bearers of change within civil society—women's movements, peasant organizations, environmental groups, pro-democracy advocates, and the like. These movements voice concerns or demands, mobilize, and apply pressure for the "new" security issues such as food, ecology, human rights, and so forth. But these groups interlink differently at the regional and global levels.

Globalization is not leveling civil societies around the world but, rather, is combining with local conditions in distinctive ways, accentuating differences, and spurring a variety of social movements seeking protection from the disruptive and polarizing effects of economic liberalism. Evidently, the state is constrained by a problem of supranationalism and subnationalism, facing pressures from above and below.

This dialectic creates the greatest difficulties in some parts of the developing world, especially Africa, where Westerners attempted to graft a Western construct—the Westphalian state—on to a different social reality, and the social organism rejected a wholesale transplant. Africa adopted the trappings of the state system, but it was never really anchored in the multiple layers of societies. It is important to remember that the colonial interlude was but a brief period in the vast expanse—the *longue durée*—of African history. A combination of precolonial, colonial, and postcolonial forms has resulted in predatory governance that relies more on brute coercion than the subtleties of consent. Paradoxically, the regional realities—the weakness of the postcolonial state coupled with cross-border flows that are truly bottom-up (communication within ethnic groups that transcend international borders, migratory movements, trading on the parallel market, and so on)—may, in some respects, put Africa at an advantage in moving toward post-Westphalian governance, a multilevel system marked by a less autonomous state amid a multiplicity of other actors. In Africa, where it is painfully evident that collapsed states do not and cannot provide the political and economic rudiments for civil life, an initial lessening of autonomy may eventually pave the way for a regrouping and a determination to build more autonomy. There is an opportunity to reconstitute the state not by shoring up its present postcolonial form, but by opening the channels of political participation to social forces at the base of domestic society working in tandem with democratic movements beyond national borders.

In a transition to an alternative form of governance, the role of international institutions would be especially important. Notwithstanding great expectations in the early 1990s about a supposed revival of the United Nations—primarily, its peacekeeping role—in the post-Cold War era, the existing set of international institutions risks becoming increasingly ineffective and obsolete, only partly because of resource shortages. In the emerging international division of power, the United Nations system attends to political crises, serving as an arena for contestation but, in the main, seeking to harmonize, rationalize, and stabilize patterns of hegemony. Meanwhile, the Group of Seven (G-7) democracies attempt to coordinate the international economy, but it is a tall order for state officials to try to harness unaccountable global market forces.[1] In light of the challenge that economic globalization poses for governance, a restructuring of international institutions will inevitably be inscribed on the policy agenda. It is an elusive task, not least because some regional or subregional movements (such as the CEA, with more than two hundred million people), are without an institutional base and disavow institutional trappings (Stewart, Cheung, and Yeung 1992).

What is to be institutionalized? Insofar as international organizations are products of change within the global political economy, their task is to project a picture of a globally conceived society, a universal vision, and to maintain the dominant world order. If so, they typically set general rules of behavior as well as facilitate regional and global hegemony (Cox 1982, 1996a). Yet international institutions are double-edged swords. In some instances—e.g., to some extent, decolonization and the anti-apartheid movement—they may promote counterhegemony. They are agents of change and do have potential for innovation, especially in the realm of ideas, although the present tendency is to institutionalize neoliberal concepts and practices.

## THE IDEA OF NEOLIBERALISM

The predominant ideas about world order from the 1980s and into the twenty-first century have been neoliberal thinking, partially a reaction to

[1] The G-7 members are all Western capitalist countries, plus Japan. Sometimes referred to as the Group of Eight, they also include Russia, deemed in a transitional stage and invited to join summits for only the political aspects of the talks.

the influence of structuralism in the 1960s and 1970s, and now widely translated into policy prescriptions. By ideas, I mean the shared meanings embodied in culture. When transmitted transnationally, they help to maintain and reproduce a social order, specifically by eliciting consent from both dominant and subordinate groups. Not only may shared meanings entrench the continuity of a given order, but inasmuch as they contain the capacity to create and invent new ways of life, universalizing values bear potential as transforming agents.

On the policy side of the equation, there appears to be a resurgence of integration projects in the South. Perplexed about how to keep up with the enormous concentrations of power and wealth in the three macroregions, the dominant strata in developing countries are attempting to establish new economies of scale. Although economic integration fell into disfavor as a development strategy in the 1970s and early 1980s, international agencies are now pumping money into regional projects. The bandwagon effect has brought aboard bilateral agencies, as well as the World Bank (Davies 1992; Seidman and Anang 1992; Thompson 1991; Mandaza 1990; Shaw 1992). In this way, neoregionalism can become a vessel for neoliberalism, although the two are incompatible under other conditions (discussed below).

Unlike strategies of collective self-reliance, the idea of neoliberalism centers on increasing involvement in the global economy. Whereas self-reliance typically leads to policies of import substitution industrialization, with goods formerly imported being produced locally, engaging the world economy implies an emphasis on export-oriented industrialization. Neoliberals claim that exports can compete with international market prices only if production is unfettered by price controls, such as tariffs. The premise is that left to its own devices, the market is a far more efficient arbiter of economic growth and development than is the state. In a globalizing world, primacy is given to extraregional markets, rather than to intraregional linkages.

Of course, there are trade-offs in the neoliberal project. Deregulation, liberalization, and privatization—a single package, all ingredients of structural adjustment programs—entail welfare losses and distributional effects, for they spread the pain unevenly. In the absence of coordination of the elements of market reforms, neoliberalism may fragment into *degenerative regionalism*. There is degeneration from a more highly organized type into a simpler one. Like the neoliberal project, this form of regionalism seeks to optimize a collectivity's position in the globalization matrix. Yet degenerate regionalism is a defensive measure against further social disintegration, the symptoms of which include widespread corruption, pervasive crime, and gangsterism, often in collusion with the upper echelons of the state bureaucracy: It is a regional attempt at curbing the consequences of shifting the burden onto the more disadvantaged parts of the population in more than one country.

Hence, twelve members of the Commonwealth of Independent States (CIS), a loose confederation established without the three Baltic nations in 1991 to harmonize interrepublican policies after the fall of the Soviet Union, have adopted diverse reform strategies and proceeded at different speeds. In market restructuring, Russia has moved rapidly; Ukraine, Belarus, Kazakhstan, Turkmenistan, and Uzbekistan have avoided shock liberalization and have maintained a high degree of state control over production and prices; and Azerbaijan, Armenia, Georgia, Moldova, and Tajikistan have deferred the question of economic reforms until ethnic rivalries and armed conflicts are settled (Grinberg, Shmelev, and Vardomsky 1994).

Moreover, the spread of the market has fostered two poles, one European and the other Central Asian, in the CIS. Russia is so big and powerful relative to the other members that some of these newly independent states fear Moscow's influence and control over their energy and mineral resources. Except for gas-rich Turkmenistan, the CIS republics are economically dependent on Russia. They seek to maintain sovereignty and achieve collective security, heretofore highly problematic.

The outbreak of civil wars (Georgia, Moldova, and Tajikistan), international clashes (Azerbaijan and Armenia), Russia's military operation in the breakaway region of Chechnya, twenty-five million "ethnic Russians" dispersed precariously in several republics, and the widespread abuse of minorities, in some cases triggering an outflow of population, belie the link between a neoliberal regional economy and liberal politics. Post-Soviet Eurasia is marked not only by chronic violence, but also by continuity in political leadership from the Soviet era, with an entrenched officialdom, or *nomenklatura*, aided by security police who have infrequently been demobilized, as well as a retreat from democratic values.

Under more auspicious political conditions, however, neoliberalism still promises economic growth, and offers flexibility in terms of policy initiatives in a dynamic and increasingly integrated world economy. The neoliberal vision rests on flexible responses to price signals and a high degree of division of labor adapted to new methods of production.

## NEOLIBERALISM AND FLEXIBLE PRODUCTION

If the new regionalism approach neglects the question of production of what and for whom, it cannot explain changes in the geography of world capitalism. If so, it would fail to constitute more than a partial and limited view of the mosaic of regional development. Coincident with the ascendance of neoliberalism is the emergence of specialized regional production systems, with their own intraregional divisions of labor both among countries and within industries.

The introduction of flexible specialization systems makes regional production networks ever more important, because a premium is placed on spatial clustering of suppliers around plants, partly to ensure timely deliveries. Notwithstanding the advent of new technologies that compress time, propinquity in certain industries still means lower costs and greater opportunities for matching needs and capabilities. Proximity to nearby suppliers and workers, installed within a production culture that encourages innovations from the shop floor, allows for fluctuations in market demand.

In the new flexible production subregions and microregions, there are several variations. Centers of flexible production have burgeoned in many Asian and Latin American NICs and near-NICs (an experience assessed in Mittelman and Pasha 1997, chapter 6). In Asia-Pacific regionalism, Japanese-led TNCs have expanded and have relied on the flexibility offered by a multiplicity of small and medium-size contracting firms. Regional complexes of industries are developing in such activities as electronics and computers. What is emerging is a regionally integrated production zone not solely based on Chinese family enterprises and networks of business, but often fueled by Japanese capital lacking such familial ties (Stubbs 1994, 372–73). As the Japanese economy has become deeply embedded in the economy of the Asia-Pacific region, it has used a web of sociocultural structures as a conduit for flows of capital. Strong bonds of kinship and culture in geographically proximate areas can reduce transaction costs and provide a level of interpersonal trust that facilitates regional business.

## FLEXIBILITY THROUGH SOCIOCULTURAL NETWORKS

The implementation of flexible specialization turns not only on a technoeconomic structure rooted in a territorially concentrated system of production, but also on the qualitative aspects of a social milieu. Most important are cultural factors grounded in civil society, including the degree of trust and consensus underpinning the market and the industrial climate for generating skills for the workplace. In other words, informal communication of ideas about building regionalism at different levels takes place within social institutions such as ethnic groups, families, clubs, and so on, some of them originating in precapitalist society (Asheim 1992; Goodman and Bamford 1989). Insofar as the flexible specialization model as a productive system requires strong relations with civil society, sociocultural institutions may represent either a constraining or a potentially enabling factor in regional development.

What needs to be added to what I have said about the role of Chinese families as transnational linkages in Asia-Pacific's explosive economic growth (Chapter 2) is the way that Japanese investment and aid set off the explosion, particularly in the Southeast Asian subregion. In fact, the expansion of the ASEAN economies cannot be understood without taking into account the geopolitics of Southeast Asia and the conjunction of the hegemonic interests of the United States and Japan.

After the United States pumped capital into Southeast and East Asia during the Korean and Vietnam wars, Japan gradually expanded its flows of capital throughout the region, but it is to the United States, and not Japan, that Southeast Asian countries export the largest portion of their manufactured goods. In the evolving triangular division of labor in Asia-Pacific regionalism, Japan, and to a lesser extent the United States, furnish investment capital, and Southeast Asia provides raw materials for Japan as well as cheap labor for the production of manufactured goods largely for the U.S. market. Japanese capital has had an uneven impact on the economies of Southeast Asia, with Singapore attracting the biggest share of direct investment on a per-capita basis. Quite clearly, Singapore has been the chief beneficiary of capital flows and the geopolitics of the subregion (Stubbs 1989, 1991).

With Japan's trade patterns shifting toward a regionally based economy, Tokyo has helped ASEAN economies enlarge their export manufacturing sectors and augment the efficiency of Japanese manufacturers relocating in Southeast Asia. The regionalization of Japanese industry has created a little-noticed incongruity in the economy of Singapore, and perhaps those of other countries. One of the few countries to identify the extent of GDP generated by foreign or foreign-controlled factors of production, Singapore releases data that show that an increasing share of its output is foreign-produced. From 1980 to 1991, foreign-produced GDP grew at a rate of 250 percent, compared to 147.5 percent for indigenous GDP. Paradoxically, the foreign-controlled sector is able to find an array of profitable opportunities for expansion and investment in Singapore, while national capital is now lending a greater part of its portfolio abroad. Doubtless, the explanation partly lies in the locally controlled sector's competitive disadvantage in technology, showing just how hard it is even for one of the more dynamic economies in the developing world to jump the elusive last hurdle to advanced-economy status (Kant 1992; Bernard and Ravenhill 1995).

The explanation also rests on the complex divisions of labor and power in the region. While Japanese direct foreign investment in Asia soared from $2 billion in 1987 to $8 billion in 1990 (two to three times as great as the U.S. total), the telling point is that the bulk of value added stays with the Japanese; smaller shares accrue to junior partners in a flexible but structured manufacturing bloc. Retaining a clear-cut technological edge, Tokyo coordinates locational decisions in a regionally articulated division of labor, offering investment, aid, and knowhow. Although there are still stand-alone Chinese conglomerates, "ethnic Chinese" throughout Southeast Asia are often partners linked to the Japanese in joint ventures. In a regional system that widely adopts Japanese methods of flexible production, big Chinese firms—the Liem group and Astra, for example—are vehicles for Japanese capital, sometimes as assembly plants or as distributors for corporations such as Fuji or Komatsu (Tabb 1994; Heng 1994).

Going beyond the interplay of Chinese family holdings and Japanese enterprises, it would be shortsighted to say merely that in regional development, culture facilitates flows of capital. The emphasis on powerful structures should not deflect attention from cultural discontinuities and the ways that these discontinuities are created. In the second phase of a Polanyian double movement, a reaction to changing material conditions on a global and regional scale, individuals are not passive occupants, but active agents who negotiate socially prescribed roles. They enter and shape decision making in national and multilateral arenas by reconstituting culture, beginning with micropractices. Strategies of countering social control in the workplace or of reorganizing the production process involve renegotiating meanings, redefining customs, and pushing up against the boundaries of old social structures in more enabling ways (Kabeer 1991). While other authors have provided graphic studies of the production-culture link at a local level, my interest here centers on regional interactions, with sociocultural institutions mediating the production process and labor supply.

## FLEXIBLE PRODUCTION AND
## FLEXIBLE LABOR MARKETS

With the emergence of macroregions, the new regionalism internalizes multiculturalism in the form of the North-South problem. In vastly different ways, APEC, the EU, and NAFTA facilitate the mobility of both capital and labor. To enhance the competitiveness of open economies, and to provide labor market flexibility, countries at various levels of economic development have joined together, a process that may be taken further by the admission of the Eastern European countries to the EU (Yamamoto 1993).

In Eastern Asia's NICs and near-NICs, high rates of economic growth for more than a decade, coupled with a rapid demographic transition, resulted in elevated wages and labor shortages. Singapore, for example, has relied on foreign labor to mitigate problems in labor supply. Malaysia, an exporter of skilled workers to Japan, was hosting about one million illegal migrants from Indonesia and others from Thailand and elsewhere until the 1997 economic downturn, which prompted the repatriation of foreign laborers. Unlike receiving countries in the subregion, the Philippines is a large supplier of contract labor and also a major exporter of skilled workers and human services. Migrants from Indochina are putting further pressure on labor markets in other parts of Eastern Asia.

In Southern Africa, the historical pattern of subregionalism was shaped by South Africa's need for cheap migrant labor and services from neighboring countries, which became parties to a highly unequal relationship. In fact, dating back to the discovery of gold in the Transvaal, migrant labor has powered the engines of the South African mining industry. For South Africa's capitalists, a migratory labor system offered several advantages. So long as South Africa paid higher wages than the hinterland territories, it was sure to have a labor reserve. By recruiting workers from beyond its borders, South Africa could keep wages in the mines depressed, ensuring that local laborers would not be diverted from home industries and farm enterprises.

In the period following 1975, when Mozambique won political independence, South Africa sought to diversify its sources of migrant labor and to reduce the magnitude, part of its destabilization campaign against hinterland countries. Thus, against a 31 percent decline in employment on member mines of the Chamber of Mines of South Africa from 1984 to 1994, the number of foreign mineworkers dropped from 204,104 to 165,808 during this period (computed from South African Institute of Race Relations 1996, 258). Nonetheless, migrant labor remains a crucial component of the post-apartheid and subregional economies. Large-scale rural-urban migration provides a labor pool for industries. Moreover, the brain drain from other parts of the region benefits South Africa. Semiskilled, skilled, and professional people are sapping the sending countries of human resources and are contributing importantly to South Africa's economy, although a high rate of unemployment is a nagging problem. Just as South Africa attempts to convert its economy from the old industries, as well as from a plethora of laws designed to regulate labor supply, so too is the new power structure trying to create competitive advantage, which entails flexible specialization and a reconstituted labor market.

## POWER RELATIONS

Looking at regionalism from the standpoint of power relations, it is clear that the neoliberal approach holds sway. In fact, there is little evidence that other projects, though important theoretical contributions, have been implemented with any degree of adherence. Autocentric regionalism and development integration schemes in the ASEAN and SADC countries have not achieved coordination of production on a subregional basis; they rarely articulate with either the industrial bourgeoisie or grassroots movements. A number of national agendas promoted by subregional organizations could have actually been instituted without international intervention. Hence, analysis of extant forms of regionalism necessarily focuses on the neoliberal variant and the interests it serves.

Concerned as it is with purportedly universal laws of development, neoliberal theory posits that, in principle, the same rules of economic development can be applied across the board from the most developed to the least developed countries. As such, the theory is overly mechanical and represents a slot-machine approach to regionalism. Taking an individualist approach, it is silent about deep structural inequalities, especially the qualitative aspects of underdevelopment lodged in the blockage of highly inegalitarian social systems. In addition, largely unnoticed is the contradiction between the openness of neoliberal regionalism and its potential antiregional thrust. Insofar as open regionalism strives for a worldwide market and hooks directly into the global economy, it can skip over regional integration. The rationale sometimes heard in business circles is that gains from trade will be maximized through an efficient international division of labor, not a regional one.

What is more, neoliberals' vision of market relations as a frictionless world of shared meanings, the uncontested adoption of the ideology of capitalism, is structurally blind to patterns of domination and hegemony. Guided by a highly developed neoliberal agenda, regional hegemony is a recurrent issue accompanying the new regionalism, conspicuously so in the macroregions: Germany in the EU, the United States in NAFTA, and the sometimes strained relationship of the United States and Japan in the Asia-Pacific cluster.

The linkages in Japan-ASEAN relations aptly illustrate this pattern of asymmetry. If all imports and exports are included, Japan is ASEAN's largest trading partner, its major direct investor, and the chief source of official development assistance (Naya and Plummer 1991, 266–67). Although the United States has become the leading recipient of ASEAN exports, the ASEAN countries are highly enmeshed in the Japanese vector of the globalization process: ASEAN is the base for production, and Japan is its core. As part of the Japanese-led integration scheme, many Japanese industries relocated in Southeast Asia, with greater coordination of home-based enterprises and their overseas firms. ASEAN became a production site for exports to the United States, Europe, and its own subregional market. The regional division of labor in such industries as automobiles has involved the coproduction of parts. Within Toyota, for example, Indonesia and Thailand concentrate on diesel engines, stamped parts, and electrical equipment; the Philippines, transmissions; and Malaysia, steering links and electrical equipment. The Singapore office coordinates and manages various transactions. While both ASEAN countries and Japan can gain from such linkages, the ASEAN economies become marginalized from decision making and more vulnerable to political and economic manipulation from Tokyo (Hamzah 1991).

In other regions, too, the specter of regional hegemony rears its head. To wit, South Africa's GDP of $136 billion in 1995 was approximately four times the total for the other eleven (later thirteen) SADC members, according to the most recent figures available (World Bank 1997b, 236–37). Moreover, by any measure, the military imbalance dwarfs such economic disparities, woven as they are in a complex web of historical interconnections. Most overseas investment in the subregion goes to South Africa as well. Its infrastructure and banking, manufacturing, trading, and service sectors make it an economic headquarters for the region.

Neoliberal theory has, of course, been put into practice in the form of adjustment policies drawn up by the World Bank and the IMF. The main beneficiaries of such neoliberal projects are capital that can quickly shift across national borders, exporters free of restrictive trade policies, industrialists at home whose productivity and prices are competitive with foreign firms, and local banks that gain from the framework of deregulation, liberalization, and privatization (Hewitt, Johnson, and Wield 1992, 195). Not covered by the neoliberal umbrella are the interests of other social forces, which must seek an alternative venue.

## THE ARCHITECTURE OF THE NEW REGIONALISM APPROACH

Having identified four responses to the pressures of global restructuring—autocentric regionalism, development integration, neoliberal regionalism, and degenerate regionalism (tendencies that can coexist)—it is important to search for signs of another conceptualization, a supplement to the new regionalism approach. The beginnings of a design for an alternative architecture may be found in the contradictory nature of globalization. Its integrative and disintegrative aspects establish a new polarity, which allows space for experimentation on a regional level.

On the one hand, a centralizing trend under globalization may provide either hegemony led by the United States or cohegemony, a form of multilateral governance directed by the triad of Europe, the United States, and Japan, perhaps with Japan serving as a junior constable for the United States (Mushakoji 1994, 25). Centralizing globalization seeks to justify itself through universalizing values. It helps shape a hierarchical regional order, and transnational capital incorporates regionalism. However, the global restructuring of power regionalizes conflict. For example, China's microregions (EPZs) compete with a subregional body, ASEAN, for investment. In turn, ASEAN is losing investment to a national unit and now a member state, Vietnam, with its low-cost manufacturing base. In a contradictory relationship propelled by neoliberalism, a number of investors from ASEAN have turned to Vietnam, contributing to its infrastructural, manufacturing, and service sectors (Kumar 1993, 36–37).

Without attempting to provide a complete inventory of such regional clusters, it is clear that focusing too heavily on the macrolevel underestimates the importance of the microissues. The microdimensions are especially important precisely because new production methods and technological conditions encourage specialization and diversification. The introduction of frontier technologies calls for small capital initiatives, not gigantic transnational R&D ventures (Mushakoji 1994, 21). Moreover, there is opposition to the emergence of certain regional processes. Opponents raise the knotty question of distribution of benefits not only in terms of the nation but also in light of ethnic and racial access—e.g., whether in Southeast Asia, Chinese Malaysians benefit disproportionately from their relationships with Chinese Singaporeans (Akrasanee 1993, 14).

While hegemony contains social conflict, it does not eliminate it altogether. The dominant interests set limits to opposition, but in transitional conjunctures created by structural transformations, fundamental challenges may be mounted. In other words, hegemony is not a stable condition; it is always being created and undermined.

At present, a counterthrust to neoliberal restructuring is emerging in what might be called the stirrings of *transformative regionalism*, i.e., a regionalism grounded in civil society, more as a future prospect than as a current phenomenon. In its embryonic form, transformative regionalism is partly a defensive reaction mounted by those left out of the mosaic of globalization, particularly in zones outside the macroregions. The political and economic program is not unlike that of the development integration model: close political cooperation at the beginning, not the end, of the project; equity and balance in relations among member states, including redistribution formulas; and increased trade based on regional industrial planning. In restructuring, the state must be an active agent in transforming integration; its main roles are to rationalize production, build infrastructure, and promote exchange. Stressing self-organizing, the alternative formulation calls for regionalism that flows from the bottom upward and is linked to new forms of cultural identity being developed by the women's movement, environmentalists, prodemocracy forces, human rights groups, and so on. At the end of the day, the possibilities and limitations of transformative regionalism rest on the strength of its links to civil society. Creative potential for bringing about sustainable growth and democracy lies in popular support and a sense of involvement of multiple strata of the population.

Although practitioners may not use the term, transformative regionalism is clearly the expression of a dialectic. Forces from above seek to entrench the neoliberal framework, but encounter resistance from social forces at the base. At issue are local control and alternative directions of development, which also comprise a struggle over different visions of regionalizing processes. The unsteady balance between a top-down thrust and a bottom-up counterthrust varies not only among regions, but also within them. Alongside the struggles in Eastern Asia and Southern Africa is the strife over Thatcherite Europe versus "social Europe."

Is transformative regionalism a pipe dream or a process given concrete expression? In 1989 in Japan, and in 1992 in Thailand, various movements and networks issued a call for a People's Plan for the Twenty-First Century (PP21). The PP21 process is an effort to promote a popular and democratic movement for social transformation. Transborder concerns—the role of migrant women in Asia's growing sex industry, the struggle against environmental degradation wrought by the construction of golf courses and other resort facilities on agricultural lands, the role of Korean workers in Japanese-owned firms operating in Korea, and so forth—are central to the agenda. There is recognition that the new vision can be best put into practice through coordinated regional action (Hart-Landsberg 1994).

Similarly, the São Paulo Forum, founded in 1990, meets annually and brings together parties and social movements from around the Americas to discuss ways to build an egalitarian form of regional unity. What animates the forum is the magnitude and consequences of neoliberal restructuring in Latin America. Neoliberal globalization—cum macroregionalism in Mexico—has displaced vast numbers of workers and peasants, pushing them into the informal sector, where they adopt survival strategies in a range of legal and illegal activities. Restructuring is depriving the state of its ability to regulate economic life, furthering the outflow and internal concentration of wealth. The social consequences are severe, with a teeming underclass barred from meaningful or productive participation in society. Although the forum has not fully detailed an alternative project, it stresses redirecting hemispheric integration away from U.S. hegemony and toward Latin American integration "with a nationalist focus and a continental perspective that addresses North-South inequalities." With the restructuring of world capitalism, the solution is not seen as withdrawal from the global economy or exclusive interaction among Latin Americans themselves. Rather, emphasis is placed on regional cooperation and collective action (Robinson 1992).

Although the Latin American experience differs in many ways from the integration process in Southern Africa, a common item on the agenda in both regions is the inclusion of social charters in integration agreements. One issue inscribed in these charters is enabling integration to serve as a mechanism for enhancing workers' rights and standards across a region. Other elements are corrective measures so that the pain of adjustment in integration does not fall heavily on the poor, the establishment of funds to invest in depressed areas, a resolution of debt, reform of immigration laws, environmental protection, some management of trade, the deepening of democratic practices, and the creation of democratic regional institutions. In the Southern African Trade Union Coordinating Conference/ Congress of South African Trade Unions/National Council of Trade Unions "Draft Social Charter," the South African trade union movement has addressed some of these points (Davies 1992). If they have to be prioritized, the last of the aforementioned challenges is the one that is likely to be the most telling: how to promote a strong regional civil society that will involve people in decision making at every level in a democratic way. Such civil-society initiatives must be considered in conjunction with the structure they encounter, namely, global hegemony, to which we now turn.

# CHAPTER 7

## Global Hegemony and Regionalism

### (COAUTHORED WITH RICHARD FALK)

HEGEMONY is a recurrent feature of regionalism, contributing to polarization and resource imbalances. Not to be confused with its non-Gramscian meaning of a preponderance of power, the concept of hegemony is used here in the Gramscian sense of a mix of coercion and consent, in which consent is the dominant element. In this usage, neoliberal hegemony is instituted under global leadership to mediate between an oligopolistic market and domestic sociopolitical forces. Since the end of the Cold War, the United States has played this central role—as the phrase "the Washington consensus" suggests—in conjunction with its partners in different regions. When ideological hegemony proves fragile or is challenged, a hegemon may use a variety of instruments, including diplomatic means of maintaining harmony and military methods of coercion.

This chapter, then, turns to politics. It explores the geopolitics of globalization, and examines links between economic and military security in the context of globalizing processes. Specifically, this chapter considers the following: Can the new regionalism be used to promote U.S. hegemony in a globalizing world order? What are the dilemmas associated with forging regional approaches to managing the globalizing pressures of a post-Cold War era?

Our core argument is that the overall U.S. approach to sustaining hegemony—i.e., ingraining the idea and practice of neoliberalism—incorporates a loose composite of regional policies that forms a patchwork. The conclusion holds that for U.S. policy makers, regionalism has nonetheless emerged as a critical, yet still tentative, and even inconsistent feature of a neoliberal multilateral order—an adhesive often used to join the political and economic dimensions of global restructuring.

We begin by delimiting the context and, then, exploring challenges to U.S. interests associated with the new regionalism. Since the United States, in effect, belongs to various regions, it is necessary to examine the three pillars on which U.S. policy rests: NAFTA, APEC, and the Atlantic Community. Other regional projects in far-flung, and in some cases marginalized, parts of the world, while of concern to Washington, are not central to this analysis, because, by the late 1980s, they had, by and large, followed suit in a competitive liberalization drive to attract foreign investment and expand international trade.

## AFTER THE COLD WAR

In a manifest sense, the collapse of the Soviet Union ended, at least temporarily, the debate about U.S. decline that had been so prominent during the 1980s. Indeed, the triumphalist mood emphasized the role of the United States as the sole surviving superpower. U.S. hegemonic diplomacy and military prowess were confirmed by the way in which the 1990–91 Persian Gulf crisis, initiated by Iraq's invasion of Kuwait, was resolved. The new era, which President George Bush christened as "the new world order," would seem to allow the United States to make use of the UN as a legitimizing support in relation to hegemonic security concerns.

But such developments associated with the end of the Cold War obscured the weaknesses of the United States as a global hegemon. Even in the Gulf War, the United States insisted on shifting the financial burden of the military action to others, prompting Japan to complain about taxation without representation. Beyond this, the weakness of the dollar, which reflected huge trade and budget deficits in the early 1990s, meant that sustaining the U.S. hegemonic position required new methods that would not create a domestic backlash within America. The firestorm of criticism directed at the United States in 1993, after eighteen Americans died in an incident in Somalia, disclosed that the multilateral frame of the Gulf War was an anomaly rather than an emergent pattern of geopolitics, and that the American public concurred with hegemony, but with few burdens on wealth and lives. The 1995 Bosnian peace agreement, forged in the heartland of the United States —Dayton, Ohio—represented a new phase of the trial-and-error dynamics with respect to shaping a hegemonic role in the overall setting of the 1990s. The diplomatic leadership of the United States now seems firm and unchallenged, but the will and wherewithal are not at all assured, giving the hegemonic stature of the United States an ambiguous and tenuous quality.

Against this background, regionalism in various formats is an important feature of *hegemonic geopolitics*. Unlike the globalist response to the Gulf crisis, the effective locus of diplomatic and military initiative increasingly was a United States-led reliance on NATO, and, to a lesser extent, the European contact group. Whether this regionalization of response can provide a pivotal moment for the *geopolitics of globalization* is not currently evident. Also, the search for a hegemonic role for the United

States in various economic settings also remains open-ended, as does the balance between reliance on unilateralist and on regionalist approaches.

We argue that the relationship between regionalism and U.S. foreign policy is eclectic and uneven. Notwithstanding NATO's 1999 bombing campaign against Slobodan Milosevic's Yugoslavia, regionalism associated with military-strategic goals is generally of questionable significance as an instrument in the hands of U.S. foreign policy makers, while economic regionalism is of increasing importance. In part, this dual pattern expresses the basic shift from an era of geopolitics to one of *geoeconomics* shaped by the logic of globalization. Regionalism for military-strategic security depends on common external or internal enemies, and in their absence is unlikely to take precedence over the tendency of states to rely on their own capabilities to uphold security, or in cases of particular threats, to seek support on a bilateral basis, as in the 1998–99 U.S. air strikes against Iraq with British participation.

In contrast, regionalism for economic purposes depends on the logic of global capital that gives states an incentive to band together to achieve market shares and augment trading and investment opportunities. Furthermore, expanding economies pose threats to weaker state systems, giving regions and subregions incentives to integrate economically to offset the threat being posed.

Since 1989, U.S. foreign policy has been casting about for a mixture of political instruments to sustain its hegemonic role in the world in a manner that minimizes fiscal and political strains. Although the overall relevance of regionalism to the U.S. global role is yet to be clearly defined, this chapter contends that for the present, U.S. foreign policy is only occasionally relying on regional military-strategic arrangements while increasing its reliance on economic regionalism.

Indeed, regionalism has become a major theme in American foreign policy. The scholarly writing and public discourse on this issue focus on questions of regional security arrangements and trading blocs. Often these two sets of concerns are kept in distinct compartments, although there are large degrees of overlap, especially in relation to Europe.

With respect to military-strategic security in the current global setting, U.S. foreign policy is, for the most part, moving away from regionalism, with the partial exception of Europe. In other regions, regional alliances of the Cold War, such as CENTO, SEATO, and ANZUS, survive merely as relics of a superseded past. During the Cold War, U.S. foreign policy, especially in the 1950s under the influence of John Foster Dulles, promoted and relied on regional security arrangements as an integral element in its overall global policy of containment directed at the expansion of Soviet bloc influence. In the contemporary phase of globalization, however, the United States has little need for such regional security arrangements. Besides, many countries seek to exercise their sovereign rights as independent states, and do not perceive themselves to be threatened by "expanding world Communism" or another systemic "menace." But there are other social forces and values that must be taken into account.

## FOREIGN POLICY CHALLENGES AND U.S. INTERESTS

Domestic factors figure prominently in the orientation of policy makers toward regionalism. In the United States during the 1990s, the politics of discontent has taken different forms—calls for a third-party candidate as an alternative in presidential elections, low voter turnout (37 percent) to enable the Republican Party to form a majority in Congress in 1994 (for the first time in forty years), and polls showing that even those who cast ballots for these Republicans did not expect meaningful change. There appears to be a sense—more than an undercurrent, but rather a sophisticated understanding among the citizenry—that electoral politics does not produce leaders with credible solutions for the country's problems. Indeed, from the perspective of some critics of the type of "process-oriented" liberal democracy in the United States, leadership choice confined to a small, managed group alongside formal freedoms cannot deal with the fundamental issues of economic power and inequality (Robinson 1996). This dissatisfaction can, to a significant degree, be associated with pressures generated by economic globalization, especially polarization of incomes and benefits. Notwithstanding substantial stock market rises during the mid- and late 1990s, the economic circumstances for many—such as reductions in welfare provisions, the need to work more than one job, and diminished employment security—grew harsh and mean-spirited.

While scholars explicate the particular set of structural changes that comprise the realignment known as globalization, the state itself is seeking adaptive strategies to manage this trend. Additionally, politicians—members of Congress, for example—are responding to these new realities in a variety of ways, including a package of benefits for business and burdens for the laboring portions of the citizenry, especially its most disadvantaged segments. One expression of this adaptive dynamic has been to shrink the resources and roles of government, especially in relation to social spending, and, in some instances, the environment.

This tendency is reinforced by the weakening of organized labor, the public ascendancy of business and finance, and the mainstream ideological consensus of a neoliberal character. President Bill Clinton, a Democrat in the White House from 1992 to 2000—despite being elected on the mandate of giving priority to the domestic economy—tilted foreign economic policy in the direction of global market forces, overriding the objections of the traditional constituencies of the Democratic Party, a process evident in the fight over the ratification of NAFTA and in the promotion of the World Trade Organization (WTO). This pattern of adjustment by nominally liberal (and, to some extent, social) democratic leadership has been repeated throughout the world, suggesting the structural impact of globalization. For various reasons, especially associated with welfare and employment traditions, the specific character of adjustment has been much more painful in some countries than in others.

This cluster of circumstances arising out of globalization has generated a series of foreign policy problems that take their distinctive shape as a result of the interactions between a high degree of unipolarity with respect to global diplomacy and military capability and a general character of tripolarity or multipolarity (G-7) when it comes to economics.

First, U.S. foreign policy makers are struggling with the issue of how to cope with transnational economic forces for which there are no effective regulatory mechanisms. As evident in the 1995 collapse of Barings Bank as a result of fraudulent trading practices of a single employee in its Singapore branch office, international finance's highly leveraged market for derivatives is global in reach, but effective regulation depends on domestic frameworks. Similarly, the growing mobility of capital, its capacity to move, makes it increasingly difficult for any state to use its policy instruments to control polluting and environmentally destructive behavior by corporations. Going one more step, to the extent that globalization—and regionalism as one of its components—extends the boundaries of unregulated or deregulated capital accumulation, it shrinks governments' capacity to be responsive to democratic pressure, and thereby constrains citizens' power to control their own economic lives. Subject to the constraining impacts of conditionality and structural adjustment, some developing countries experience this loss of control to a larger degree and in more blatant ways than do developed countries, but even a country as rich and powerful as the United States is increasingly a casualty of globalization, at least as far as governmental policy on public goods is concerned.

Next, in practice, foreign policy makers in Washington, like their counterparts elsewhere, encounter a matrix of zones highly integrated into globalization, and others increasingly marginalized from it. A fundamental feature of a globalizing world, this sharp polarization threatens to produce instability and recurrent eruptions of regional conflict.

The third challenge is the contradiction between the globalization of markets and assertions of a community of values not premised on neoliberalism. Put differently, the issue is really one of moral order: Beyond gauging human worth in terms of market criteria and the amount of consumer goods one possesses, what is the moral component of globalization? At bottom, this is the challenge of an alternative globalization project—resurgent Islam, whose image is tarnished in Western media, but one dimension of which powerfully challenges the absence of an ethical dimension in neoliberal globalization and condemns the cultural consequences of the consumerist ethos (Pasha and Samatar 1996).

Finally, in the face of globalizing forces that it cannot harness, the state surrenders a slice of sovereignty partly as a defensive measure and partly to reflect the globalized outlook of the governing stratum. Taking the most institutionalized form of regionalism, the EU is not the "United States of Europe" envisaged by its founders, but is often perceived as a new externalized authority structure that determines how much farmers can grow, specifies conditions for equity in pensions, allocates funds for economic development in poor regions, stops some national subsidies deemed anticompetitive, and requires countries to admit products they do not want. The EU is empowered to enforce rules on the environment, on mergers and acquisitions, and on standards in the workplace. In fact, EU decisions can supersede national law on a scale reflected by the eighteen thousand bureaucrats now employed in Brussels. Hence, the state is not so much a casualty of regionalism as it is a willing, even enthusiastic, partner in this process. While the state is pushing outward to adapt, because of its outlook, it is also coping with the disruptive pulls of subnationalism both at home and abroad, a second, countervailing process that can be partially understood as a backlash against globalization.

In formulating a response to these challenges, Washington can draw on its military superiority, its great diplomatic leverage, its status as the world's largest national economy, its vast resources in technological innovation and the knowledge industry, and the country's magnetic culture that is so attractive to the youth of the world. The United States is the world's leading trader, and its GNP is almost 1.5 times as large as the one in second place—Japan's—according to the most recent figures available (World Bank 1997b, 214–15). As is well known, however, the United States shifted from being the world's major creditor nation to being the chief debtor, and its share of world output dropped from one-third in the 1950s and 1960s to one-fifth in the early 1990s (Bach 1993, 11–12; Nye 1990). Yet, since hegemony cannot be fully measured in the appurtenances of overt power and wealth, there is also the matter of shared values, intersubjective meanings, a leadership role with considerable diplomatic assets. Hegemony is about the way that consent is produced. Machiavelli's sage advice that the ruler cannot rule by brute force alone is germane to a post-Cold War world. And the insight of his compatriot,

Antonio Gramsci, that hegemonic structures embrace not only interests, but also rationality in the form of consent, may be extended by noting that the amalgam of coercion and consent is always changing; it is uneven and continually needs to be adjusted in response to challenges.

To refurbish hegemony after the Cold War, and to overcome the challenges of globalization, the United States, above all, seeks to institutionalize the neoliberal idea that the basic building blocks of order are individuals rather than economic or social structures. And related to the tenet that left to their own devices, markets will lead to an efficient allocation of resources is the notion of flexibility such that both producers and consumers can readily respond to price signals. Of course, neoliberalism is not merely an economic model that trumpets the primacy of markets, but it is also a means of action that translates into policies for opening markets. The impact is not neutral to different groups, but favors certain forces: large firms, big investors, and the major capitalist countries. The ideology of neoliberalism is also associated with the decline of the economic sovereignty of states, reductions in social welfare, and a transformation of state capitalism into free-market capitalism.

Adopting neoliberalism as a cornerstone of foreign policy, Washington has enshrined flexibility as a hallmark of its post-Cold War strategy. In "reinventing government," the rubric of Vice President Al Gore's proposals for reducing the size of government and making it more efficient, policy makers employed a principle, flexibility, drawn right from the market economy—"flexible production," a system of organization designed for competitive strength in the globalized world economy. As an approach to regionalism, flexibility means a series of hub-spoke relations between the United States and its partners, sometimes reflecting a shallow form of interstate association and, in other cases, deeper interactions involving the protection of worker rights and civil society, but in all instances determined by trial and error in different zones of the global political economy, ranging from Europe and the Americas to the Pacific. Not a member of the EU, though maintaining diplomatic and cultural ties as well as a huge economic presence, the United States has sought to rely on regionalism in North America and the Pacific Rim, with NAFTA providing the boldest move in the search for a template that would integrate regional arrangements with an overall response to globalization.

## RECONSTITUTING HEMISPHERIC HEGEMONY

Historically, the United States has experimented with various initiatives to build hegemony in Latin America, dating back to the Monroe Doctrine in the nineteenth century, while establishing strong historical, military, trading, and cultural ties. Although it is beyond the compass of this chapter to detail the provisions of the precursors to NAFTA, it would be remiss not to note the importance of previous bilateral and multilateral hemispheric arrangements spearheaded by Washington. In many respects, NAFTA and plans for future liberalization in the Western Hemisphere flow from historical patterns that crystallized in the 1980s and 1990s.

President Ronald Reagan's 1982 Caribbean Basin Initiative was motivated in significant part by his administration's desire to bolster rightist regimes in Central America, isolate and undermine the Sandinista government in Nicaragua, and exert further pressure on Fidel Castro's Cuba. Far from a narrow security or geopolitical concern, backing for the contras was in fact tendered in a sustained move to eradicate the Sandinistas' attempt to offer a second regional alternative to the neoliberal project. At the same time, the Reagan team offered expanded aid, investment incentives, and duty-free access to the American market in return for the political consent of the Central American countries and the Caribbean nations. Although there were many compromises in this legislation and its implementation, the link between U.S. expectations and rewards was patent, even though Cold War considerations were intertwined with the attempted regionalization of economic activity.

The carrot-and-stick model of consent formation was applied in other instances as well, though perhaps not as brazenly, and was continued by Reagan's successors. Although Canada differs in most ways from developing countries in the Western Hemisphere, Canada is similarly highly dependent on the U.S. market and its investors. Here too, U.S. power—and hence the provisions of the U.S.-Canada Free Trade Agreement of 1988—was used to push liberalization for foreign investors. From the point of view of business interests, the objective was to facilitate capital mobility. In Canada, regionalism was presented as a necessary means to protect and expand access to the U.S. market (Fishlow and Haggard 1992, 21). Turning south, the United States sought to maintain political stability, slow illegal immigration, and cement a neoliberal economy. Hence, the United States-Mexico Free Trade Agreement, which President George Bush presented to Congress in 1990, guaranteed Mexico access to the North American market, locked in neoliberal domestic reforms, and reassured private investors that new flows of foreign capital would be forthcoming. Finally, President Bush's 1991 Enterprise for the Americas Initiative opened channels for a hemispheric free trade arrangement. Liberalization included investment promotion, privatization, debt reduction, and the removal of trade barriers (Fishlow and Haggard 1992, 22–25).

With these spokes radiating from the hub, the pattern for NAFTA was set in motion. All that remained was to systematize a set of bilateral and multilateral policies that had been put in place over the past decade. For U.S. business, represented by Democratic President Bill Clinton, who championed a Republican stance on economic regionalism even though it was opposed by his party's labor constituency, hegemonic regionalism meant instilling confidence in the neoliberal model. More than a set of trade provisions, NAFTA became an emblem of neoliberalism, a means of action, and a method for forging transnational consent and establishing investor confidence in the irreversibility of the arrangements. Along with U.S. capital, business and the state in both Canada and Mexico came to recognize that NAFTA was an instrument to pry open the U.S. economy, but with worrisome effects on labor and environmental conditions.

For all practical purposes, the North American triangle is a misnomer. Since the U.S. economy dwarfs those of its neighbors, the legs are of vastly unequal lengths. In fact, the third leg, that between Canada and Mexico, does not really exist. Internalizing the North-South problem, NAFTA incorporates wide discrepancies in income distribution and policy congruence. The asymmetry is so pronounced that NAFTA not only is a free trade zone, but also inevitably functions as a sphere of ideological and political influence for the United States (Poitras 1995, 9). Less clearly perceived by most policy makers, but anticipated by some commentators, was the degree to which NAFTA created a danger zone for the United States, an embrace that imposed responsibility to rescue the weak member (Castaneda 1995). Pre-NAFTA, it would have been inconceivable for the United States to put together a rescue package to restore investor confidence in the Mexican economy; post-NAFTA, it was inconceivable not to try.

While business and finance on both sides of the two borders supported the agreement, opposition came especially from U.S. laborers who feared "runaway shops" and environmentalists aware of weaker standards in Mexico, but also from ultranationalists on the right, such as Ross Perot and Pat Buchanan. Human rights groups pointed to widespread abuses in Mexico and accused the Clinton administration of delinking the moral component of foreign policy from economic gain. When it was agreed in 1994 to admit Chile soon afterward as a member of NAFTA, the Caribbean countries complained that their minuscule economies could be hurt by rapid market liberalizations. Also, there has been a move in Latin America to find alternatives to NAFTA, some of them southern-based versions of neoliberalism—a Southern Cone Common Market among Argentina, Brazil, Uruguay, and Paraguay, signed in 1991, as well as a revival of the Andean Common Market.

In order to prepare Mexico for NAFTA, the government of Carlos Salinas de Gortari embraced neoliberal reforms to allow the division of *ejidos*, land communally owned by peasants, making it easier for individuals to sell their property to more efficient large holders, who would be better equipped to compete with American and Canadian producers. This process dislodged many poor peasants and helped fuel the Zapatista uprising in the state of Chiapas that symbolically was timed to coincide with the day of the inauguration of NAFTA on 1 January 1994. The actual impact of NAFTA policies includes the loss of 41,201 manufacturing jobs in the United States, documented by the U.S. Labor Department, which is far below the number of Mexicans put out of work. This labor shedding is variously attributed to trade liberalization and a continuing trend of a drop in manufacturing employment in the Mexican economy since September 1990 (DePalma 1995; Cornelius 1995). Liberalization, deregulation, and the integration of capital markets mean increasing economic insecurity for low-income earners and people of color. Just as there is growing income inequality between Mexico and the United States, economic polarization within Mexico is also on the rise, a notable development in light of the already vast disparities in income and wealth. The displacement of workers and farmers in all three countries has accelerated migration. Yet the escape valve of emigration to the United States is a less effective outlet, given the increasing resistance to newcomers in California and other states.

Fifteen months after the adoption of NAFTA, Washington stepped in to respond to Mexico's chaotic financial markets, providing a $52 billion guarantee program. While cutting back on welfare at home, the U.S. government came to the rescue of private investors, both Americans and Mexicans, who had knowingly taken a risk on an "emerging market"—Mexican equities—but were saved from suffering the consequences of placing a bad bet. For all practical purposes, the U.S. government and the IMF became the central bank in Mexico, suggesting the burden side of regionalism as an hegemonic instrument for the United States. Also, expediency, as might be expected in the crunch, superseded neoliberal ideology. In a classic Polanyian move, the utopia of the self-regulating free market was silently sacrificed on the altar of massive state intervention.

In spite of this debacle, the long-term goal is to liberalize and integrate capital markets from Arctic Canada to near-Antarctic Chile. The aim is to enlarge and replace NAFTA by a Western Hemisphere Free Trade Area, with the United States paramount in its hegemonic role. In Asia, by comparison, the United States encounters a highly diverse region with much stronger states, ones with their own agendas for regionalism. Asian regionalism relies less on formal agreements and intergovernmental institutions and more on a web of bilateral economic relationships, but with a regional overlay.

## RETHINKING HEGEMONIC REGIONALISM
## IN THE ASIA-PACIFIC ARENA

Important to reconfiguring hegemony in accordance with post-Cold War conditions and neoliberal globalization are the competing ideas propounded by American policy intellectuals. Their proposals and explanations are influential, providing a key contribution to setting the policy agenda. One thesis that temporarily attracted widespread attention was put forward by Francis Fukuyama (1989), a former State Department official, who held that with the end of communism, the dialectic of history had come to a conclusion marked by the permanent triumph of capitalism, pluralist politics, and constitutionalism. Having reached the ultimate synthesis, the focus for political leaders should be on expanding prosperity and helping some laggard societies to integrate into the liberal economic system. Another, and perhaps more durable, facet of the hegemonic discourse is represented by Samuel Huntington (1993), whose article "The Clash of Civilizations?" argued that Cold War rivalries have been supplanted by the "fault lines of civilizations," including the identities of religion and culture, especially pitting Islam and Confucian elements against the West. For Huntington, post-Cold War conflicts and competition come down to two poles, namely, "the West and the rest." Not only do these representations disclose the thinking of major organic intellectuals apropos of American hegemony, but they also presume that there is only one neoliberal project. This is not so, however, in the Asia-Pacific region.

There is a dominant neoliberal scenario, which is an inclusive version, as well as an alternative neoliberal option, a more exclusive mode. APEC, the inclusive grouping, envelops all of the subregional bodies (e.g., ASEAN) and microregional experiments (e.g., EPZs) in the Pacific Basin. Its Asian flank subsumes two of the world's three largest economies, China and Japan; four countries heralded as NICs; two near-NICs, Malaysia and Thailand, with the Philippines and Indonesia trailing behind; and countries as different as Canada, Chile, and Papua New Guinea. Just as APEC must deal with ASEAN's fear of domination by Japan and the United States, so too it must try to encapsulate China and Taiwan in a single organizational structure. This structure is, of course, only a consultative forum without any rule-making organ, although in 1994 it was decided to create a free trade area (AFTA) for the ASEAN six by 2003; but whether such a horizon is to be understood as a literal commitment is as yet unclear.

The rationale for regional deepening flows from a series of circumstances compressed into a short time span—the dynamism of some Asian economies until 1997, the powerful thrust of globalization, and the end of the Cold War. In many respects, the economic crisis of the late 1990s added to this rationale. In the wake of an attack by currency speculators and herdlike behavior among foreign investors, a contagion affected Thailand, Korea, Indonesia, Malaysia, and, to a lesser degree, other Asian countries. When the policy agenda turned to economic recovery, it became increasingly evident that at present, most of Asian capitalism, while variegated, and irrespective of whether an IMF program is adopted de jure or de facto, is dependent on broad conformity to the U.S.-guided model of development. There followed many proposals and modest initiatives for new forms of subregional unity.

For both the American and Asian wings of APEC, one incentive to deepen the regional structure is the potential gain from expanding trade and investment. Asia is now North America's primary market, and trans-Pacific trade exceeds trans-Atlantic trade. The eighteen members of APEC account for a growing share of worldwide production and trade—almost 60 percent of global GDP and 46 percent of all exports in 1993, up from 38 percent in 1983 (Higgott and Stubbs 1995; "APEC: The Opening of Asia" 1994). But which deepening agenda will prevail? What are the deep integration issues?

The Asian wing of APEC is wary that deepening will be a means for the United States to impose its notion of fair trade. The smaller, developing countries fear that the United States will seek to reshape tried and proven domestic economic policies that rely on large-scale state intervention, and insist on social issues—human rights as well as labor and environmental standards (though not of the sort demanded by some NGOs). Also, the effort to imagine or construct an Asian identity poses broad and nettle-some questions about conflicts between different value systems, not in Huntington's sense of intercivilizational tensions, but in terms of the moral content of a neoliberal regional project. In this vein, two observers strike a chord that resonates in some quarters in Asia: "APEC . . . is clearly the child of western-educated, international trade economists steeped in the methodology of positivism and utility maximizing rational-ism" (Higgott and Stubbs 1995, 531). Implicitly, the point is that if neo-liberalism is a facsimile of neoclassical economics, does it respond to the deeper yearnings of ancient Asian civilizations caught in the vortex of rapid globalization? Also, is it compatible with a range of coercive politi-cal styles and structures?

An alternative, alluded to in chapter 6, is the Asianization of APEC. Proposed by Malaysia's prime minister in 1990, an EAEG would consist of Japan, China, the East Asian NICs, and the rest of ASEAN as a strong counterweight to the EU and a U.S.-centered regionalism; Australia, New Zealand, Canada, and the United States would be omitted. In other words, in comparison to the Pacific scenario, the Asian scenario calls for a more exclusive membership, and emphasizes the cultural dimension—identity—of regionalism as a central feature of deepening. Although the modalities of this arrangement were never set forth in detail, the United States, not surprisingly, opposed it from the very outset. The United States wanted to maintain its leadership role in the region, and could play its trump cards—guarantor of military security, container of China, and sheer market size—to deflect the Malaysian expression of frustration with the dominant neoliberal agenda. Outright U.S. opposition to Mahathir's idea resulted in its dilution, becoming only a weak Asian caucus within the larger Pacific formation, at least for now. There is but one other tripartite system to consider, with Europe as the third sphere of influence.

## REVITALIZING HEGEMONIC REGIONALISM IN THE ATLANTIC COMMUNITY

Heretofore, North Atlantic relations have been based on substantial historical and cultural ties, a high degree of market interpenetration, a central military alliance (NATO), and a series of bilateral relationships. Yet, after the Cold War, all parties needed to take account of changed conditions. Also, the United States is confronted by a strong regional organization to which it does not belong, although some sort of participation cannot be ruled out entirely.

While Europeans with myriad visions debate a deeper integration agenda, it is necessary to invent more flexible strategies to cope with the needs of a community of thirty to thirty-five members early in the new millennium and the social implications of a single market, including the absorption of immigrants, high levels of unemployment, pronounced ethnic cleavages, and polarization between rich and poor. Within Europe, there is a difference of opinion over whether there should be: (1) an advance guard of member states moving ahead to deepen regionalism, with the provision that other countries could follow later; (2) a prerequisite of all willing countries first subscribing to common goals; (3) a two-track system between those preferring and capable of adapting to tight integration and those favoring a looser framework, all within an umbrella of cooperation; or (4) an á la carte menu of integration options (Barber 1995). To change the metaphor, certain choices might have a bootstrap effect on regionalism in general. Additionally, there could of course be transitional arrangements from one tier of regional deepening to another.

Responding to this drive to further regionalism in Europe, U.S. officials have emphasized that insofar as it has proven itself the guarantor of European freedom and stability, America is a European power (Holbrooke 1995). The U.S. effort to refashion hegemonic regionalism in this sphere thus rests on the premises that Europe still does not have the capacity to meet its security needs, that the American connection is based on a strong foundation of common interests and values that survived the long test of the Cold War, that without America a more objectionable German hegemony would result, and that Russia might soon again pose a challenge that could not be confidently met unless America remains enmeshed in Europe. Here is the rub: Since Europe failed in its response to aggression and genocide in Bosnia, the United States, which refused to dispatch its own troops during the ordeal of "ethnic cleansing," nevertheless has questioned whether Europeans have the bona fide capacity to bring peoples closer together. Beyond rhetorical flourishes, is there a genuine willingness to make the sacrifices necessary to sustain a community when its most basic values are under attack? The diplomatic end-game in Bosnia, as well as the Kosovo sequel, emphasized the reassertion of an American hegemonic role in relation to European security. Also, the shift from the UN to NATO as the body responsible for peacekeeping in Bosnia and for safeguarding Kosovo both reinforced the remarginalization of the UN in relation to global security and the perception of a reaffirmation of U.S. leadership in Europe. Although NATO is European in its locus of operations, it remains a regional arrangement dominated by the United States, a point reinforced by the way in which Washington insisted on having the final word with respect to the selection of the new NATO secretary general after the discrediting of Willy Claes in 1995. Yet it remains highly questionable as to whether the U.S. military-strategic role in Europe can be parlayed into a comparable role in relation to European economic affairs. It would seem definitely not, at least within the present conjuncture.

Just as there are limits to protecting professed ideals, so too are there palpable bounds to formal regionalism. Not only counterhegemonic forces, but also hegemonic actors, will avail themselves of informal or unofficial regionalism. Paradoxically, informal regionalism is often exercised through extraregional forums—the G-7, the Paris and London clubs for international financial issues, the WEF, the Trilateral Commission, and so on—which can be more effective in fastening down hegemonic nuts and bolts. Clearly, these forums may be public or private associations adept in their flexible management of both consent and structural forms of coercion. Both regional and extraregional vehicles are compatible with reconstructing U.S. hegemony so long as they are attuned to a multilateral world order, although they are encountering substantial barriers on the road to neoliberalizing ends.

## TOWARD A GLOBAL STRATEGY OF REGIONALISM

In sum, in an effort to sustain hegemony, the United States, as the hub power, has attempted to radiate a series of regional spokes, all within the wheel of neoliberalism. Does it turn smoothly in the sense of successfully managing the foreign policy challenges noted above? We think not. Although regionalism can be a potent selective instrument in controlling agendas, cornering markets, and policing certain areas and activities, the United States has often not used it prudently or wisely, partly because there are sharp contrasts and tensions between different spheres. Cooperation is deepest between the United States and its NAFTA partners, but even here far more problematic than expected, due to economic distress that has resulted for Mexico and Canada; shallower, weaker, and less institutionalized across the Pacific; and more uncertain in the North Atlantic because of the growing salience of the other two zones (Haggard 1994).

Hence, the United States has used a differentiated approach to regionalism, abandoning its adherence to neoliberalism when decision makers have deemed interventionary actions to be more efficient. The U.S. bailout of the Mexican economy serves as a spectacular reminder of such an expedient willingness to rescue market forces, as does U.S. support for comparable bailouts in such countries as Indonesia and Brazil.

Quite clearly, the speed at which global markets have evolved over the last thirty years has been much faster than the capacity of states and regional organizations to manage the effects, or even directions, of change. The structural impact of globalization has narrowed the range of policy choice available to the state. This overarching reality has made it imperative for policy makers to reconcile globalization and regionalism to the extent possible.

Regionalism is far from being monolithic, calling attention to political forces within formal groupings or transnational movements that consider it possible to convert regionalism into a shield against hegemony. Just as regionalism functions as a hegemonic strategy for the United States, it may also provide space for a variety of counterhegemonic projects. Regionalism is thus not only a component and reflection of globalization, but also acts as a modifying response to it.

Whatever the American approach to regionalism in a given time and place, powerful forces—such as nationalism, religion, ethnicity, and language—not only bind communities, but also continue to pull peoples apart and even set loose a destructive chain reaction. Counteracting U.S. strategy has generated global strife, much of it violent. Expanding regionalism may not be powerful enough to neutralize other differences, many of them stymied and disguised by repressive states and bloc politics during the Cold War, but since 1989 substantially liberated from the geopolitical discipline of bipolarity.

Given these problems in developing a coherent and effective policy on regionalism, why does the United States persist? Why not discard this approach and stick to state-centered, power-oriented tactics? Why not link directly to the global economy and skip the intermediate layer of regionalism? For one thing, the United States is, of course, pursuing both statist and regional strategies, although finite resources limit the capability to invest in two projects for the same ends. Moreover, with a changed power configuration and the reorganization of the global economy along regional lines, new modes of competition impel states, firms, and banks to use regionalism as one essential means to reposition themselves vis-à-vis their competitors. If globalization entails a reduction in control at the national level, then the best option for many states, including the United States, may be regional fallbacks (Crone 1993). But, as argued, the current picture is clouded, especially since the European and Pacific regional arenas remain fluid and contradictory with respect to the United States' role as insider or outsider. It is likely that U.S. hegemonic ambitions will be realized to the extent that Washington's security contributions to these regions remain salient and are perceived by important member states as indispensable. If the European and Asia-Pacific macroregions can reduce, or eliminate, their military-strategic dependence on the United States, then it is likely that its economic participation will be more scrutinized, and likely constrained, thereby eroding hegemonic capacity. At present, there are two overriding and unresolved considerations that bear upon the reliance on regionalism as a means to sustain hegemony: Can traditional security factors be converted into influence in economic domains? Will regional tendencies be neutralized by globalizing pressures and by intraregional disruptions and unevenness? The next chapter examines some of these intraregional patterns of unevenness in the form of distinctive subregional responses to globalization.

# CHAPTER 8

# Subregional Responses to Globalization

TAKING NOTE of the upsurge of the new regionalism, observers have largely focused on the most conspicuous sign of this trend: the rise of, and relations among, the three macroregions the Asia-Pacific, the EU, and NAFTA. This chapter will, rather, center on another and neglected question: What are the major interactions that constitute the dialectic of globalization and subregionalism? In the main, this interplay is both shaped by and constitutive of neoliberalism's drive to open economies and societies to global markets. In other words, the dominant subregional response to globalization is to accommodate this set of processes, to embrace it, or even to become a component of it. The less pronounced and embryonic trend is resistance to globalization (to be examined in Part III).

Subregional patterns form within globalization, constituting a distinctive subset of power relations internal to a macroregion. They also intensify the interactions among nodes (states or parts of states) that transcend national borders within and beyond a macroregion. In the face of globalization, there is now a range of distinctive subregional processes. The best known is the constellation of NICs in Eastern Asia that first pounced on the advantages of a robust and globalizing economy in the 1960s, and are part of a regional grid of production organization, investment, and trade. This formation may be differentiated into (1) the super-NICs of South Korea and Taiwan, (2) the city-states and entrepôts of Singapore and Hong Kong (although politically absorbed by China in 1997, an entity that continues to hook out on its own into the global economy), and (3) the near-NICs, a second generation of supposedly more nimble Asian rivals (at different times, said to include Malaysia, Thailand, Indonesia, and the Philippines, with some of their neighbors in tow). Other important subregional reactions to globalization, and also components of globalization, are (4) growth triangles, sometimes referred to as polygons, and (5) transfrontier resource areas.

To varying degrees market-driven, state-sponsored, or society-induced, these possible responses have arisen in a period of intense experimentation with subregionalism. There are several permutations and combinations, which lead to the question, In what respects are subregional processes vehicles for neoliberal globalization? Put differently, are they embedded or disembedded from social forces on the ground? Implicit in this formulation is the importance of both formal organizations and the more latent aspects of production organization, politics, and culture. In other words, subregionalist activities embody both top-down and bottom-up initiatives, with different forces from above and below contesting the direction of the reactions to globalization.

As we have seen, other studies have often taken the EU as the exemplar of the new regionalism. But this chapter constructs its framework from the varied experiences of Eastern Asia and Southern Africa. At the risk of imbalance, here I will give somewhat more attention to Eastern Asia, only because ideas about organizing in response to globalization seem to travel more readily from there to Southern Africa, and the transportation of these concepts does not appear to be moving in the reverse direction, although, of course, both have their indigenous roots. The aim in this chapter, then, is not to attempt a systematic comparison of the two subregions, but to derive illustrations from their experiences, with Southern Africa serving mainly as a salutary check on, or a disclaimer about, attempts to graft lessons from the Asian context. For example, after examining the achievements and problems of subregionalism in Eastern Asia, one becomes alert to the specific factors shaping this configuration as well as the consequences. Apart from long historical processes (flows of population, ethnic distribution across borders, and the informal economy), in the recent globalizing phase of capitalism, the impulse toward subregionalism has been weaker in Southern Africa, for which it is extremely useful to try to understand the Asian experience.

Rather than organizing this chapter in the most obvious way—i.e., into sections that focus on the overt aspects of subregionalism (the forms themselves, which are the different generations of NICs, growth areas, and transfrontier parks)—more can be gained by centering attention on *explanations* for what meets the eye and then turning to manifestations. Hence, the first three sections of this chapter address competing interpretations of the NIC model—the neoliberal, culturalist, and statist approaches. Next is an examination of a paradigm shift behind the creation of transborder networks, followed by discussion of their upward, downward, and lateral thrusts. The conclusion returns to the theme of the interactions between subregionalism and changing global structures, and builds on the concept of *embeddedness* as an alternative explanation for the linkages.

## NEOLIBERAL ACCOUNTS OF THE "MIRACLE"

After an Asian power, Japan, constructed the world's second largest economy, much attention was lavished on the "miracle" wrought by the four tigers as a paradigmatic strategy for moving up the value-added ladder. No longer mere suppliers of primary commodities and cheap labor, a handful of developing countries became highly competitive in the global marketplace. Spurred by deindustrialization in the North and the relocation of manufacturing in the South, the NICs are now producers of capital-intensive and some technology-intensive products.

Neoliberal estimations for the emergence of these "miracle" economies differ in their emphases, yet share a common perspective. Within the neoclassical framework, there are several elegant formulations. Abstracting from the specific characteristics of Japan and the Asian NICs, Paul Kuznets (1988) delimited "an East Asian model of development" characterized by high investment ratios, small public sectors, competitive labor markets, export expansion, and government intervention in the economy. For neoclassical authors, the success of the Asian NICs reflected the fullest extent of the workings of the law of comparative advantage. Stressing national endowments or the virtue of an open international economy or both, they claim that the Asian NICs tied economic growth to the logic of the market (Lim 1994; Lal 1983).

Further to this argument, the key to success was an export-promotion strategy, designed to maximize the advantages of cheaply produced manufactured goods, and few controls over the movement of capital and goods: Outward-oriented economies perform better than inward-looking economies (Greenaway and Chong 1988). An export-led growth strategy not only increased national income, but also led to structural transformation of the tigers' economies (Chow 1987). Keeping their economies ajar, mixing ratios of labor and capital in optimum quantities, following commands from the pricing system, and demonstrating remarkable degrees of enterprise, risk, and management, the NICs have behaved like Schumpeterian firms eager and able to maximize the opportunities presented by a globalizing economy.

Betting on the right superpower during the Cold War also ensured access to Western investment, technology, and markets. As noted, deindustrialization in the advanced countries and the relocation of manufacturing industry in the South, too, played an important role. But, from a neoliberal perspective, it was mainly the ingenuity and élan within their national contexts that permitted the abundance of riches.

The failure of import substitution in Latin America in previous decades also reinforced the rationale for export-oriented strategies as the desirable route. Yet surely the distinctive historical conditions and social structures in Latin America are in sharp contrast to those in Eastern Asia. Complicating the comparison is the question of timing, the different points of instituting specific policies. Without these considerations, it would be misleading to derive lessons about the pitfalls of import substitution or the virtues of export-led industrialization.

Moreover, it is appropriate to confront the logic of an export-oriented strategy under conditions of severe indebtedness and structural adjustment. Without generating internal demand, the NIC approach fails to redress a major challenge in some subregions, including Southern Africa: the viability of export-led industrialization dependent primarily or wholly upon the expansion of the global economy and the capriciousness of the market (Broad and Cavanagh 1988). In addition, there is the matter of culture, an explanation for long-term growth that neoclassical economists undertheorize but, in some analyses, nevertheless attempt to relate to the NIC route.

## THE CULTURALIST CASE

Sometimes incorporated in the neoliberal thesis of privileging markets is a culturalist argument: The rise of the Asian NICs may be attributed partly to their exceptional cultural resources. According to this view, Confucian values of temperance, collective purpose, and sacrifice are delimited as distinctive features underpinning East Asian development. A work ethic and obedience to authority are designated as hallmarks of societies infused with Confucian values (Baum 1982). These societies are characterized by filial piety (Hamilton and Cheung-Shu 1987), a collectivist ethos, and respect for hierarchy, which provide the bedrock of entrepreneurship (Berger and Hsin-Huang 1988). Unlike their counterparts elsewhere in the South, the tigers are said to embody Weberian correlates of capitalist achievement (Hamilton and Cheung-Shu 1987).

For the sake of brevity, I will not travel down this avenue of inquiry at length, because its conceptual potholes are readily apparent. Just as the NICs' economic growth is now attributed to a Confucian heritage, it must be recalled that before the 1960s, the lack of economic advancement in countries such as Taiwan, South Korea, and China was also explicated in terms of Confucian values. It was argued that Confucianism blocked the emergence of a modern economy. But culture is neither static nor homogeneous. In fact, East (and Eastern) Asian cultures are diverse, often syncretic, and historically contingent.

## THE STATIST CONSTRUCTION

As an alternative to the neoliberal and culturalist approaches, the state is widely accorded special status in elucidating East Asia's remarkable economic growth (Appelbaum and Henderson 1992; Johnson 1982; Deyo

1987; Bienefeld 1988; Stein 1995; White 1988; Haggard 1990). Although there are several variants of this theme, the emphasis here is on a Japanese-styled developmental state, imbued with purpose and capacity to turn the adversity of underdevelopment to advantage. Providing stability, guidance, infrastructural investment, especially in education, and government intervention in strategic sectors (Johnson 1986, 565), the developmental state, it is claimed, was the author of unprecedented economic growth. Often getting the prices "wrong" rather than trusting the price system, the developmental state assigned priority to "learning" from the advanced capitalist countries, particularly Japan, how to propel industrialization (Amsden 1989). Fundamental to this strategy were labor control, political exclusion, and outright repression (Deyo 1987). In the absence of a credible threat from organized labor, the tigers were able to fast-track their economies. An expanding global economy may have provided a propitious climate, but from this perspective, the key to success was the role of the state.

Focusing on South Korea and Taiwan, some scholars advance this statist view as a counterpoint to the neoclassical argument. They note that state-induced development touched on all sectors of the economy, especially agriculture: "small-holder-based" agriculture was "fostered by means of heavy state involvement, which integrated the rural sector into the national economy and allowed the supply price of rural labor to be raised progressively" (Bienefeld 1988, 20). Highlighting the role of a "coherent national development strategy that created a relatively stable domestic investment climate," Bienefeld (1988, 19–20) argues: "a dynamic and heavily state-directed process of accumulation could become the basis of an ambitious and long-term oriented process of industrialisation and technical change." Inverting the neoclassical view that elevates liberalization as the basis of growth, Bienefeld (1988, 20) maintains that state-directed links with the global economy were the primary factor in the NICs' surge. The role of the state is also essential for creating or facilitating the conditions that attract TNCs and foreign investment (Carnoy 1993; Nolan 1990).

Although they capture an important facet of the Eastern Asian experience, the statists do not give sufficient credence to the ways that the world has changed since the 1960s, when the NICs began their upward mobility in the GDLP. What the statists downplay are the difficulties that the "miracles" and "near-miracles" have encountered in jumping the elusive last hurdle from capital-intensive to technology-intensive economies. Moreover, the global-economy powers, including the IMF, hope that the economic crisis that rocked Asia in the late 1990s betokens the demise of the state-led model of development. There is no denying that in this nexus, the state felt the brunt of market discipline. In light of the capital controls applied by Malaysia, Taiwan, and some other countries, however, there is a possibility that Asians and some of their governments may see in mercantilism a means of defense against the depletion of their resources and weakening of their institutions by global finance and TNCs.

What may have been relevant for Eastern Asia's role in the global political economy, especially in an earlier phase, is less plausible in Southern Africa and elsewhere today. To be sure, innovations in transportation and communications, the globalization of production and finance, and numerous cross-border flows provide unparalleled opportunities matched by formidable risks and burdens. At the same time, they do not permit the same choices that were open to the NICs. Partly due to new technologies that easily transcend territorial boundaries, the ability of statist interventions to safeguard domestic societies and economies from the outside world is highly circumscribed. For even the most powerful states, harnessing global forces is implausible. Far more acutely, the least economically developed countries feel the pinch of this loss of control.

The statist option has receded because the state itself is becoming globalized, its performance in good part measured in terms of how "successful" it is in promoting access to footloose capital. However, impoverished and debt-ridden countries in subregions such as Southern Africa face structural limits to creating the right conditions for exploiting the global market and selecting more nationally oriented strategies for sustainable growth. Globalization *conditions but does not eliminate* possibilities for national development. Put differently, it is politically and economically wise to engage in globalization planning, not traditional national development planning.

In addition, a changing context for state interventions includes a shift away from a geopolitical environment characterized by superpower rivalry, military alliances, and proxy wars. At one time, this system gave reprieve from human rights standards to undemocratic rulers in South Korea and Taiwan. Brutal measures to silence discontent were adopted, and a certain path of economic development rationalized in terms of security against a perceived communist threat. In the wake of the Cold War, however, autocratic leaders experience difficulty finding sponsorship, and persistent, or mounting (in cases such as Indonesia), pressures from social forces at home constrain authoritarian rule. Within the compass of a global political economy in flux, many developing countries are the scene of homegrown tensions rooted in their varied historical landscapes.

## A PARADIGM SHIFT TO A TRANSBORDER NETWORK:
## TRIANGLES AND POLYGONS

These political and economic transformations have opened space for subregional initiatives. The evolving GDLP encompasses various subregionally integrated activities in a de facto free-trade regime. Following the accession of Vietnam, Laos, Myanmar, and Cambodia as new members, ASEAN represents a market of more than 450 million consumers. The de jure form, AFTA, is on the agenda for deepening the process of subregionalism, with a target date for full implementation for the ASEAN six, Vietnam, Laos, and Myanmar (with Cambodia, admitted in 1999, presumably to be added) by 2008, but the subregional patterns shaped by private capital and cultural practices do not depend on this form of political support (Rasiah and Haflah 1998, 4; Lim 1996).

The four tigers' dynamic economies registered spectacular growth rates, elevated from the 1960s until they encountered market turbulence in 1997, and, after 1985, became wealthier by investing in their Asian neighbors, which in turn received investment, technology, and jobs. In the 1990s, the tigers invested more in the ASEAN countries than did either Japan or the United States. In addition, they purchased the biggest share of ASEAN exports and constituted the largest market for China's products (Legler 1995).

Given integrated, cross-border investment and industrialization, both labor markets and capital markets reflected regional momentum within the ambit of economic globalization. The more ambitious concept of outer globalization, known as a "crescent of prosperity," is a subregional scheme for joint utilization of resources. A bigger version of the growth triangle, the crescent would encompass Korea, Japan, China, Taiwan, and the ASEAN countries (Vatikiotis et al. 1991). With the emergence of both integrated regional production and trade networks, a triangular pattern has involved industrial relocation from Japan and the NICs to ASEAN. The ASEAN countries import machinery, equipment, parts, and supplies from the Asian home countries of foreign investors, using them to manufacture goods, which are then exported to Western markets. Added to this triangular form of trade, other types of growth triangles are developing.

What emerged was a patchwork of smaller subregional subgroupings, variously known not only as growth triangles but also as growth polygons: transnational economic zones spaced over defined geographical areas and involving three or more countries (Sato 1996). Designed as ways to shape hypercompetition, these geometric forms are conduits of, and responses to, globalization. A propellant for economic growth, the growth triangle and polygon widen the manufacturing base, with different factor endowments in each node, and thus offer an incentive for TNCs to consider the subregion as a whole for investment. Although the first growth triangle briefly entered into the discussion in chapters 2 and 6, it is useful here to map the different forms and to elaborate so as to pinpoint the conjunction between globalization and subregionalism.

The best known among them is the Southern China Growth Triangle, also referred to as the Greater China Economic Zone, a subregional expanse primarily delimited by flows of private capital, in which the states concerned act as facilitators. With the inauguration of China's "open door policy" in 1979 and the establishment of SEZs, the new subregionalism has been based on the development of industry in the Pearl River Delta, allowing easy access for Hong Kong's industries to take advantage of cultural affinities: a common language, Cantonese, and family ties across the border. In the early 1990s, 90 percent of the southern province of Guangdong's external trade was with Hong Kong, and Guangdong's foreign enterprises represented more than 37 percent of the industrial output of all foreign-owned enterprises in China. Similarly, Taiwanese investment has flowed into Fujian Province (Goodman 1994, 32–33).

Next to emerge was the Indonesia-Malaysia-Singapore, formerly known as the Singapore-Johor-Riau (SIJORI), Growth Triangle. It represents a distinctive blend of FDI, private sector initiative in steering activities and deciding on location, and state participation in developing infrastructure and expediting capital flows. Introduced in 1990, there are signs that this triangle is attracting foreign investment and causing the migration of industries in search of specific factors of production. Problems associated with integration, however, include the potential enlargement of disparities in income and the emergence of a shanty economy on the fringes of industrial townships, especially with an inflow of workers of diverse ethnic backgrounds in (and from) Indonesia and of young female workers to staff assembly operations. Moreover, SIJORI seems to rest on two legs, Singapore-Johor and Singapore-Riau, without a viable third link between Johor and Riau, both providers of cheap labor and land. To the extent that Singapore suffers an industrial hollowing out, with an exodus of industrial investment exceeding the rate of entry, there will be an increasing need to replace an aging population with foreign workers (Kumar and Lee 1991).

A third growth area is the Tumen River Delta in Northeast Asia, where the borders of China's Jilin Province, Siberia, and the Democratic People's Republic of Korea (DPRK) converge. Backed by the UN, the concept is to pool the abundant natural resources of Siberia and Mongolia with the processing facilities in China and the DPRK, along with technology and capital from South Korea and Japan. In addition, there are increasing calls for accelerated, subregional cooperation around the Sea of Japan and the Yellow Sea.

The proliferation of these triangles has stimulated experiments elsewhere in Asia. Supported by the Asian Development Bank (ADB), the new growth polygons include the six countries comprising the Greater Mekong Subregion—Cambodia, Laos, Myanmar, Thailand, Vietnam, and China's Yunnan Province—all engaged in building infrastructure and promoting economic growth. A counterpart to the other growth areas, the Brunei-Indonesia-Malaysia-Philippines Growth Area is composed of East and West Kalimantan and North Sulawesi in Indonesia; Sabah, Sarawak, and Labuan in Malaysia; Brunei Darussalam; and Mindanao and Palawan in the Philippines. This East ASEAN Growth Area was set up to expand transborder trade, to help secure the openness of the economies by removing barriers to flows of input and capital, and to facilitate the movement of people as well as services. Finally, another subregional initiative is the Indonesia-Malaysia-Thailand Growth Triangle, or the North ASEAN Growth Area, which encompasses North Sumatra and Aceh in Indonesia; the northern states of Kedah, Perak, Penang (known as "Silicon Island," in light of its sizable semiconductor manufacturing base), and Perlis in peninsular Malaysia; and the southern provinces of Satun, Songkhla, Yala, Narathiwat, and Pattani in Thailand. The concept is to optimize the complementarities of these provinces to boost certain industries and economic activities, including the establishment of two SEZs.

Although some evidence on the actual performance of these growth areas is available (e.g., Lee 1991), it is early to assess the results. It is possible, however, to make some general observations. On the whole, they are private sector-led, market-driven, state-assisted, and informal with little institutionalization. Compared to regionwide forms of integration, these subregional responses to globalization are decentralized with fewer partners, looser, and more flexible, offering greater scope for experimentation and speed in changing operations. But they could complicate wider or deeper forms of regionalism, heighten disparities within a region, compete economically with one another, and spur political conflicts between levels of jurisdiction, for there is no prescribed mechanism for coordination or dispute resolution. Indeed, this spindly web is already being rewoven.

There is a shift in emphasis from economies of scale to economies of network: deploying various stages of value-chain activities, usually in the production process, not by centralizing them within countries but spreading across regions or countries (Kondo 1996). The paradigm shifts from a "center-periphery" framework to a mode of analysis that obliterates the distinction between "center" and "periphery." Nippon Denso-Thailand is as important as Nippon Denso-Australia or even Nippon Denso in Japan. It is not the center, but the total network, that must rely completely on every unit and that generates value added for the global market. Small and medium-sized corporations in a subregion, which formerly served as subcontractors for firms such as Toyota, now participate more directly in a globalized market (Kondo 1996).

## THE UPWARD, DOWNWARD, AND LATERAL THRUST
## OF TRANSBORDER PRODUCTION

Mapping these subregional networks is an inherently difficult exercise, for some of them are submerged in the unwritten norms, as well as the tacit understandings constituting corporate and cultural practices. However, it does appear that growth triangles or polygons, which intersect with and even embody segments of private-sector and family networks, are being re-formed into "growth corridors." Companies forge links within a growth area and then merge them to establish a corridor. In the future, these corridors may in fact coordinate their activities or even integrate (Kondo 1996).

More certain is subregionalism's downward thrust to the local level, because, as noted, it embraces SEZs, also known as EPZs. These zones were introduced in Shannon, Ireland, in 1959 and expanded to Taiwan, Mexico, Brazil, the Philippines, and India by the late 1960s (Crane 1990, 8–9). Although the zones are often regarded as microregional activities (i.e., industrial enclaves within nation-states, physically and legally fenced off from the rest of the home country), they appear to be part of multifaceted, cross-border strategies. Indeed, there are subregional strategies of zonal development that explicitly contain EPZs.

In some countries of Eastern Asia, SEZs, or EPZs, have attracted foreign investment but are now drawing less interest. China, for example, has begun to reduce its established SEZs. Although China is undergoing a transition from central planning to a market economy, the state sector in the SEZs is mushrooming and imposes many regulations, substantially driving down investment in the mid-1990s. On the other hand, there is a move away from industry in the coastal cities toward establishing de facto SEZs, as in Shanghai's Pudong, as well as overtures to foreign insurance companies, accountancies, and law firms, all subject to financial reforms, in select cities.

Ching Kwan Lee's (1995) comparative ethnographic study of manufacturing production in two factories in south China details gender hierarchies in the plants in Shenzen and Hong Kong. The major difference between the two workforces is that most of the laborers in the Hong Kong company are middle-aged mothers, whereas those in the facility in Shenzen tend to be young single women who have recently moved to the city from rural areas—a "floating population" of migrants. The wage rate for an assembly worker in Shenzen in 1993 was less than one U.S. dollar per day and around 1/16 of that in Hong Kong (Ching 1995, 382). Ching's research (1995, 383, 385–86) shows that control in the Shenzen factory is "overt, visible, punishment-oriented, and publicly displayed," whereas the managers in Hong Kong are more apt to use the "covert and inconspicuous" aspects of gender hierarchy embedded in familial and local authority structures.

In light of such experience, the social and political effects of EPZs are under scrutiny in other subregions, including in Southern Africa, where SADC is charged with responsibility for coordinating and assisting cross-border industrial projects. Already some SADC members have launched EPZs. Influenced by the experiences of such countries as Singapore and Taiwan, Mauritius, as early as 1970 (before SADC was formed), passed an EPZ act, paving the way for foreign investors and new enterprises. In 1994, Zimbabwe followed suit, adopting its EPZ act and establishing the Zimbabwe Export Processing Zone Authority. Next came Namibia's 1995 EPZ act and Mozambique's "Industrial Free Zones." Debates in post-apartheid South Africa center on whether full and formal EPZs should be set up, given the country's distinctive history. Conditions in the decentralized industrial areas constituting the apartheid homelands (before 1994, supposedly "sovereign" countries) are tantamount to disguised EPZs (Jauch, Keet, and Pretorius 1996, 35).

On one side of the ledger are the EPZs' standard attractions: employment creation, technology, and capital. On the other are concerns over the potential environmental consequences (not least in the workplace), violations of trade union rights, and the implications for labor in general: What types of jobs would be created in "industrial monocultures" dominated by a few and very specific labor-intensive industries? Would there be protection for workers' rights? Given the general quality of EPZ employment, what are the effects of zonal jobs on the social status and economic power of women? Would these industrial monocultures augment vulnerability to global market forces? Would backward linkages to the host economy be established? Could the EPZs be subordinated to society-directed attempts to refashion the national and subregional projects (Jauch, Keet, and Pretorius 1996)?

In the final analysis, the debate over the costs and benefits of EPZs comes down to a matter of the opportunities of and risks in globalization itself. The wide range of subregional responses to globalization reflects the diversity of geographic and socioeconomic conditions under which they arise, especially striking in a subregion where the combined GDP of the twelve SADC members, not including the two 1997 entrants, is about that of Finland (see Introduction). In Southern Africa, the search for development generators has emphasized corridors, understood to mean geographical linkages created to spur economic growth within countries and across borders. As in Eastern Asia, inter- and intraregional markets have propelled corridor development to the forefront. With corporations, governments, and international agencies serving as *vendors* for the concept, it gives rise to such projects as the Maputo Development Corridor, whose raison d'être is to build an integrated infrastructure network and to upgrade the port of Maputo into a multimodal access point, with vast multisectoral potential for linking Southern African markets to the global economy, encouraging cross-border ties, and improving environmental resource management (Interim Coordinating Committee for the Maputo Development Corridor 1996).

With an overall lack of skills, infrastructure, and finance, SADC countries have made an important conceptual shift toward creating transfrontier resource areas. The idea is to join existing national parks and nature reserves in a vast conservation zone. Core areas in four countries—Mozambique, South Africa, Swaziland, and Zimbabwe—have been identified along the borders. For example, on the Mozambique-Natal (South Africa) boundary, these areas would be attached to national parks and nature reserves such as Ndumu, Tembe Elephant Reserve, the Coastal Forest Reserve, the Maputo Elephant Reserve, and possibly in association with the forest areas northwest of the Maputo River and the sand veld areas between the Mozi and Maputo rivers. Other areas that transcend national borders have been targeted to serve as buffers between centers of conservation and nodes of development (Tinley and Van Riet 1991). More than mere bumpers, however, they are also meant to provide access to global capital, and represent a subregionally distinctive form of adjustment to the globalization trend.

## SUBREGIONAL EMBEDDEDNESS IN GLOBALIZATION

Given the wide range of subregional responses to globalization, it is not sufficient to dichotomize them as either "from above" or "from below." Globalization has not spawned such ideal types but, rather, a mix of contested subregional projects: strategies, in various degrees spontaneous or deliberate, home-grown or emulated. These include different generations or iterations of the NIC model, growth triangles and polygons often encompassing EPZs, development corridors, and transfrontier growth areas.

In large measure in response to the formation of the EU, itself an aspect of global restructuring, Asians and Africans have sought to take steps appropriate to their own conditions. In the quest for development, the dominant pattern in both subregions—Eastern Asia and Southern Africa—is to embrace neoliberal globalization. Yet subregional responses for economically auspicious conditions differ from those in a marginalized zone. The Asians achieved upward mobility in the GDLP when the world economy was robust and during the Korean and Vietnam wars such that geopolitics favored this subset of countries.

Notwithstanding the sudden economic downturn in the late 1990s, the NIC formula is still regarded as a standard for developing countries to adopt. But the NIC construct—by and large, a grouping on a gradational scale of statistical indices—must be seen as a descriptive category. Underestimated by purveyors of this model, even by enthusiasts who advance the culturalist explanation, is that subregional strategies are linked to historical and social structures with their own dynamics. Today, developing countries seeking to climb to a higher position in the GDLP are all embedded in a series of powerful structures collectively constituting globalization. To suggest otherwise is to misapprehend the most basic transitions under way in the global political economy. History is in fact a nonlinear, spasmodic process replete with friction and tensions, now shifting from what is quaintly called international relations to a post-Westphalian system composed of several levels and multiple actors.

A focus on NIC strategies of export promotion may offer solace—imaginings about gaining riches for all—to those exceptional economies in the South perched to ascend the GDLP. But this vision is structurally blind to the costs of NIC-hood (environmental abuses, deterioration of the agricultural sector, and in some cases political authoritarianism), as well as the historical and social embeddedness of the NIC experience. The capabilities and limitations of a particular strategy in a given zone of the global political economy are neither reducible to the domestic characteristics of individual countries nor to engineering, wherein temporal factors take a back seat. To suggest otherwise is to pluck possibilities and choices out of an historical stream without really mapping the relentless currents wending through the globalization landscape.

Although the culturalist account of the rise of the NICs is reductionist, one may recast this explanation in terms of cultural embeddedness. Clearly, with the growth of a multicultural workforce in many countries, lives are reshaped and identities are reimagined in different ways. Increasingly, class is overlaid with ethnic, racial, religious, and gendered divisions of labor. In the context of globalization, cultural adaptations to economic growth provide intersubjective meanings and mediate inequalities arising from a changing division of labor and power.

On balance, the NIC model is too static, either as a representation of the changing nature of a subset of the global political economy or as a prototype for other economies. Perhaps the most important ingredient of the NIC experience is the efforts of a handful of countries to hitch their economies to the world market for local advantage, with the state acting as a spacer between the domestic and international spheres. In the teeth of globalization, however, the state can no longer maintain the same type of barriers. There is no point attempting to repel structural forces over which there is limited control. By shrinking the state, political authorities are, in fact, acting out the logic of globalization, trying to convert a structural force into a virtue.

The NIC model is more likely to serve as an ideological and political tool in the neoliberal kit than help to build economic power. Globalization's reach already betrays severe shortcomings in the "miracle" economies. Long-standing social compacts are eroding. Increasing labor costs and the rise of new social movements challenge the foundations of the super-NICs (Mittelman and Pasha 1997). Triggered by financial speculation, herdlike behavior, and a contagion effect, along with cronyism and misguided policies at home, the turmoil that upset Eastern Asian economies in the late 1990s showed the extent of their vulnerability. This is not to exaggerate their drawbacks, but to note countervailing factors that make the NIC model a less likely candidate for emulation. Above all, these developments underscore the contingent nature of the NIC experience.

In the throes of a historical transition, more so than at other times, ideas about subregionalism are contested and unevenly embraced. They are less institutionalized in Eastern Asia and Southern Africa than they are in Europe. Subregionalism is subject to a paradigm shift—expressed in practice in such innovations as cross-border development corridors, growth triangles and polygons, EPZs, and transfrontier parks—which reflect not only interests but also, as emphasized, culture and values. Notwithstanding Singapore's senior minister Lee Kuan Yew's and other leaders' case for "Asian values," wherein the collective, not the individual, is supposedly the ordering unit in society, in fact Asia's NICs offer diminishing levels of social protection, such as pensions, unemployment insurance, and health care for their citizens (Zakaria 1994). Few people are shielded against the jagged edges of the market. In comparison to the West, Asian governments transfer little spending from one class of taxpayers to another. Inasmuch as public institutions in the NICs do not really make allowance for absorbing the market's shocks, the family must play this role, but, with globalization, this form of solidarity, like other aspects of community, is increasingly atomized and thus eroded.

In short, the ways in which the market, the state, and civil society interact and react to the challenges of globalization are crucial in constituting subregional outcomes. Under very different conditions, there will be diverse configurations. But in all instances, subregionalism is an historically contingent phenomenon at the crossroads of globalization and the need to cope, in one manner or another, with this megaprocess. Although there are a variety of ways to accommodate globalization, sometimes resistance is either the preferred choice or the only option.

# Part Three

## RESISTANCE TO GLOBALIZATION

# CHAPTER 9

# Conceptualizing Resistance to Globalization

## (COAUTHORED WITH CHRISTINE B. N. CHIN)

ASSESSMENTS of resistance to globalization are necessarily influenced by the manner in which one conceptualizes resistance. Too often, this term is used promiscuously, sometimes as a synonym for challenges, protests, intransigence, or even evasions. Hence, we seek to juxtapose alternative explanations of resistance and highlight the complexities of theorizing it. The purpose of this chapter, then, is to explore the question, What is the meaning of resistance in the context of globalization?

One way to approach this issue is with the proposition that a major asymmetry in the globalization trend is between its economic and political levels. Although it would be wrong to concede the neoclassical premise that economics and politics are separable realms, it is clear, at least in analytical terms, that globalization's hegemonic project is neoliberalism and that liberal democracy has not kept pace with its spread. In the space opened by this disjuncture, resistance to globalization is on the rise. But it cannot solely be understood as a political reaction. Rather, in the teeth of globalizing tendencies, resistance movements shape and are constitutive of cultural processes. This is the main thesis to be developed in this chapter.

There is no dearth of culturally laden manifestations of resistance to globalization. Culminating in the election of a Government of National Unity, led by the African National Congress (ANC) in 1994, the worldwide anti-apartheid movement against a racial monopoly of the means of production is one of the foremost examples of a mobilization against globalization from above. This was *a movement from below against globalization from above* in the sense that South Africa was, and is, the site of substantial foreign investment and where many TNCs have touched down; their role in maintaining the white redoubt was successfully contested by large-scale collective action at home, including armed struggle, in conjunction with a transnational network of support groups. The demise of apartheid may also be understood as a *movement from above against globalization from above* inasmuch as it was facilitated by a split in South African capitalism, in which the modernizers and globalizers abandoned an obsolescent capitalism based on an increasingly less profitable form of racial segregation. Thus in 1985, Gavin W. H. Relly, the retired chairman of the Anglo American Corporation, the largest conglomerate in South Africa, defied official government policy and led a delegation of business leaders to meet privately with the banned ANC in Lusaka, Zambia, where they discussed the transition to a new order. In addition, there are numerous illustrations of more localized resistance, including the Zapatista armed uprising among the Maya Indians against the Mexican government's neoliberal reforms, a struggle in which the rebels quickly turned to modern technologies, including the Internet, to rally transnational support. But it would be facile to conceptualize resistance only as declared organized opposition to institutionalized economic and military power. One must dig deep to excavate the everyday individual and collective activities that fall short of open opposition. To grasp resistance to globalization, one must also examine the subtexts of political and cultural life, the possibilities and potential for structural transformation.

We begin to delve into the constitutive role of power in shaping cultural critiques of economic globalization as well as patterns of struggle by revisiting the works of three master theorists of resistance, even if their writings were not explicitly directed at the contemporary phase of globalization: Antonio Gramsci's concept of counterhegemony, Karl Polanyi's notion of countermovements, and James C. Scott's idea of infrapolitics. For the sake of brevity, our scope is limited to these authors—other conceptualizations would take us too far afield; empirical referents are provided in chapters 10 and 11. We hold that the trilogy of Gramsci-Polanyi-Scott, set forth through a critical evaluation of each author's work in the next three sections of this chapter, offers a sound basis for reconceptualizing resistance. The conclusion then probes the convergence and contrasting emphases within this triad, and also suggests directions for further study and exploratory research.

## RESISTANCE AS COUNTERHEGEMONY

Ostensibly, Gramsci's analysis of social change as explicated in *Selections from the Prison Notebooks* (1971) could neither have anticipated nor accounted for globalization. The notes were written between 1929 and 1935 while Gramsci, a member of parliament and the general secretary of the Communist Party, was imprisoned by the fascist regime in Italy. In his discussions of state-society relations, Gramsci was concerned particularly with orthodox Marxist and bourgeois liberal theoretical frameworks that privileged economism by reducing transformations in all aspects of social life to economic determinants. His theoretical efforts to transcend economism are applicable to conceptualizing resistance at the turn of the millennium. To replace economism, Gramsci developed the concept of hegemony, which encompasses whole ways of life. For Gramsci, hegemony is a dynamic lived process in which social identities, relations, organizations, and structures based on asymmetrical distributions of power and influence are constituted by the dominant classes. Hegemony, then, is as much economic as it is "ethico-political" in shaping relations of domination and subordination.

The institutions of civil society, such as the church, family, schools, media, and trade unions, give meaning and organization to everyday life so that the need for the application of force is reduced. Hegemony is established when power and control over social life are perceived as emanating from "self-government" (i.e., self-government of individuals embedded in communities) as opposed to an external source(s) such as the state or the dominant strata (Gramsci 1971, 268). Since hegemony is a lived process, different historical contexts will produce different forums of hegemony with different sets of actors, such as the nineteenth-century "passive revolution" of the Risorgimento, in which the bourgeoisie in Italy attained power without fundamental restructuring from below, and the early twentieth-century proletarian revolutionary leadership in Russia.

The processes of establishing hegemony, however, can never be complete because a hegemonic project presumes and requires the participation of subordinate groups. While hegemony is being implemented, maintained, and defended, it can be challenged and resisted in the interlocking realms of civil society, political society, and the state. Different forms and dimensions of resistance to hegemony are subsumed under the rubric of counterhegemony. Implicit in a counterhegemonic project are "wars of movement" and "wars of position," in which people engage in openly declared collective action against the state. Wars of movement are frontal assaults against the state (e.g., labor strikes or even military action), whereas wars of position can be read as nonviolent resistance, e.g., boycotts that are designed to impede everyday functions of the state (Gramsci 1971, 229–30).[1] The objective of both types of war is to seize control of the state. Wars of movement and position are expressions of counterhegemonic consciousness at the collective level. They represent moments in history when individuals come together in violent and nonviolent confrontations with the state. The question nevertheless arises: Why and how does counterhegemonic consciousness emerge in everyday life, leading to openly declared collective action?

[1] Gramsci (1971, 106–20) also linked wars of position to "passive revolution" of the dominant classes—i.e., revolution from above—that sidesteps the need for fundamental restructuring from below.

Gramsci's discussion of common sense in the development of counter-hegemonic consciousness is crucial to explaining historical and/or contemporary forms of resistance. Common sense that is held and practiced in everyday life is neither linear nor unitary; it is the product of an individual's relationship to and position in a variety of social groups:

> In acquiring one's conception of the world one always belongs to a particular grouping which is that of all the social elements which share the same mode of thinking and acting. We are all conformists of some conformism or other. . . . *When one's conception of the world is not critical and coherent but disjointed and episodic, one belongs simultaneously to a multiplicity of mass human groups.* . . . The starting-point of critical elaboration is the consciousness of what one really is, and is "knowing thyself" as a product of the historical process to date which has deposited in you an infinity of traces, without leaving an inventory. (Gramsci 1971, 324; emphasis added)

Importantly, the coexistence of conformity and resistance in common sense can give rise to inconsistencies between thought and action, which help explain contradictory behavior on the part of a subaltern group which may embrace its "own conception of the world" while still adopting conceptions borrowed from dominant classes (Gramsci 1971, 326–27). By arguing that individuals and groups possess critical consciousness—albeit "in flashes"—of their subordinate positions in society, Gramsci acknowledged the ambiguity of resistance and dismissed the overly deterministic and unidimensional explanation of false consciousness.

Nevertheless, in the discussion of thought and action, Gramsci was careful not to suggest that submission in the face of domination is the simple product of the subaltern's rational calculation of costs and benefits (in the sense that resistance would be futile at best, or would elicit retaliatory action, at worst). The fragmentation of social identity that characterizes and is characterized by simultaneous membership in different groups means that it is possible, if not probable, that the subaltern can be progressive on certain issues and reactionary on others in the same instance.

A Gramscian reading of resistance would have to explicate the development of counterhegemonic consciousness that informs wars of movement and position, as well as national-popular actions led by organic intellectuals from all walks of life who can meld theory and praxis to construct and embed a new common sense that binds disparate voices and consciousness into a coherent program of change. In his time, Gramsci called for organic intellectuals to infuse common sense with a philosophy of praxis that encourages subaltern groups' critical understanding of their subordination in society. The objective is a "national-popular" movement constituted by alliances between the leaders (in league with their organic intellectuals) and the led (subaltern). Whereas wars of movement and position aim to capture the state, the national-popular movement provides the new basis for whole ways of life.

Gramsci did not offer programmatic ways that a philosophy of praxis could transcend the fragmentation of identity and interests. With contemporary globalization, the interpenetration of forces at the local, national, regional, and world levels implies that different peoples enter into alliances that can be and are ever more contradictory: e.g., low-wage female factory workers in EPZs who also are members or supporters of Islamist movements in Southeast Asia. A new common sense has to address effectively or make coherent women's critical understanding of the tensions, limitations, and opportunities inherent in their identities as daughters or wives in the household, as low-wage workers on the factory floor, as citizens, and as Muslims in the local, national, and transnational Islamic communities.

Moreover, globalization begets openly declared forms of resistance that may or may not have the state as a target. Rotating the holders of state power may not alleviate the problems that ignited resistance in the first place. In a context in which liberal, authoritarian, and ex-communist states-in-transition alike are often becoming facilitators for transnational capital, if and when it occurs, the driving force(s) of openly declared resistance against the state must be analyzed within a larger framework. At issue are the contradictory ways in which state structures and policies assume "educative" functions that nurture a new kind of citizenry and civilization commensurate with the requirements of transnational capital, while trying to maintain the legitimacy with which to govern (Chin 1998). In this connection, one can profitably invoke Gramsci's insights into civil society and resistance, about which he offered many pointers, although they are not always congruent with one another. Additionally, Gramsci's concepts can be pushed beyond the domestic realm to world order, and scholars have begun to extend the framework in this manner (especially Cox 1986, 1987, 1999; Augelli and Murphy 1988, 1997).

Although wars of movement and position may still be discerned, sometimes in nascent form, the compression of time and space has created new venues of and for *collective resistance transcending national borders.* Contemporary social movements simultaneously occupy local, national, transnational, and global space as a result of innovations in, and applications of, technologies such as the Internet, facsimile machines, cellular mobile phones, and globalized media, which produce instantaneous communication across traditional frontiers. The Gramscian framework of resistance thus must be stretched to encompass new actors and spaces from which counterhegemonic consciousness is expressed. In the following section, we discuss the possibility of further considering social movements as a form of resistance.

## RESISTANCE AS COUNTERMOVEMENTS

A different emphasis in regard to resistance may be found in Polanyi's notion of the double *movement*. To add to what has been said in previous chapters about his notion of how, during the eighteenth and nineteenth centuries, the state-supported drive to install and expand the "self-regulating" market sparked protective measures or countermovements to reassert social control over the market, it is important to bear in mind that Polanyi understood resistance in the form of countermovements as having arisen from, and affecting, different ways of life. Protecting workers from the commodification process implies defending the social relations and institutions of which they are a part:

> *In disposing of a man's labor power the system would, incidently, dispose of the physical, psychological, and moral entity "man" attached to that tag. Robbed of the protective covering of cultural institutions, human beings would perish from the effects of social exposure*; they would die as victims of acute social dislocation through vice, perversion, crime, and starvation. . . . [N]o society could stand the effects of such a system of crude fictions even for the shortest stretch of time unless its human and natural substance as well as its business organization was protected against the ravages of this satanic mill. (Polanyi 1957, 73; emphasis added)

The movement-countermovement framework thus allows one to conceptualize contemporary social movements as a form of resistance since the latter are, in the main, defined as "a form of collective action (a) based on solidarity, (b) carrying on a conflict, (c) breaking the limits of the system in which action occurs" (Melucci 1985, 795). The level of analysis would have to be extended from the national to the transnational and/or global since some contemporary social movements, e.g., those that concern environmental destruction, women's rights, and indigenous peoples' rights, appear to go beyond the state in search of transnational or global solutions.

There are two implicit problems in the counter/social movement framework. Collectivity is assumed in the notion "movement" and this has the effect of constructing counter/social movements as united fronts in and of themselves. In the past decade or so, the fragmented nature of the feminist movement is evidenced in the internal conflict and domination generated from differences of race, religion, class, and nationality in spite of, and because of, attempts to address national and global patriarchy (Hooks 1981, 1984; Mohanty, Russo, and Torres 1991).

Also imputed in counter/social movements is the presence of organizational structure. This may be the case with some social movements (e.g.,

Greenpeace and Friends of the Earth in the environmental realm), but "submerged networks" with no clearly defined organizational structure too have formed in an era of globalization. Participants in submerged networks live their everyday lives mostly without engaging in openly declared contestations: "They question definition of codes, nomination of reality. They don't ask, they offer. They offer by their own existence other ways of defining the meaning of individual and collective action. They act as new media: they enlighten what every system doesn't say of itself, the amount of silence, violence, irrationality which is always hidden in dominant codes" (Melucci 1985, 812).

The presence of submerged networks gives new meaning to resistance. Even though participants can mobilize to protest state policies, open engagement or confrontation with the state or even TNCs is not the immediate, or even ultimate, objective. In the absence of openly declared collective action, resistance has to be read as the ways in which peoples live their everyday lives. Submerged networks affirm that even though resistance can be manifestly political and economic, it is shaped by and shapes ways of life. In advanced industrialized societies, examples of submerged networks are those in which families and their friends make it a point—in their consumption habits—to refuse to buy tuna fish caught using methods that destroy entire dolphin populations, or to purchase consumer products only from companies that actively practice environmental conservationism. Such acts have economic consequences in the corporate world, and political consequences for policy makers. Significantly, submerged networks are sites of emerging alternative values and life styles.

In Egypt, for example, submerged networks exist in the popular quarters and among the common people, known as the *sha'b*.[2] Networks radiate from the family—the basic unit of social organization in the *sha'b*—to include ties that transcend class, occupation, and kin. The "familial ethos" governs the allocation and distribution of material and symbolic resources in the *sha'b*. In the present unspoken pact between the Egyptian state and the *sha'b*, state legitimacy is maintained by the distribution of basic goods and services to the *sha'b* in return for political acquiescence. Participants of the *sha'b* acquiesce to, as much as they engage in, resistance against the state. Members of the Islamist movement, who also are members of the *sha'b*, have been known to and can draw on submerged network ties to smuggle arms and, on occasion, to mobilize and organize mass protests against the state.

The notion of the Polanyian double movement thus has a distinct advantage of neatly encapsulating openly declared demands on the na-

[2] "While the noun, the *sha'b*, refers to a collective people, populace, or folk and has an implicit collective connotation to it, as an adjective *sha'bi* demarcates a wide range of indigenous practices, tastes, and patterns in everyday life" (Singerman 1995, 10–11).

tional, transnational, and global levels for protective measures against various dimensions in the implementation and expansion of the self-regulating market. As discussed, however, the movement-countermovement framework neither advances analysis of differences within countermovements nor adequately anticipates undeclared forms of resistance, both of which have emerged and must be addressed in conceptualizing collective resistance to globalization.

## RESISTANCE AS INFRAPOLITICS

In 1990, James C. Scott introduced the idea of "infrapolitics" as everyday forms of resistance conducted singularly and collectively, but which fall short of openly declared contestations. What began as his attempt to understand the conditions for peasant rebellions in Southeast Asia and the absence of openly declared resistance in a village in rapidly industrializing Malaysia gradually led to the conceptualization of infrapolitics: a way to explain the changing meaning of politics and resistance in most forms of day-to-day, dominant-subordinate relations (Scott 1976, 1985, 1990). Scott warned that, in the context of increasingly complex societies, the absence of openly declared contestations should not be mistaken for acquiescence. It is in the realm of informal assemblages such as the parallel market, workplace, household, and local community, when people negotiate resources and values on an everyday basis, that "counterhegemonic consciousness is elaborated" (Scott 1990, 200). These are the sites of infrapolitical activities that range from foot-dragging, squatting, and gossip to the development of dissident subcultures.

Taken at face value, such activities cannot tell us anything about counterhegemonic discourse until we account for the conditions from which they emerge. Infrapolitics is identified by juxtaposing what Scott calls the "public" and "hidden transcripts." Public transcripts are verbal and non-verbal acts carried out by the dominant party or, "to put it crudely, the *self*-portrait of dominant elites as they would have themselves seen" (Scott 1990, 18; emphasis in original). They are the public record of superior-subordinate relations in which the latter appears to acquiesce willingly to the stated and unstated expectations of the former. Hidden transcripts, on the other hand, consist of what subordinate parties say and do beyond the realm of the public transcript or the observation of the dominant. In the context of surveillance structures set up by the dominant class(es) or the state, hidden transcripts record infrapolitical activities that surreptitiously challenge practices of economic, status, and ideological domination.

The study of infrapolitics, we believe, is premised on what sociologists call ontological narratives (Somers 1994). Ontological narrativity does not refer to the mode of representation or the traditional "story-telling" method of historians (i.e., a method of presenting historical knowledge) considered nonexplanatory and atheoretical by mainstream social scientists. Rather, ontological narratives are the stories that social actors tell, and in the process they come to define themselves or to construct their identities and perceive conditions that promote and/or mitigate the possibility for change (see, especially, Butler and Scott 1992; Geertz 1983; Taylor 1989).

Even though hidden transcripts record contestations over material and symbolic resources and values in everyday life, they do not occur in a localized vacuum. Infrapolitical activities are the product of interactions between structure and agency: the ways that real and perceived constraints and opportunities affect the behavior of subordinate groups. Scott's analysis of infrapolitical activities thus falls short of capturing the complexities inherent in undeclared forms of everyday resistance. In his study of landlord-peasant relations in a rural Malay village, Scott asserted that analyses of state structures and policies were important *only* to the extent that they impinged on local class relations (1985, xix). Especially during the 1980s and in the context of national agricultural development policies and fluctuating global prices of commodities, landlord-peasant relations were shaped by impingements on, and interactions among, the rural community, state structures and policies, as well as the transformations marking a globalizing economic system.

Superior-subordinate relations, such as those of the landlord-peasant, manager-worker, husband-wife, and state official-squatter, are embedded in the ways of life, of which state structures and policies play an important part. Take, for instance, policies designed to normalize the patriarchal nuclear family form as most natural in and for the expansion and maintenance of capitalist free markets, and/or that privilege scientific and other technical education at the expense of the humanities. Such policies frame worldviews insofar as they directly and indirectly affect all aspects of social life from the rate of urbanization, housing development, and employment opportunities, to the control and distribution of resources in the household. In increasingly complex social contexts, subalterns do not have an unproblematic unitary identity. Nor can their behavior be explained by implicit reference to the economic model of the self-interested utility maximizer. Put simply, infrapolitical activities are not the mere product of subaltern decisions to conduct undeclared resistance in the face of surveillance structures set up by the dominant strata.

Class is but one important modality of identity in landlord-peasant or other forms of dominant-subordinate relations. The different and possibly conflicting modalities of subaltern identity can be as real, and under certain conditions, as constraining on behavior as the actual or perceived futility and fear of openly declared resistance in the face of domination. By putting a unidimensional face on resistance, Scott inadvertently assigned a similar unidimensional countenance to domination, even though he analytically distinguished economic, status, and ideological domination. In this connection, Gramsci reminded us that subaltern identities are embedded in complex overlapping social networks in which individuals simultaneously assume positions of domination and subordination (perhaps as a husband or wife, an elder or junior, a manager or office clerk, and a donor or recipient of aid). Analysis of the manner in which particular combinations of identity are expressed in the context of structural constraints can help explain why, given systems of surveillance (in which rewards and punishments inhere), some conform while others engage in infrapolitical activities of different types. Conversely, this approach also deepens analysis of the changing nature of domination.

Hidden transcripts have the potential to facilitate understanding of the internal politics of subaltern groups. The phenomenon of "domination within domination" occurs in cases in which contradictory alliances are formed between the dominant and the subordinate that, in turn, dominate others. Although Scott acknowledges this point, his emphasis on class without a sufficiently subtle exploration of the interactions between class and nonclass forces undermines the efficacy of the infrapolitical framework. The immediate focus on class presumes that the development of class consciousness stands apart exclusively from other modalities of identity. It is, indeed, possible to argue that class contests in the context of surveillance can and do lead to infrapolitical activities that are grounded in material life. This argument is made possible *only* after having considered how and why the class dimension comes to be privileged and expressed over other modalities of identity. To do otherwise would reaffirm what Gramsci called "economism," and subsequently relegate noneconomic considerations to the ambit of superstructure.

Infrapolitics is embedded in whole ways of life, part of which is the material dimension. They embody contestations over the processes of grounded identity construction, maintenance, and transformation, of which the symbolic and material dimensions of class are intertwined with other modalities of identity, such as age, gender, race-ethnicity, religion, and nationality. The identification, juxtaposition, and analyses of public and hidden transcripts can highlight the conditions in which certain dimensions of counterhegemonic consciousness develop, and how different or even conflicting perspectives within hidden transcripts are negotiated and/or (not) resolved in everyday life.

Resistance conceptualized as infrapolitical activities offers a possible avenue for generating theoretically grounded studies of everyday responses to globalizing structures and processes. If conducted with sensitivity to the complex interplay between or among multiple identities in the context of structural constraints, the study of public and hidden transcripts may reveal changing notions and practices of work, family, and politics, for example, as peoples seek to negotiate a semblance of social control over the expansion of market forces in diverse spheres of their everyday lives. At the same time, one should not overwork the broad category of infrapolitics by imagining that every sort of reaction to globalizing structures is resistance. Whereas Scott carefully argues that diverse modes of resistance may or may not coalesce into opposition to authority structures, it is important to avoid treating resistance as an omnibus category.

## AN EMERGING FRAMEWORK

The conduct and meaning of resistance are culturally embedded. This foundational proposition is no less applicable or relevant in conceptualizing contemporary resistance to globalization, as it was to Gramsci, Polanyi, and Scott's analyses of social change in different historical periods. The three master theorists acknowledged, implicitly and explicitly, that resistance arises from and is constitutive of specific ways of life. From this elemental proposition, however, the theorists diverged in their respective discussions of the forms and dimensions of resistance. Gramsci and Polanyi focused on the collective level, whereas Scott drew attention more to the level of the individual, as well as class, in everyday life. As delineated in Table 9.1, the main targets and modes of resistance differ from one theorist to another: Gramscian wars of movement and position against the state (though not to the neglect of change within civil society short of toppling the state), Polanyian countermovements against market forces, and Scott's infrapolitical activities in the face of everyday domination.

Differences in levels of analysis, main targets, and modes of resistance should not be reasoned only by way of the intellectual proclivities of each theorist per se. Rather, the conceptual tensions among the theorists correspond to, and reflect, the changing conditions of social life: From Gramsci to Polanyi to Scott, as societies became more complex, so too did the targets and modes of resistance. Contemporary transformations in social life in general, and state-society relations in particular, imply that all three major targets and modes of resistance coexist and are modified in globalizing processes.

This important conversation among the theorists forms a grid that may be profitably fastened to neoliberal globalization. The emerging framework helps to identify possibilities for contesting forms of domination,

### TABLE 9.1
Three Analyses of Resistance

|  | Main Target | Mode of Resistance |
|---|---|---|
| Gramsci | State apparatuses (understood as an instrument of education) | Wars of movement and position |
| Polanyi | Market forces (and their legitimation) | Countermovements aimed at self-protection |
| Scott | Ideologies (public transcripts) | Counterdiscourses |

expanding political space, and opening new venues—hence redefinitions of politics. Seen from the observation points of this triad, a conceptualization of contemporary resistance to globalization sensitizes one to the ontological shift suggested below.

### Forms of Resistance

As certain dimensions of political and economic power become more diffuse and less institutionalized, so too will forms of resistance. Undeclared forms of resistance conducted individually and collectively in submerged networks parallel openly declared forms of resistance embodied in wars of movement and position, and countermovements. Depending on the context, everyday activities, such as what one wears (e.g., the veil in Muslim societies or the dashiki in the African-American community), buys, or consumes, may qualify as resistance—as much as that of organized strikes, boycotts, and even armed insurgencies against states and TNCs throughout the world. One of the key challenges here is to problematize the absence of openly declared forms of resistance. Doing so can explicate the changing meaning of politics as a result of interactions between forces of change on the local, national, regional, and global levels.

### Agents of Resistance

In the past, agents of resistance were synonymous mostly with union workers, armed rebels (many of them peasants), and political dissidents, including students and certain intellectuals, as class contestations assumed overt political and, in some cases, military dimensions. At present, agents of resistance are not restricted to such actors. They range from blue-collar and white-collar workers to clerics, homemakers, and middle managers. It is important to note that even state functionaries can resist the wholesale implementation of neoliberal development paths (especially the veneer of liberal democratic politics), such as those who insist on "Asian-style democracy" in the midst of establishing open markets and free trade. It is the complex ways in which symbolic resources and values articulate with the material conditions of life in different societies that produce a variety of organic intellectuals, a more encompassing group in the current phase of globalization. Class contests only partly form the basis of resistance. Instead, agents of resistance emerge from interactions between structure and agency that lead to the contextual privileging of particular intersections of different modes of identity, i.e., class-nationality-gender-race/ethnicity-religion-sexual orientation. Implicit in the designation of diverse peoples as agents of resistance is an expansion of the boundaries associated with the traditional sites of political life.

### Sites of Resistance

Resistance is localized, regionalized, and globalized at the same time that economic globalization slices across geopolitical borders. What this means, in part, is that the "public-private" dichotomy no longer holds, for most, albeit not all, dimensions of social life are affected in varying and interconnected ways by globalizing forces. Everyday life in the household and the informal market can facilitate, as well as resist, such forces in distinctly material and symbolic ways. Another closely related phenomenon is the development of cyberspace, a site at which resistance finds its instantaneous audience via the Internet or World Wide Web. Counterdiscourse is a mode of globalized resistance in cyberspace. One has to bear in mind, however, that although states in general are incapable of effectively monitoring and censoring cyberspatial counterdiscourse, this particular means of resistance is open only to those who have access to computers, modems, and the Internet.

### Strategies of Resistance

By strategies, we refer to the actual ways that people, whose modes of existence are threatened by globalization (e.g., through job loss, encroachment on community lands, or undermining of cultural integrity), respond in a sustained manner toward achieving certain objectives. While forms of struggle differ, groups may adopt varied means to contest, and link objectively and subjectively to their counterparts in other countries or regions. Local movements become transnational or global with sustained access to communication technologies that construct and maintain communities of like-minded individuals. For example, community activists and scholars meet at different forums for the exchange of information and plans. An emerging strategy of "borderless solidarity" is to link single issues such as environmental degradation, women's rights, and racism, and to highlight the interconnectedness of varied dimensions of social life. Analyses of this may bring to bear the conditions and methods by which commonality can be achieved in spite, of and because of, the fragmentation of identities and interests while economic and political life is being globalized. Nonetheless, evolving global strategies of resistance do not necessarily sidetrack the state. Under certain circumstances, strategies of resistance can, and do, pit state agencies against one another (e.g., in the case of shipping toxic waste to the developing world, state agencies in charge of environmental protection may join in protests, while their counterparts responsible for industrial development continue to encourage the kind and methods of industrialization that cause environmental damage). Studies of global, transnational, and local resistance must then take into account transformations in state structures, whether or not strategies of resistance manifestly engage the state.

Quite clearly, an ontology of resistance to globalization requires grounding. When contextualized, the elements of *forms, agents, sites,* and *strategies* may be viewed in terms of their interactions so as to delimit durable patterns and the potential for structural transformation. The Gramsci-Polanyi-Scott triad calls for conceptual frameworks that link different levels of analysis. Integration of the local and the global can bring to the fore the conditions in which diverse forms, agents, sites, and strategies of resistance emerge from the conjunctures and disjunctures in the global political economy, as shown in the following chapters, which are intended to exemplify the intricacy and the variability of *combinations* of resistance from above and below. The next chapter threads the categories and propositions developed here through the environmental realm, and the penultimate chapter complicates the analysis by bringing to light a very different kind of resistance, one that emulates the market by adopting its logic, yet interfering with neoliberal rules, and profoundly affecting the nature of political life.

# CHAPTER 10

# Environmental Resistance Politics

NOT ALL types of environmental degradation are of recent origin or global in scope—some are long-established and local. Even so, unsustainable transformation of the environment under globalization differs from environmental harm in previous epochs. Although contemporary environmental abuses have their antecedents in earlier periods of history, globalization coincides with new environmental problems such as global warming, depletion of the ozone layer, acute loss of biodiversity, and forms of transborder pollution (e.g., acid rain). These problems have emerged not singly, but together. Moreover, some ecological problems are clearly the result of global cross-border flows, as with certain kinds of groundwater contamination, leaching, and long-term health threats traceable to importing hazardous wastes.

Large-scale growth in world economic output since the 1970s has not only quickened the breakdown of the global resource base, but also has upset the planet's regenerative system, including its equilibrium among different forms of life and their support structures. A large part of the explanation is that deregulation and liberalization mean more global pressure to lower environmental standards, albeit there are, of course, counterpressures to shift from environmentally destructive activities to cleaner technologies. In the absence of stringent regulations and effective enforcement mechanisms, fear and insecurity about the planet's future are on the rise.

With hypercompetition for profits, the market is trespassing nature's limits (Shiva 1992, 211, 216). Yet nature's protest, its signals of breakdown, provide an opening. Rather than reify the environment, it is important to resist the ontological distinction between humans and nature, a dualism rooted in modern thought since Descartes. If so, humankind and nature may be viewed interactively as "a single causal stream" (Rosenau 1997, 190–91; also Goldblatt 1996). The environment may then be understood as political space, a critical venue where civil society is voicing its concerns. As such, the environment represents a marker where, to varying degrees, popular resistance to globalization is manifest. Slicing across party, class, religion, gender, race, and ethnicity, environmental politics offers a useful entry point for assessing counterglobalization.

Accordingly, the questions that frame this chapter are: What are the specific sites of environmental resistance to globalization? Who are the agents of resistance? What strategies are adopted? And to what extent are they localized or regionalized and globalized? In other words, is there evidence to demonstrate the stirrings of counterglobalization?

In attempting to answer these questions, I will show the complex layering of different modes of resistance politics. My chief concern is organized environmental responses to globalization, though not to the exclusion of other types of resistance. For reasons that will be elaborated in the next section, I am especially interested in direct environmental initiatives—solid patterns and cumulative action—but also in the soft, or latent, forms of protest that may or may not sufficiently harden so as eventually to challenge global structures. Attention will be given to submerged forms of resistance insofar as they are emerging into networks. Networks are important here because they may serve as venues for resistance, and also because global capitalism is not at all singular (Yearley 1996; Heng 1997; Hefner 1998). Rather, capitalism is organized in multiple ways. For example, "network capitalism" is widely recognized in the Japanese and transnational Chinese forms of ties originating at universities and continuing in professional circles, information exchange, and government-business collaboration.

A major goal in this chapter, then, is to present evidence for exploring the politics of resistance in light of the theoretical propositions already set forth on modes of resistance (chapter 9) and to bring to light the diversity of environmental politics in encounters with globalizing processes. The evidential material adduced here centers on transboundary problems, illustrates the myriad ways that environmental groups operate, and offers fresh and original examples of the emerging and varying consciousness of resistance.[1] For the purposes of academic research, it would be desirable to separate the domain of resistance to globalization from resistance to other forms of hierarchical power relations, but they cannot be neatly

[1] An irony in completing the empirical research for this chapter and recording my findings is that I did so in Hanoi, where I temporarily became an environmental refugee, escaping the effects of choking haze that blanketed six countries and reached "hazardous" levels on the official air pollution index in 1997. Ostensibly caused by uncontrolled forest fires in Indonesia, drought brought about by El Niño patterns in the oceans, and winds that swept the smoke into neighboring countries, including Malaysia, where I was living, the problem of course had other causes: the slash-and-burn techniques practiced by transnational agribusiness, the lack of a political will to deal with some of the domestic sources of pollution in countries engaged in high-speed economic growth, and ways that special interests outside and inside the state stymie strong remedial action. The immediate impact of the environmental crisis was deaths linked to respiratory illnesses, a welter of ancillary health problems overcrowding the hospitals, accidents attributable to poor visibility, and enormous direct economic costs, especially in tourism, agriculture, education, and industries that had to cut back. Plainly, the magnitude of this crisis reached major regional and global proportions. A salutary effect of the haze was that it alerted the public to the systemic consequences of unbridled economic growth and of looking exclusively to government for solutions.

divided. Rather, spheres of resistance surrounding the environment, labor standards, women's issues, human rights, and the like merge and interpenetrate. One can, however, identify certain emphases in consciousness and action as a basis for analyzing potential transformations in world order (Mittelman 1997b).

To enter the crucible of resistance politics, I first explore the characteristics of environmental resistance politics. The next section turns to the forms and sources of popular resistance, followed by a discussion of the agents challenging macrostructures. Inquiry then focuses on the sites of resistance and, finally, weighs the efficacy of multilayered strategies.

## CHARACTERISTICS OF ENVIRONMENTAL RESISTANCE POLITICS

The environment is not a single phenomenon, and, as implied above, may be viewed through different prisms: a series of interactions between the physical and human worlds; a site of resistance; and a social construction that is contested. In terms of the latter approach, attitudes to nature are always changing, are linked to time and place, and initially reflect the dominant culture. In fact, the relationship between nature and culture has been rapidly and variously transformed around the world. This is not new, but technological innovations and hypercompetition accelerate the trend. Moreover, a hallmark of globalization is the outburst of cultural pluralism, and some cultural conflicts tied to imbalances in power relations find expression in environmental ideologies, understood as systems of representation of a definite group or class.

A graphic example of the social construction of the environment is the Eurocentric conservation ideology that developed in Southern Africa. In the mid-twentieth century, there emerged an extension of the colonial paradigm, a conservation ideology based on a wildlife-centered, preservationist approach that buttressed white privilege and power in the subcontinent (Khan 1994). The story of game and nature reserves in Southern Africa is embedded in the mythology surrounding Kruger National Park and symbolized by the portrayal of Paul Kruger as a visionary who championed wildlife protection. Environmental historians have deconstructed this romantic myth, showing that Kruger actually opposed stricter game protection laws and supported the legal right of whites to continue to hunt. But the icon of "Paul Kruger's dream" was appropriated by the purveyors of an emergent Afrikaner nationalism and manipulated to gain the support of poor whites; it helped to unite opposed factions and classes in Afrikaner society in the post-World War I period. After 1948, the apartheid regime revived the Kruger wildlife, protectionist myth in an attempt not only to rouse patriotism, but also to gain international respectability for the pariah state among its critics overseas (Carruthers 1995; Khan 1990).

Racial discrimination in the application of conservation policies, such as stock culling, forged anticonservation attitudes. The marginalization of blacks generated a negative attitude toward government decisions concerning the environment, which were seen as imposed by an unjust system that denied meaningful representation or participation to people who believed that they had a rightful claim to the land. Africans engaged in poaching, withheld their services, and lived clandestinely in the game reserves—all expressions of freedom of action. Popular resistance gave rise to initiatives such as the Native Farmers Association (NFA), the first black organization in South Africa to record a formal environmental ethic and thereby contribute to a counterideology opposed to the culture of the park as being white, pristine, and scientist. The NFA, in fact, called for a paradigmatic shift toward socially responsive policies (Khan 1994). What many white South Africans and Westerners came to regard as a science—conservation and park, or more generally, environmental management—others came to interpret as a disguised form of resource control.

This illustration indicates that the environment may be construed as a set of alternative moral forces forming ideological representations. It demonstrates that submerged responses to environmental use (or abuse) may in turn be transformed into organized political resistance that props up its counterideologies. It also implicates the basic categories of analysis used by the master theorists of resistance—Gramsci, Polanyi, and Scott—discussed in chapter 9. At this juncture, I will not revisit what was said there, but want to position myself within this triad so as to forge a link to environmental resistance politics.

Needless to say, all three frameworks advanced by these authors have great explanatory power. Their merits do not require elaboration in this chapter, but a few critical comments are in order. A Marxist who subscribed to the view that class conflict is the motor of history, Gramsci differed from Marx in allowing considerable autonomy for consciousness, which helps to understand the cultural dimensions of resistance. Nonetheless, Gramsci's two-pronged conceptualization of wars of movement and position must be stretched to include a range of other actors and different spaces in which, at the turn of the millennium, consciousness develops.

Like Gramsci, Scott turns attention to the culture of resistance. His emphasis on "infrapolitical" activities offers a subtle way to probe everyday responses to globalizing processes. Indeed, there are valuable empirical studies documenting the microrelations of encounters between local and global conditions. For example, Aihwa Ong (1987) details spirit possession episodes, when Malay factory women become violent and scream abuses as a symptom of their loss of autonomy at work. Nevertheless, the limitation to Scott's probing of covert acts is that the wide gamut of forms of resistance he suggests is a catchall. Not only are they highly diffuse, but they also may make little overall impact on power relations. This problem in Scott's framework is revealed in the very first line of his 1990 book. The aphorism he selects to open it is an Ethiopian proverb: "When the great lord passes the wise peasant bows deeply and farts." Yet how much political impact does farting really have? How much effect do foot-dragging, squatting, gossip, and other forms of uncoordinated resistance actually have on environmental problems such as global warming and deterioration of the ozone layer? Where is the evidence to demonstrate that countless microscopic activities will ultimately amount to a shift in macrostructures?[2]

Although, as Scott cautions, these acts, even when multiplied, may not topple regimes, they often signal weaknesses in a regime's legitimacy and can help undermine faith in authority. Indeed, it might be argued that numerous subversive measures do add up, for they are cumulative. But it seems fair to ask, If the consequences are fully felt only in the *longue durée*, how long will that be? As the eruption of multiple environmental crises patently shows, nature is already vetoing its subordination to the market economy (Harries-Jones, Rotstein, and Timmerman 1992).[3] By all indications, it will not wait for the *longue durée* to resolve the matter. Whereas it is right to be alert to the subtexts of resistance, and this the seeds of potential transformation, the question is, How, and under what conditions, do submerged forms of resistance coalesce and genuinely contest globalizing structures? Conversely, it is important to specify the conditions that prevent the crystallization of resistance politics. What factors facilitate and hinder the stiffening of resistance?

Few contemporary scholars (with notable exceptions, including Walker 1994; Shaw 1994; Murphy 1994; Sklair 1994, 1997; Smith, Chatfield, and Pagnucco 1997; Keck and Sikkink 1998) have attempted to theorize the connections between social movements and world politics. It should be recalled that master thinkers such as Gramsci and Polanyi offered traces of a finely grained analysis of the emergence of social movements within the global political economy of their times. Turning attention to the Owenites and Chartists of his day, Polanyi underlined that

---

[2] In this vein, Adas concludes his research findings on peasant resistance with a helpful formulation: "Avoidance protest in its many forms can protect, win specific concessions or exact revenge, but it cannot reform in major ways or transform unjust socio-political systems. Only modes of confrontational protest can achieve the latter" (1986, 83).

[3] This phrasing embodies a departure from the dualism contained in the distinction between humankind and nature.

"both movements comprised hundreds of thousands of craftsmen and artisans, laborers and working people, and with their vast following ranked among the biggest *social movements* in modern history" (1957, 167; emphasis added). It was Polanyi's insight that the dialectic of movement and countermovement advances understanding of resistance but only if concrete political, economic, and social institutions are brought into an analysis of historical transformation. Polanyi was, above all, concerned with the specific institutional arrangements by which particular societies ensure their livelihood. Following from Polanyi's contribution, an area of inquiry that needs to be extended is: As societies try to protect themselves against the traumatic effects of the market, including what he regarded as "the disintegration of the cultural environment " (1957, 157), how do submerged expressions of resistance solidify and actually take shape as countermovements? In this vein, a Polanyian framework may be readily applied to the relationship between political economy and ecology (Bernard 1997). In fact, writing more than a half century ago, Polanyi ([1944] 1957) himself registered grave concern over the disembeddedness of markets not only from society, but also from nature.

An ecological reading of Polanyi requires a grasp of his critique of classical political economy and liberalism. In opposition to Adam Smith's emphasis on individual economic gains over an appreciation for embeddedness in social relations, and in contrast to Smith's response to the Physiocrats' proclivity for agriculture, Polanyi held that it is an error to exclude nature from political economy. Similarly, he pronounced Ricardo guilty of the commodity fiction of treating land as only a factor of production and detaching it from social institutions. Marx, too, came under fire for one-sidedly judging the character of an economy in terms of the labor process. According to Polanyi, always the economic historian and anthropologist, nineteenth-century society differed from its forerunners in the way that economic gain became preeminent in organizing, or reorganizing, human life. For Polanyi, both Marxism and liberalism erroneously posited that the dominant pattern in their societies was dominant throughout history (Block and Somers 1984, 63). Adopting a wider, historical frame, Polanyi delimited forms of integration of humans and nature in premarket society, and showed that the economy had been governed by basic institutions of society, and not vice versa. The institutional mechanisms had included reciprocity, redistribution, and household relations (Polanyi 1968).

To extrapolate from Polanyi, the error of economic rationalism is to vest an economistic culture with an economistic logic. A science of economics subordinates the science of nature. This relationship turns on one's understanding of the "economic," which cannot be taken for granted. One definition commonly used is formal, and centers on scarcity. It is to be distinguished from a second, the substantive sense, which involves "the fundamental fact that human beings, like all other living things, cannot exist for any length of time without a physical environment that sustains them; this is the origin of the substantive definition of *economic*" (Polanyi 1977, 19; emphasis in original). The interactions between humans and their natural surroundings thus carry "meanings," and there may be counteracting forces at work.

For a condition in which economics subordinates both nature and society, and hence creates market society, the antidote is re-embedding. But in practice, what does it really mean to reground economics in nature and social relations? Posing this question underscores the elemental dilemma in resistance politics today. The challenge is even greater than in Polanyi's time—and requires an extension of his framework—because of the increasing integration of national economies. The search for a formula for re-embedding has clearly given rise to different political projects, and is a contested issue. To examine these projects, let us first identify *forms* and sources of popular environmental resistance so that we can then delineate the work of *agents* for change, especially the politically organized wings of civil society, the *sites* at which they operate, and the principal *strategies* of resistance. What must then be taken into account is whether these wings of resistance fall into any sort of formation.

## FORMS AND SOURCES OF POPULAR ENVIRONMENTAL RESISTANCE

Forms of environmental degradation are diverse and have several root causes. The main problems pertain to the home environment, the workplace, and nature, and are to be found in different sectors of the economy, especially energy, agriculture, mining, and manufacturing. The sources have both objective and subjective dimensions, and may be mapped as a combination of factors:

- hypercompetition;
- social inequality and poverty;
- unsustainable levels of exploitation of resources;
- occupation of land and its conversion into commercial and industrial projects;
- migration and overcrowding;
- fears of displacement;
- debt structures, which in turn further resource exploitation; and
- criminalizing the customary use of resources (or a perception thereof) and a lack of accountability.

Rather than speak only of a list of discrete sources, one must also trace distinctive historical trajectories culminating in environmental abuse.

These constitute interactive webs of social relations. Some of the sources noted above originated in the preglobalization periods, but globalization intensifies these processes. There are also new forms of age-old problems, such as debt. Consider, for example, the environmental impact of structural adjustment programs. Greater austerity at home, coupled with the need to meet heightened interest payments required by international financial institutions, often result in more emphasis on the export of natural resources to earn foreign exchange. The exploitation of resources and big projects, such as the construction of dams, displace people. Most often, it is poor people who become internal migrants (Freedom from Debt Coalition 1996). On Mindanao, the southernmost island in the Philippines, TNCs—for instance, big pineapple concerns such as Dole—have gained possession of lowlands, eroding the soil and driving peasant farmers upland. Amid a sharp conflict between lowlanders and uplanders, indigenous peoples—"tribal groups"—battle to protect their cultural integrity and "ancestral domain."

While not a mountainous terrain, the landscape of eastern Zimbabwe straddling the Mozambican border is the scene of a similar form of encounter. With Cargill—a transnational food processing conglomerate—controlling large tracts of land, and with the erosion of the soil, internal migration is on the rise. Ethnic groups, or subdivisions of them, are competing for resources and coming into conflict with one another. In this case, it is difficult to distinguish internal from international migration, for local peoples regularly cross the border with impunity. They do so partly to evade laws—for example, Zimbabwean rural dwellers drive elephants, which destroy crops, over the border into Mozambique, and kill them there. The attitude among these peasant farmers is that borders are a nuisance that interfere with both their livelihood and relations with kin, redound to the advantage of the well-to-do, and are another way in which the political authorities seek to impose control. In this instance, the state is seen as constraining cross-border flows—of fish, ivory, meat, marijuana, and spirits—rooted in culture and economy. From this perspective, borders are instruments of coercion and sites of conflict. Such visions are underpinned by divisions of labor and power at the national, regional, and global levels. In both the Philippines and Zimbabwe, not only are there pressures on poor people to become migrants, but to survive, they must also destroy resources.

Hence, the targets of environmental resistance may be direct and take on a tangible form, or be indirect in the sense of process. The issue, at bottom, is control: control of land, species, forests, marine life, labor, and ideology. These aspects of control may be inscribed in law and enforced by the state. The resisters are ultimately motivated by the desire for access, and in varied measures, react against layers of structural power. One aspect of such opposition, increasingly apparent among different power positions, is the disjuncture between environmental ideologies (Nazarea-Sandoval 1995). Evident under varied guises in both Eastern Asia and Southern Africa is a clash between a modern-day, trickle-down approach, which holds that the first task is to grow the economy without, at the same time, attending to distribution and equity, and alternatives that stress the need for community-based development and the linkage between economic reform and social policy (e.g., "social forestry"). In other words, access to resources is reinforced or challenged by different ideologies; but the dominant one is reform understood as growth before equity. Although from one interview to another, my interviewees' terminology differed, this same point was made several times over. In a joint interview that centered on forestry, an interviewee punctuated his remarks by proclaiming: "The root causes [of environmental abuse] are in social structures reinforced by the development paradigm. The paradigm is the villain" (del Castillo 1996; Rebugio 1996).

The resisters adopt time and space perspectives consonant with their own sense of dignity and interests, which at present is a matter of sheer survival for many. The specific forms that reactions take turn on the type and degree of environmental abuse, as well as the strategies available to the resisters (Peluso 1992, 13; Scott 1985). The recourse may be outward in the sense of striking at an external phenomenon, inward in taking on local forms of control, or both inasmuch as layers of outsiders and insiders become so interwoven that structures of resistance seek to break both down in either a simultaneous or a sequential manner (Peluso 1992, 13, 16–17; Scott 1985). This then begs the question, What are the sites at which agents resist globalizing structures and craft alternative strategies?

## SITES OF RESISTANCE

Aside from self-help societies and local charities, a dense web of private, associational life was not available as a site of resistance—it did not exist in Japan and most other areas outside the West—before the 1960s and 1970s. In fact, it is generally absent in Vietnam today, where environmentalists work with a ministry but do not find a scope for private initiatives outside the state. There is only a handful of Vietnamese environmental NGOs, each one small, based in Hanoi, and lacking autonomy. Environmental groups also face severe constraints in Singapore and Malaysia, but the conditions differ and beget a distinctive mix of strategies.

There have been tentative attempts by Singaporean environmentalists—a multiclass group, but mainly professionals, administrators, and managers—to open up political space and test the state's rhetoric about tolerance. Most notably, the Nature Society of Singapore (NSS), founded more than thirty years ago as the Singapore branch of the Malayan Nature Society, has contested government policy within stringent parameters. Inasmuch as NGOs in Singapore are subject to restraining legislation, such as the Societies Act and deregistration, which effectively bans their operations, as well as court proceedings, the NSS has represented its actions as "constructive dialogue." Composed of about two thousand members, the NSS has engaged in letter-writing campaigns, designed a master plan for conservation, and commissioned its own environmental impact assessments (Ho 1997b). The NSS also takes the initiative and submits proposals to the government, even though most of them—99 percent—are rejected. The most extreme move involved enlisting up to 25,000 signatures for a petition and submitting it to the appropriate authority. A major constraint is that the NSS and Singapore's few other environmental groups, which are mainly involved in school activities, risk losing credibility with the state—and thus facing sanctions—if they work with NGOs in other countries. Apart from sharing information, there is little transnational collaboration. Even so, tussles over environmental projects have contributed to important changes in land use: converting eighty-seven hectares zoned for an agro-technology park to a bird sanctuary at Sungei Buloh, shelving plans for a golf course at the Lower Pierce reserve catchment area, and the diversion of a proposed mass rapid transit line so that it would not disrupt the natural habitat of bird life in Senoko (Ho 1997a; Rodan 1996, 106–7; Kong 1994). Notwithstanding coercive rule and cooptation wrought by a postcolonial transformation from poverty to economic well-being, and despite a culture that values "consensus," not dissent, clearly there are fledgling attempts to expand civil society and, however tenuously, to foster resistance.

As in Singapore, civil society in Malaysia is constrained by economic cooptation, draconian laws such as the Internal Security Act (a relic of colonialism that permits detention without trial), and intimidation against environmental activism, including Prime Minister Mahathir Mohamad's rhetoric about "green imperialism." So, too, the state requires NGO registration, controls access to the media, and is dominated by one party, which not only penetrates deeply into society, but also is extremely shrewd in mixing coercion and consent (as emphasized, the ingredients of hegemony so long as the latter is the main component). The holders of state power have nipped off elements of checks and balances—e.g., by eroding the prerogatives of farmers associations and other semiautonomous structures in the rural areas. Ideological representations—issues of race, language, and religion—have deflected attention from critical problems, including environmental degradation. Nevertheless, there have been bottom-up actions by environmentalists—mobilization in *kampung* (villages) around acid pollution, protests over radioactive waste, residence issues concerning trees in Cheras, and logging blockades in Sarawak (Singh 1997). A handful of environmental organizations—including the Environmental Protection Society; the Malayan Nature Society; Sahabat Alam Malaysia; the Centre for Environment, Technology, and Development, Malaysia; as well as various consumer associations—have established space for low-key agitation and "critical collaboration" with the government.

In contrast, a robust civil society has developed in countries such as the Philippines and South Africa, and there are vibrant activities elsewhere—for example, in Thailand and South Korea. Highly politicized Philippine and South African civil societies emerged in the context of mobilization: in one case, through armed struggles against Spanish colonialism, U.S. domination, and martial rule, while, in the other, against the apartheid regime. Among the different kinds of civil society activities illustrated above, countries such as Zimbabwe are in an intermediate position: Environmentalists and other activists push the limits but are ever mindful of the consequences of not respecting them. In all instances, the concrete institutions of civil society, specific to countries and regions, are crucial.

## THE AGENTS

The spectrum of environmental institutions does not form a continuum running left and right. Rather, the environmental movement may be likened to a broad tree with many branches and shoots of varying degrees of maturity. The thickness changes from the roots to the different sides and levels. With the thickening of civil society, its treelike growth may still be a matter more of twigs than boughs.

In practice, this structure consists of several institutions—such as churches, trade unions, the business sector, peasant associations, and student groups—that have participated, and often joined together, in rallying around environmental issues. All these institutions are part of civil society. It is civil society that is the main vector in environmental resistance. Within civil society, there appear to be five layers of environmental resistance to globalization. Without underestimating the silent struggle of poaching, killing animals, cutting fences, burning fields, and so on, it is direct and organized action at these five levels that seems to have the greatest impact and bears the most potential for gaining momentum.

First, there are a host of international environmental organizations, such as Greenpeace, Friends of the Earth, and the World Wildlife Fund, that work closely with indigenous groups or have local affiliates under their aegis (see Wapner 1996). Most of the former are based in the West, and may or may not have the same agenda as their partners in the developing world (Brosius 1997; Eccleston 1996; Eccleston and Potter 1996). In some cases, those on the ground express reservations about the discrepant priorities of external bodies, and, at times, seek to fuse indigenous values with Western environmental concerns (Lee and So 1999, 291). At the second level of generality come national coalitions or networks, such as the Caucus of Development NGO Networks, an umbrella organization of fourteen major NGO networks in the Philippines. Its objective is to serve as a network of networks (Songco 1996). Together, these coalitions encompass nearly three thousand individual organizations. An important research need is to map these coalition structures. Essentially, this is a weblike realm of functionally specialized organizations that link many NGOs, associations, societies, and so on, as well as share a common agenda and set of priorities.

Third, individual NGOs at a national level play multiple roles. They are catalysts that strive to facilitate action, often by advocacy, mobilizing resources, and providing expertise: skills in local administration, legal drafting, accounting, and other forms of training, as well as research on specific issues. Swept up in transformations of their livelihoods and modes of existence, leaders of civil society are searching for an understanding of these conditions. In honing their mission and carrying out research, NGOs require, and indeed seek, analytical paradigms. Notions such as trickle-down economics, participatory development, and community organizing are all born out of paradigms. Yet, with globalization, more compelling explanations are sought, especially to help generate means of action.

Next, although the idiom varies from one region and country to another, grassroots organizations are engaged in the actual implementation of projects. POs and CBOs are grassroots organizations involved in collective action. They may or may not seek the assistance of NGOs. Finally, civil society also includes a large swath of unheard masses who are unorganized but not unconcerned citizens, for they too are stakeholders. They can be mobilized around issues of severe environmental degradation, and have been incited to join campaigns to block activities such as illegal logging and the dumping of toxic wastes. Religious leaders, from Catholic bishops to the mufti, have indeed implored their followers to stop ecological destruction. The influence of Buddhism, Christianity, Confucianism, Islam, Judaism, and other religions runs deep in environmental resistance politics, but extends farther down in some contexts than in others.

The Catholic Church, for example, sometimes serves as an alternative power structure or helps to establish one. Hence, in 1988, the Catholic Bishops Conference of the Philippines issued a signed pastoral letter that lamented the damage done to the forests, rivers, and corals attributable to "human greed and relentless drive of our plunder economy." The bishops also praised the efforts of the local people of Bukidnon and Zamboanga del Sur, who "defended what remains of their forest with their own bodies," and urged the people to "organize around local ecological issues" (as quoted in Magno 1993, 15). Through their sermons, parish priests have rallied the masses to self-organize and take action, such as blocking illegal logging in the Philippine countryside. They have made moral and practical appeals, explaining that "God created the trees, but the trees are being cut down." One priest even called on the people to revive their tradition of headhunting, and this threat was used against the loggers and their collaborators in local government (de Guzman 1996; Dacumos 1996). Similarly, Zimbabwean environmentalists draw on ancestral rights as well as entreat churchgoers that if one cuts a tree, one is cutting the body of Jesus Christ; and if one plants a tree, one is healing the body of Jesus Christ (Matowanyika 1996).

In South Africa, Earthlife Africa has catalyzed protests by unemployed and working-class people against the building of toxic waste dumps adjacent to black townships by arranging for blacks, many in these communities unemployed and with little formal education, to visit residents of other such townships near toxic dumps (Earthlife Africa, Toxics Group 1996). Not restricted to instances of environmental racism, which places a disproportionate burden on the most marginalized sector of the population, such cross-visits are used in the face of various environmental abuses in other poverty-stricken communities as well.

Drawing on different support bases of privileged and underprivileged elements, civil society crosscuts class structures, but the roots of the contemporary environmental movement, at least in the more economically advanced areas, are implanted in the privileged sector. Again, it is important to underscore the wide variation from one context to another. In Japan, for example, lawyers, some of them doing pro bono work in other countries in Eastern Asia, as well as intellectuals, have played a leading role in the environmental movement, although the middle classes and many working-class people have mobilized around consumer issues. In some other Eastern Asian countries and throughout Southern Africa, environmental politics for the many is linked to matters of livelihood and, thus, social justice, not ecocentric causes—conserving nature for its own sake—as in parts of what is known as the developed world (although eco-*dhamma*, or Green Buddhism, in Thailand may be an exception).

Nowhere in my research was the link, or the impediments to linkage, between the environmental movement and class structure more apparent than in interviews with working-class black South Africans. Pelelo Magane (1996), a union organizer, noted that although the black community faces multiple problems such as consumer waste, toxins, pollution, and safety issues, there is a stigma to organizing around environmental issues: "The environment is looked at as a liberal phenomenon that doesn't interest working-class people." In the wake of the anti-apartheid mobilizations around race, an implication of this statement is that the environment is the concern of those who can afford the luxury. Similarly, in the black townships adjacent to Cape Town, respondents stressed the class barriers to organizing around the environment, given the dire need for jobs, housing, health care, and protection against crime. In Langa township, whose residents migrated there as a result of forced removals (a feature of the Group Areas Act), Tsoga, an environmental movement, encounters the perception that the environment is "a white thing." Hence, in the view of its director, local people see but two worlds—"the advantaged and the disadvantaged" (Dilima 1996).

A power structure has emerged within the environmental movement. Groups are arrayed according to size of staff as well as the number of projects undertaken; scope and type of activities; and human and financial resources. In terms of access to resources in both Eastern Asia and Southern Africa, the organs of civil society have little connection to regional international organizations. An exception, perhaps, is the convening of workshops on matters of environmental concern and the building of a wildlife college—to be sure, not a grassroots activity, but a registered SADC project funded by Germany and a consortium of local donors. Such forms of regionalism, some of them under a SADC unit, Environment and Land Management Systems (ELMS), are only beginning to emerge. ELMS is mainly donor-driven, and has established some NGO focal points in various countries. Formed as a defense against apartheid, SADC remains a loose organization without much capacity vested in it. For the most part, the formal regional infrastructure to support civil society projects is weak.

Both SADC and ASEAN are largely remote from the day-to-day activities of civil society. Part of the explanation is that different political coalitions are operative in each country and embrace diverse paradigms, some of which discourage the development of civil society. Another factor is the power relationship between North and South. In civil society in Eastern Asia and Southern Africa, ties to Northern governmental and nongovernmental institutions are stronger than links within the subregions themselves. Surely, regional and subregional international organizations have not developed clear environmental policies, and the United Nations Environmental Programme has had little capacity to connect to civil society.

In the practice of environmental resistance politics, several problems have arisen. A large NGO bureaucracy has mushroomed, and individual NGOs have established a sense of territoriality. There is no formal code of ethics that governs or mitigates competition among NGOs. More conversation among different institutions in civil society is a good thing, but can there be too much diversity? Sometimes schisms emerge—for example, between the conservationists and those who stress the link between environment and development—over fundamental aims or resources. Bilateral and multilateral donors generally offer an environmental package. Implementation of their projects on the ground produces an island effect: isolated initiatives that are not effectively interrelated. Embeddedness in the local social structure is often lacking. Nationally based NGOs can serve as proxies for international agencies, with little or no organic connection to the roots of society. Frequently, there is a "pizza" effect as well: Environmental programs are spread on top of one another without any overall design (Braganza 1996). In fact, some of the institutions in civil society are not really civil-society-driven, but corporate- or state-driven, for they are held accountable to their sponsors and have little autonomy.

Closely related is the question of cooptation. Under what conditions do or should grassroots movements accept or rebuff funding, and who is setting the agenda? In a proposed reversal of the classical dependency syndrome built into aid packages and structural adjustment programs, some organs of civil society have proposed systematically monitoring international agencies and other donors. There is also the ethical dilemma, anticipated by Gramsci more than half a century ago, of whether to contest elections in government and become part of the state, rather than serve as a countervailing source of pressure and perhaps as a social conscience that raises ethical issues. Even if leaders of civil society do not take government posts, the dangers of state substitution and parallelism arise. Government agencies and interstate organizations are essentially subcontracting some of their work to NGOs. The institutions of civil society thus perform certain functions normally executed by the state, and sometimes carry them out more efficiently than do the politicians and bureaucrats.

To mitigate these tensions, techniques of negotiation within civil society are, of course, used to solve problems. Forums such as the Environment Liaison Forum, formally launched in Zimbabwe in 1996, and the Consultative National Environmental Policy Process in South Africa, set in motion by the post-apartheid government in collaboration with the myriad institutions of civil society, are bringing diverse stakeholders together in an ongoing process of attempting to find common ground. Nonetheless, there are serious differences over strategies appropriate for contesting globalization, a wide variety of which have been deployed.

## CORE STRATEGIES OF RESISTANCE

The resistance employs both old and new strategies. There is nothing new about counterbalancing state power; plying symbols such as placards, posters, and leaflets; relying on the residual power to refuse; or networking in order to galvanize the efforts of different groups up against a variety of forms of environmental degradation, as occurred at the 1992 United Nations Conference on Environment and Development in Rio de Janeiro. These tested strategies remain important, and as Robin Broad points out: "[N]o unified strategy on how to build a sustainable alternative has yet emerged" (1993, 146). There is not one single model of resistance.

Yet globalization is transforming the parameters, redefining the constraints, and upping the environmental ante, especially for future generations. Innovative strategies specifically crafted to resist globalization are not merely stabs in the dark at an amorphous phenomenon. Some—but by no means all—groups that are self-organizing have engaged in self-conscious strategizing about countering globalization. These resisters have thought out the question, What kind of political interventions can be adopted to subject neoliberal globalization, often mediated by national and local programs, to social control? Five core strategies seem most important, and are being employed individually or in combination.

First is a social compact devised to curb such abuses as the destruction and erosion of watershed areas, frequently through "legal" or illegal activities carried out by transnational corporations, as in North-Central Mindanao, which includes the Autonomous Region of Muslim Mindanao, as well as the Cagayan de Oro-Iligan Growth Corridor. A social compact is a formal understanding among all concerned parties about objectives and methods. It entails a public pledge and commitment among the signatories for the attainment of the common social good. It is based on consensual solutions and cooperation among people of different faiths (Albaran 1996). In other words, in the teeth of top-down globalization, the concept of a social compact is designed to promote democratic control from the bottom in localities. It requires technical capacity in the form of a monitoring body to ensure that all parties abide by the agreement.

Inasmuch as globalization embraces, and is facilitated by, technological advances, resistance involves developing new knowledge structures.

Simply put, a precondition for resisting globalization is to understand it. Hence the importance of the chain of education-research-information. In the view of Zukiswa Shibane, a Zimbabwean activist: "Desperate people won't fight globalization unless they are educated" (Environmental Justice Networking Forum [EJNF] 1996, 17). What some educators are striving to reclaim and transmit is indigenous and traditional knowledge about the environment, which is seen as but one part of building research capacity through networks in an effort to comprehend the dynamics of globalization. The objective of environmental education is to generate information for action, share it with the public, and channel it to the media in order to challenge globalizing forces that jeopardize the public interest. Not only is this an aspiration but one with broader implications: Providing access to information regarding municipal zoning and the risks encountered with toxic materials clearly affected the mobilization of a number of communities around Chloorkop, South Africa. In a rich case study of Chloorkop, a researcher observes: "[I]mportant is the fact that the development of an environmental consciousness, a precursor to environmental mobilisation, stemmed from both organisational activity and access to information" (Buchler 1995, 72). In short, an appreciation of the strategic importance of knowledge generation is not new, but what is novel are the linkages suggested in knowledge production and diffusion, as well as perhaps the method to point toward an alternative paradigm. If only in a very preliminary way, it may be possible to piece together a method of developing knowledge for resistance politics: deciphering the codes of domination, exposing the fault lines of power structures, identifying the pressure points for action, and fashioning images for counteridentification (Zawiah 1994, 16–18).

The third core strategy is scaling up: an increase in the scope of operations. More specifically, it is a process whereby groups within civil society broaden their impact by building links with other sectors and extending their reach beyond the local area. Asked what scaling up means in practice, two leaders in civil society, interviewed jointly, stressed "expanding the level of operations in the field" and "having a strong voice at the policy level to influence government" (Morales 1996; Serrano 1996). Another activist explained scaling-up resistance in terms of the different time horizons of globalization. Unlike the resistance that seeks to strike immediately at concrete manifestations of globalization, scaling up takes a longer span of time. It involves synergizing different skills and capacities, as well as building spaces to contest globalization (dela Torre 1996; for a concrete illustration and analysis, see Kelly 1997).

Translated into practice, scaling up can entail establishing multisectoral forums beyond the *barangay*, the basic unit in the Philippines, or coordinating among several sectors in order to paralyze a city or stop plans for, say, opening casinos. Operationally, however, it seems that when resisters try to scale up, the parametric transformation wrought by globalization, especially the ideology of neoliberalism, obfuscates its dynamics. Insofar as globalization's architecture is perceived as too big for local life, it causes disorientation. In some cases, the ambiguity rendered by globalizing structures precipitates a paradoxical reaction, which is not to scale up but to scale down. This backlash is an attempt to erect a fortress around the community, to localize rather than to engage the forces of globalization. Indeed, there is good reason to try to assert local control, particularly in places and spheres of activity where globalization involves the most acute forms of loss of control. To be sure, the more local groups extend to the global arena, the greater the temptation to conform to global norms. Nonetheless, the quickening speed of environmental degradation, its irreversibility in some cases, and its transnational reach suggest that by itself, scaling down is not a sufficient means to protect nature's endowment.

Fourth, resisters seek to thrust out in order to gain wider latitude for direct voluntary action. Earlier, reference was made to top-down forms of market-driven and state-led regionalism. In response, regionalism at the base may be either bilateral or multilateral among organizations and movements, and may thrust globally to forge links with civil societies in other regions as well. Although sometimes circumspect about "going regional" or "going global" because of fear of being eclipsed or losing control, especially to large Northern partners, Southern NGOs are increasingly aware of the potential advantages of transnational collaboration (Eccleston 1996, 82). Earthlife Africa, for example, now has branches not only in South Africa, but also in Namibia and Uganda. And trade unions in the region share information and mount joint educational workshops to provide training. In Eastern Asia, the strategy of thrusting out draws significantly on the experience of the Philippines, given the density and relative maturity of civil society there. Its NGO sector has been invited to share experiences with its counterparts in other countries. In dialogue with the representatives of civil society elsewhere, Philippine NGOs have also been involved in monitoring international financial institutions such as the ADB and the World Bank, with the goal of fashioning sustainable and alternative policies.

In the discussion of alternatives to neoliberal regionalism in chapter 6, brief mention was made of the PP21, a process that began in Japan in 1989. A coalition of grassroots movements and action groups brought together 360 activists from various countries to meet with thousands of members of Japanese civil society. They sought to establish goals and strategies based on modeling alternative social relations, not direct struggle with state structures. Following a meeting with representatives from six Central American countries, a second PP21 forum was held in Thailand in 1992, and basic concepts were hammered out. Efforts are under way to breathe life into the idea of "transborder participatory democracy," and consideration is being given to the implications of living according to the strictures of a "single, global division of labor," a hierarchy that spawns "inter-people conflicts and antagonism." As well as conferences, workshops, and electronic communication, the PP21 process includes a secretariat based in Tokyo and a quarterly review, *AMPO* (Muto 1994, 1996; Inoue 1996).

Engaging regional processes is a space that popular movements in Eastern Asia have sought to establish. For example, environmental organizations in Indonesia, Malaysia, and the Philippines have set up the Climate Action Network, with its own secretariat. In 1995–96, environmental NGOs requested observer status in ASEAN, and were rebuffed on the ground that there was no such mechanism. When this bid was scotched, the NGOs argued that inasmuch as other international institutions, including the UN, provide access for people's organizations, ASEAN should do so too. Then in 1997, the members of the Climate Action Network wrote to the ministers of the environment in their respective countries asking for the opportunity to address them, but were told that the officials did not have time for a hearing (Singh 1997).

Popular movements in Eastern Asia have also targeted the APEC process of summitry and its agenda of deepening and broadening liberalization policies. Working across borders, people's movements took aim at the 1996 APEC summit in Manila. First, they held a preparatory meeting in Kyoto, and mounted parallel NGO forums in various countries, yielding specific resolutions and action points designed to oppose member governments' trade and investment regimes that damage the environment and transgress people's rights. Preparations entailed pre-summit fact-finding missions to various locales so that delegates themselves could study precisely how forms of integration affect communities and their modes of livelihood. The documentation included a critique of "the breakneck pace and unilateral character" of blanket liberalization, especially in terms of its impact on the most vulnerable sectors and the environment, and took issue with the way that the APEC provisions "dissociate economic issues from their social implications and effects" ("Proposed Philippine PO-NGO Position" 1996). Women have contested "APEC opportunities that will fast track our rapidly shifting economic environment" (National Council of Women of the Philippines 1996). In light of a labor market structured along gender lines and the consequences for women and children, delegates called for, among other things, government financing for "a social welfare agenda to soften globalization's adverse effects" (Women's Forum 1996). Although probably unintentional, the pre-summit forum's message seemed to bear shrill—hardly modulated—overtones of a Polanyian analysis; it assailed APEC for its "anti-democratic, unaccountable and untransparent" free trade practices, and stressed the need to protect the people from "the ravages of market forces" (Manila People's Forum on APEC 1996).

Without exaggerating the importance of the above instance—amplified in a forum of NGOs, known as the Asia Pacific Peoples' Assembly, at the 1998 APEC meeting in Kuala Lumpur—there are important lessons to be derived. APEC, a market-driven, state-led process, has catalyzed intercourse among resistance movements in different countries, and grassroots organizations have set a regional agenda, one very different from that of state power holders. For example, in contrast to the latter's thrust, grassroots groups emphasize the need to link trade and investment on the one hand, and social policy on the other. Additionally, this process of resistance not only ties the substate level to the state level, but also elucidates key relationships between regionalism and globalization.

In Southern Africa, the impetus for thrusting out at the regional level and beyond comes from different pressure points, but the program of one environmental movement stands out for its level of resistance activities, especially those that highlight the contradictions between professed policies and the lack of implementation. Its green stance implicitly contests economic policy as well. The Environmental Justice Networking Forum includes more than 550 organizations that embrace common values, and largely represents the underprivileged sector of society. It seeks to identify spurs to regionalization, and engages in bridge building with other movements (Albertyn and Coworkers 1996).

Landmark resistance activities have centered on chemicals. The case of Thor Chemicals, a British-based corporation that imports waste from the U.S. company American Cyanamid, came to the fore in 1990, when large concentrations of highly toxic mercury were found in the Umgeweni River not far from its Cato Ridge plant near Durban. Earthlife Africa (a member of EJNF), the Chemical Workers Industrial Union, local residents under their chief, and white commercial farmers pursued the question, Why did Thor build the world's largest toxic mercury recycling plant in a remote location in South Africa? An alliance of trade unions, rural peasants, and green groups from different countries mounted demonstrations at Thor and at Cyanamid's plant in the United States. This joint action within civil society put pressure on the Department of Water Affairs, which ordered Thor Chemicals to suspend its operations (Crompton and Erwin 1991).

The toxic waste issue, however, did not go away. Rather, South Africa's Department of Trade and Industry was reluctant to endorse a ban on movements of toxic waste among African, Caribbean, and Pacific (ACP) countries. It became apparent that there is a regional trade, a thriving industry, in toxic waste. The EJNF expressed outrage at the revelations that post-apartheid South Africa imported waste for recycling from several African countries, and that Pretoria feared losing the income if it were to sign Article 39 of the Lomé Convention, which stipulates that "the ACP States shall prohibit the direct or indirect import into their territory of such waste from the Community or from any other country" (Fourth ACP-EEC Convention 1990, 1). The government agreed to sign the Basel Convention on the Transboundary Movements of Hazardous Waste and Their Disposal, adopted by sixty-five countries in 1989 and implemented in 1992. This international accord bans all movement of hazardous waste from industrial to developing countries from January 1998, but does not apply to traffic in toxins within Southern Africa. Hence, EJNF exposed a possible backdoor route for bringing in lucrative materials through neighboring countries (Koch 1996a, 1996b, 1996c). It became evident that state officials were trading off the regime's progressive agenda against neoliberal economic pressures. Resistance to the government's original policy contributed to the decision to reverse its position and include Article 39 of the Lomé Convention in its final trade and development agreement with the EU. Gathering information and access to the media were important aspects of the resistance strategy. A strategy of thrusting out involved developing links with the transnational green movement so that vital information could flow back to South Africa. Again, illuminating the specific links between the regional issue and globalization was crucial.

Another strategy of resistance builds innovative relationships between social movements in order to directly engage the market and establish an alternative, sustainable ecological system. In 1986, farmers from Negros Island in the Philippines and Japanese consumer cooperatives, large organizations whose members sought a substitute for the chemically laden products sold on the market, began to trade with one another. Negros grassroots communities sought a basis to transform the island's sugar-monoculture plantation economy into an integrated system of agriculture, industry, and finance. They have fundamentally attempted to remake the economy through the mutual exchange of products and services in a cyclic manner. This project includes a transborder North-South trading system, whereby an autonomous association of small farmers delivers chemical-free bananas to Japanese consumer associations of nearly one million people. The Negros growers have developed organic agriculture and set the price of bananas three times higher than the market price of bananas produced by TNCs on Mindanao Island. The elevated price, which consumers gladly pay for chemical-free products, amounts to a reverse transfer of value from the North to the South (Hotta 1996; Muto and Kothari undated).

At a Tokyo meeting of representatives of the two organizations, I was struck by their class membership—small farmers from Negros, Japanese workers (many of them in the service sector), and mostly the lower reaches of the middle class. Together, these groups have sought to resist not the market economy, but market society. They have established an alternative circuit of capital under social control—what Polanyi regarded as re-embedding the market in society and nature. This project includes cross-visits between the two communities so that social and political ties are generalized beyond trading relations. The strategy is a transboundary initiative that breaks out of the cage of the nation-state, and so do other initiatives by risk takers who strive to build social capital.

Community forestry is another example of movement-to-movement relationships that are meant to offer a sustainable alternative to the conventional market system. To substitute nontimber products such as rattan, vines, and river resources for wood, links are being forged between corporations, NGOs, and associations of direct producers (Tengco 1996). Without going into more detail, it is apparent that collective resistance is intensifying, giving rise to multilayering strategies employed according to the varied ways that globalizing trends affect individual countries and regions. Such efforts may be suggestive in terms of alternative means of governing the environment.

## FLEDGLING TENDENCIES

The research findings show that, in ways that I had not anticipated before undertaking this fieldwork, the three analytical frames—those of Gramsci, Polanyi, and Scott—overlap, deepen understanding of environmental resistance politics, and may be integrated. Yes, Polanyi provides an overall theoretical thrust for exploring resistance to globalization in the environmental realm. Approaching resistance in a Polanyian manner as an attempt to re-embed the economy in society *and* nature is extremely valuable, and the probings of Gramsci and Scott enhance this inquiry. For example, fieldwork on strategies of resistance led to the notion of "deciphering codes of domination," and here, Scott's concept of infrapolitics provides the most explanatory power. Gramsci's insights on environmental ideology as a means to secure consent so as to lessen reliance on more costly forms of coercion are also a strong tool for understanding resistance politics. The concrete evidence drawn from Eastern Asia and Southern Africa demonstrates how the three frames are integral to understanding environmental resistance, and this in turn helps to sharpen the theoretical perspective.

By all indications, the data indicate an expansion of space for resistance to neoliberal globalization, but thus far, resistant nonstate politics has had a limited impact. Within civil society, one of the reasons for forming coalitions and networks is to foster more democratic politics. However, upscaling and linking these associations does not, of course, solve the problem of hierarchical power relations integral to top-down globalization. As a political vehicle countering globalization, environmental resistance movements run on many engines. They can both follow and lead the state.

On the basis of the foregoing research findings, it is possible to identify five trends, all microcounterglobalizing tendencies: (1) In light of the diversity of experiences and contexts, many environmental initiatives are issue-oriented and subject-specific. At present, most environmental struggles are localized. (2) Nonetheless, there is a putting together of modest resistance activities based on the forging of overlapping alliances and networks within and between regions. (3) Environmental movements have implicitly adopted a policy of parallelism—i.e., replicating in one context resistance strategies that have proven successful elsewhere. (4) The core strategies are positive, not a negation, in the sense of engagement; they do not evade—delink from—either the market or the state. (5) The resistance is accumulating critical venues, such as cultural integrity and ancestral domain, and finding more openings.

Clearly, it would be wrong to celebrate these Polanyian counterforces. One might even call them what Polanyi regarded as a "move" rather than movements to indicate the protoforms by which social forces "waxed and waned" before ultimately giving birth to a political organization that begot a transformation of a particular type (Polanyi 1957, 239). Although some of them are federating, today's environmental counterforces are anything but coherent. Perhaps a high level of coherence is a desideratum that should be balanced against another consideration, namely that civil society feeds on diversity. Also, given the impediments to organizing, regional and interregional solidarity from below is a way off. Regional and global civil society are, at best, nascent and highly uneven.

At bottom, the impetus for resistance politics is not only material or technological, but also decidedly intertwined with the environmental ethic of protecting people and their diverse ways of life against quickening market forces. The words of a Jesuit priest engaged in environmental struggles in the Philippines give pause: "Spirituality is associated with suffering. This landscape bleeds. This is a suffering landscape" (Walpole

1996). The force of this message drives a powerful spiritual question in the path of globalization: Must the environment be experienced negatively, as a constraint, in terms of destruction, rather than as beauty to be relished and preserved? Posing the dilemma in this way raises the political issue of who should be entrusted, or empowered, to look after the public good. Determining which horn of this dilemma will or should bend is fundamentally about the nature and impact of interventions in evolving global structures, and we now turn to intervention in another realm—organized crime.

# CHAPTER 11

# Global Organized Crime

## (COAUTHORED WITH ROBERT JOHNSTON)

ORGANIZED crime groups may be best understood as both embodiments of certain features of neoliberal globalization and, at the same time, resistance movements, insofar as they operate outside neoliberal structures of legitimate authority and power and undermine what are generally regarded as the licit channels of the market. To be sure, organized crime has become a rapidly growing transnational phenomenon; it has spread exponentially, though unevenly, throughout all world regions, tunneling deeply to the roots of civil society. The magnitude of this problem has assumed huge proportions, with annual earnings from global organized crime reaching $1 trillion in 1996 (Boland 1997). How this movement has taken place is an interesting story, one that other scholars and journalists are documenting. Increasingly sophisticated studies of this trend are appearing (e.g., Williams 1994; Shelley 1995; Fiorentini and Peltzman 1995; Friman and Andreas 1999).[1]

Leaving aside popular books and articles, most of the literature on the spread of organized crime reflects the concerns of criminology; area studies; to some extent, the American and comparative quadrants of political science; and, very largely, applied research in police administration, government intelligence agencies, international organizations, and conservative think tanks used for fighting terrorism and other forms of unlawful behavior. In terms of globalization and global governance, however, organized crime is an understudied issue. No wonder, given that scholarly exploration of these themes is of recent vintage, at least in the formulations that take account of the distinctive historical transformations in the late twentieth century, as documented in other chapters of this book and constituting a set of megaprocesses analyzed in the international relations and international political economy literature (e.g., Rosenau and Czempiel 1992; Cox 1996a; Rosenau 1997). Quite clearly, the relationship between political economy and organized crime has not been a central

---

[1] Fiorentini and Peltzman look mainly at domestic issues. Various books and articles focus on aspects of global organized crime such as drug trade, the mafia, or Russian organized crime, but it is hard to find an academically rigorous book on global organized crime writ large.

concern in the social sciences, especially in terms of bringing a theoretical framework to bear. The political economy of global organized crime is an issue that warrants critical scrutiny.

This chapter, then, is an attempt to both shift and sharpen the intellectual focus in order to draw out the theoretical implications of the globalization of organized crime. In so doing, we employ historical materials, as well as contemporary documentary evidence, to identify continuities—and also the marked discontinuities—in the constitution of organized crime at the turn of the millennium. Although this analysis touches on national security issues and fighting crime, policy prescriptions are not the objective of our work. Rather, the purpose of this chapter is to examine the specific linkages between the dynamics of globalization and organized crime.

We first explore the theoretical underpinnings for understanding global organized crime. It is argued that while a Polanyian double movement offers a fruitful approach to the links between globalization and organized crime, binary categories, including the *legal* and the *criminal*, can also be analytically limiting. The next section identifies the characteristics of transnational organized crime groups, and is followed by a discussion of the ways in which they are embedding themselves in neoliberal globalization. We then probe the nexus between globalizing crime organizations and changing state structures, especially the courtesan role. This policy orientation is closely related to another aspect of globalization, namely, the corruption of civil society, partly a result of the inability of the state to carry out some of its key functions. The conclusion considers the implications for the transformation of civil society, particularly shifts in power relations and conflicts erupting within it.

## POLANYI AND GLOBAL ORGANIZED CRIME

In his seminal analysis of why the twentieth century has been ravaged by organized violence, Polanyi (1957) found the key not in assigning blame on aggressor nations or primarily on the Great Depression (which provided a fertile climate for expansionist, military action), but rather in the history of the Industrial Revolution and the events that followed it, beginning in nineteenth-century Great Britain, yet enveloping other countries as well. Although the Concert of Europe was able to manage a balance of power after 1815, it could not forestall a domestic response to the changing relationship between the economy and society, notably the subordination of the latter to the former. Not only did the working classes seek protection from market forces in the form of the first trade unions, but the middle classes also pressed for political participation. Nationalism and welfarism emerged from this crisis as political interventions to stave off social disintegration precipitated by the rise of the self-regulating market system. But Polanyi held that this attempt at a modus vivendi actually established the conditions for the onset of World War I. Not only did nationalism pit states against one another, but it was also combined with notions of social Darwinism that extended ideas about natural selection to nations. In short, the massive reorganization of capital, the state, and social relations, traced by Polanyi, spiraled into increased competition, arms races, hostility, and eventually in not one, but two world wars (Lipschutz 1997, 302).

When Polanyi's book *The Great Transformation* was first published in 1944, it coincided with the dawn of the Bretton Woods agreement, which launched the Allies' plan for reorganizing the world economy. But the postwar order that John Maynard Keynes and others designed did not take Polanyi's message to heart. In the last chapter of *The Great Transformation*, Polanyi argued that the propellant of the destruction of society was neither the devastation of war nor the revolt of the proletariat or a fascist lower middle class. Rather, "the conflict between the market and the elementary requirements of an organized social life" eventually destroyed that system (Polanyi 1957, 249). External wars merely accelerated the process.

At this juncture, it is worth noting several reasons why the Polanyian double movement is instructive in explaining global organized crime. Without neglecting the role of the state, Polanyi focuses on nonstate actors, especially market forces. So, too, in the context of globalization, transnational organized crime groups respond to market incentives, but outside the structures of legitimate authority and power. Moreover, Polanyi's emphasis on top-down, market-driven, and state-abetted behavior as well as bottom-up, resistance politics resonates in the international relations literature. For example, in line with this interpretation, Richard Falk (1993, 1997) was perhaps the first scholar to make the distinction adopted here: i.e., between globalization-from-above, the activities associated with the collaboration between leading states and the agents of free-market economic liberalism, and globalization-from-below, which embodies communities' attempts to regain the resources they need, to nurture their environment, and to democratize decision-making processes. Going one step further, Robert Cox (1999) shows that these tendencies are becoming less distinct and also problematizes the border between "legal" and "illegal" by positing a space between the state and nascent civil society filled by the "covert world": intelligence services, organized crime, terrorist groups, the arms trade, money-laundering banks, hermetic religious cults, and secret societies. These diverse elements, ranging from government agencies to substrata of society, constitute a sphere of politics and substitute for legitimate authority in the context of a deregulated economy. To be sure, a realm of cooperative and conflictual relationships blurs the lines between the legal and illegal. For example, in order to collect "actionable" information that leads to arrests and interdictions, intelligence services must cooperate with and attempt to recruit defectors from organized crime groups and terrorist organizations. This process often means turning a blind eye to the past and present activities of individuals who may have broken laws, but are the only ones with firsthand experience and insight into the opaque world of the terrorist groups, organized crime gangs, and other illicit groups with which they are associated.

This brings us to the issue of war, too often detached from one-dimensional accounts of globalization that stress markets and business strategies, as do the sponsors and intellectual champions of this trend who neglect political struggles, social structure, and culture (e.g., Ohmae 1990; Porter 1990). Polanyi's work sensitizes one to the interactions between the reorganization of markets and the outbreak of war. In this vein, one might claim, as does Pino Arlacchi (1986, 216), that in fact an undeclared and subterranean form of warfare has erupted among organized crime groups, sometimes with the involvement of states, over wresting control of the world's illegal markets.

Transnational organized crime groups cannot operate without some cooperative relationships over such matters as transportation and distribution, but remain at odds with one another because of ethnic differences, mistrust, and different business styles (Fiorentini and Peltzman 1995). Still, these differences seldom disrupt illegal market activities, which are too profitable to jeopardize (Nicaso and Lamothe 1995). If there is warfare among crime groups, it usually takes place within a country or between an organized crime group and the state (as in Colombia). Yet globalization blurs the line between the internal and external realms. With an acceleration in global arms sales, the marketing of nuclear materials, and the prospect of nuclear blackmail, it is no exaggeration to speak of these contemporary levels of structural violence as a form of war. Indeed, if international relations is an anarchical system, then a peaceful and stable form of coexistence with criminal power, another type of anarchy, is a likely source of structural conflict. Underlining this tension, Susan Strange (1996, 121; emphasis in original) holds that the emergence of transnational organized crime is "perhaps *the* major threat to the world system in the 1990s and beyond."

Our approach to the "why" question—explaining these massive changes and the challenges posed to global governance—thus stems from Polanyi's insights, which largely (though not exclusively) were oriented to the national unit, and pushes his mode of analysis to very different forms of market relations now taking shape at the global level. Adding the contributions of contemporary political economists and international relations theorists such as Falk, Cox, and Strange enables one to account for, if only in a preliminary manner, the quantum shift in the loci, scale, and indeed the dynamics of global organized crime. From these diverse perspectives, undergirding the spread and deepening of the market is a reformation of social power relations, with new beneficiaries and victims, especially in the marginalized zones of the global political economy.[2] In this scenario—what Yoshikazu Sakamoto (1994), picking up on Polanyi, calls a "global transformation"—the state's autonomy is reduced by numerous cross-border flows: legal and illegal migrants, lawful and unlawful forms of trade, sought-after information and knowledge, violations of copyright, and pornography. A neoliberal global consensus in favor of deregulation has further reduced state autonomy. Accompanying these pressures on the state, the market exercises disciplinary power over it, applied through the medium of structural adjustment programs, credit rating agencies such as Moody's and Standard and Poor's, and the actions of currency speculators, as in the grip of the financial crisis of the late 1990s in Eastern Asia.

Consequently, there are vast areas of activities that fall between the cracks of traditional realms of jurisdiction in national and international law. Crucially, there are whole new types of crime, some of them taking place in electronic space, where, with instantaneous transaction speeds, state institutions with territorial scope, such as central banks, are perforce unable to exercise extraterritorial control—say, over the foreign currency market, now a $1.5 trillion a-day business. Sanctioned agencies supposed to hold a legitimate monopoly to enforce compliance within their own domains are proceeding helter-skelter to devise novel forms of cooperation with their counterparts elsewhere, but they appear to be stymied by increasing deterritorialization in matters of economic governance. In the international arena, there is no dearth of proposals for strong institutionalization, for example, for a "new financial architecture." International organizations such as the Bretton Woods institutions are, of course, elements of the interstate system, and, despite their substantial reach, are not really vested with the power to transgress sovereignty in the sense of legitimately filling the void in, what Rosenau (1997, 39–41) aptly calls "spheres of authority," which may or may not correspond to territorial domains and which may employ informal rather than formal mechanisms. In this hiatus, the quickening of globalization obscures the boundaries of permissibility and impermissibility, problems pertaining to basic

[2] In delineating the changes in market dynamics since Polanyi's time, the business literature, especially on strategic management, is especially helpful—e.g., D'Aveni 1994.

legal and ethical dimensions of the global political economy, preeminently so in the case of financial speculation. The subject of considerable controversy in Eastern Asia's economic crisis is whether George Soros and other currency traders are playing by the rules or not, this controversy itself betokening a malfunction in the putative control panels of global governance. But in the main, globalization grants many more opportunities for illegal actions. The dominant tendency is for criminal organizations to step into the breach wrought by globalizing tendencies, offering security when police and other authorities are implicated in crime, as well as when the state fails to ensure the rudiments of safety, justice, or equity. These are the very conditions under which civil society can become corrupt.

As evidence from Eastern Asia and Southern Africa shows, the thrust of the market in a globalizing economy is causing not only local economies, but also the illegal economic activities of organized crime, to become disembedded from their sociocultural context. Reproduced outside their original environment, the resultant transnational crime groups not only encroach on the state, but also become lodged within it, and may hinder the growth of civil society, in some cases rendering chaos in its path.

## THE NEW CRIMINALITY

Clearly, there is a long history of organized crime transcending national borders; however, traditional patterns explain only part of the surge of illegal activities today. Globalizing tendencies emerging since the 1970s are transforming organized crime. There are newly prominent forms of illegality, such as computer crimes, money laundering, stealing nuclear materials mainly from the former Soviet Union, and "sophisticated fraud" (technological complexity among several parties using counterfeit bank instruments, credit cards, letters of credit, computer intrusion, and ingenuity of design—such as stock market "pump and dump" scams and pyramid schemes) that crop up between the established codes of international law, challenge existing norms, infiltrate licit businesses, and extend into international finance. Although some types of crime remain localized, what drives organized crime groups increasingly are efforts to exploit the growth mechanisms of globalization.

To take a single example of these dynamics at work, consider Chinese emigration to the United States. Triads (Chinese criminal networks) have smuggled people to America since the California gold rush in the 1840s. Moreover, there is a tradition of Chinese from the coastal province of Fujian, across from Taiwan, to draw on their extended families in California and other states and to move to America. As many as 90 percent of Chinese boat people originate in Fujian and in Guangdong province immediately to the south, where the major smuggling groups are concentrated.

The problem of the boat people—which captured public attention in 1993 when would-be Chinese immigrants died aboard the Panamanian vessel *Golden Venture*, a rusty old freighter that ran aground on a sandbar in sight of New York City—is largely rooted in China's explosive economic growth in recent years. The transition to a market economy, which in China has been likened to a runaway train, has sparked uneven gains and losses in income, with the rural areas, especially those in the interior, lagging far behind the urban centers and coastal regions. In the first phase of a classic Polanyian double movement, millions of low-income farm workers, have been pushed off the land to make way for large-scale industrial and commercial projects, triggering massive internal migration that coastal municipalities, now surrounded by burgeoning shantytowns, cannot absorb. China's labor supply is of enormous proportions—452 million "surplus" workers, according to the Chinese Ministry of Labor ("Pointers" 1997, 10). This crisis has fueled rural resentment and peasant uprisings in some parts of China, perhaps constituting an early stage of a Polanyian backlash.

A response to the poverty trap of the relative decline of incomes in the countryside and limited opportunities for finding legal employment in the cities is to break the cycle by seeking emigration "services" that meet the demand from a desperate and impoverished sector of the economy. Where poverty is severe, criminal gangs flourish. In China today, smuggling groups feed on a marginalized layer of people, substrata subject to an overheated market economy, and are globalizing their spatial domain (Canadian Security Intelligence Service 1994).

The smuggling operations would not be possible, however, without the involvement of powerful and wealthy criminals, who have the resources to corrupt state officials. The corruption of political authorities is the crucible in which customs officers, police, and tax inspectors assist in criminal operations or merely look the other way. This is true of not only alien smuggling, but also drug smuggling, intellectual property counterfeiting, illegal currency transactions, and other black- and gray-market activities. In this web of criminals, the rich, and politicians, the holders of public office provide "legal" protection for their partners, as with the Golden Triangle—at the intersection of the borders of Laos, Thailand, and Myanmar—during the Cold War (an example of what Cox calls the machinations of the "covert world"). The high risk and high demand involved in these operations offer potentially large profits, creating incentives for the shrewdest and most ruthless criminal organizations to "supply" their services.

These trends are explicable in terms of the nexus of organized crime and globalization. The rise of transnational organized crime groups is spurred by technological innovations, especially advances in commercial airline travel, telecommunications, and the use of computers in business, allowing for increased mobility of people—some of them carriers of contraband—and the flow of illicit goods. Central to this process are innovations in satellite technology, fiber-optic cable, and the miniaturization of computers, all of which facilitate operations across frontiers (Shelley 1995, 465). Hypercompetition is accelerating these cross-border flows. Deregulation, in turn, furthers this tendency, because it lowers state barriers to free flows of capital, goods, services, and labor.

Like global firms, transnational organized crime groups operate both above and below the state. Above the state, they capitalize on the globalizing tendencies of permeable borders and deregulation. Embracing the processes of globalization, these groups create demand for their services. They become actors in their own right in the GDLP, organized along zonal or regional and subregional lines, such as in the Golden Triangle, a major production and distribution site for morphine and heroin.

At the same time, transnational organized crime groups operate below as well as beside the state by offering incentives to the marginalized segments of the population trying to cope with the adjustment costs of globalization. These groups reach down and out to the lower rungs of social structures—the impoverished—a substratum that does not lend itself to the easy strategies prescribed by the state and interstate institutions. These strategies are often cloaked as part of the national development project, but today are overtaken by the globalization process (McMichael 1996a). The marginalized represent labor supply in the form of social forces participating in the parallel economy of organized (and unorganized) crime and *impairing the licit channels of neoliberalism.* The supply side, then, may be regarded as a *disguised form of resistance* to the dominant mode of globalization. Triads, a phenomenon noted earlier, bring this dynamic into stark relief. They originated as resistance movements battling to overthrow alien invaders who dominated the Manchu Qing Dynasty during the seventeenth century. At the end of Qing rule in 1911, these groups did not dissolve, but instead evolved into criminal societies, with some of the newest and most potent ones responding to the recurrent lack of order and social disruptions in China (Bolz 1995, 148; Deron and Pons 1997). Nowadays, from their main base in Hong Kong, the triads engage several "ethnic Chinese" and Thai groups linked to opium producers in Myanmar, and also deal with their affiliated gangs in cities in the United States, Western Europe, and across the Pacific Rim.

Insofar as the purpose of organized crime is to make money, these groups are typically regarded as predominantly economic actors. Their profit comes not merely from theft, but also today from emulating market mechanisms—forming strategic alliances, investing (and laundering) their capital, plowing it into new growth areas (e.g., dumping toxic wastes that abuse the environment in developing countries and then negotiating lucrative contracts for the cleanup industry), directing a share of their returns into R&D, adopting modern accounting systems, using global information networks that have no frontiers, and insuring (protecting) themselves against risks or threats to their organizations. Whereas these groups may have ostensibly economic objectives, to the extent that they undermine the main actors in the globalization process—transborder firms and dominant states that acquiesce to it—then transnational organized crime groups are both a political component of, and a response to, globalization.

Crime groups are similar to legitimate businesses in that they embrace the logic of the market, show great flexibility in initiative, and are also hierarchically structured. For example, the Hong Kong triads provide leadership, while the commercial *tongs* (merchants' guilds), many of them based in Chinatowns, act as local subsidiaries (Williams 1994, 103–4). Enhanced by *guanxi* (connections) in Eastern Asia, which has its counterpart in other cultures, this fluidity suggests that organized crime can also be disorganized.

Although some crime groups, such as the Cali cartels in Colombia, are highly centralized, they typically draw on loose networks of familial and ethnic relations. These networks reduce the transaction costs of acquiring information about illegal activities and provide a framework of trust. Hence, operating where there are neither clear rules nor laws, new entrants such as Nigerian organizations, which first joined the ranks of major transnational crime groups in the 1980s, arise. They have relied on family and ethnic ties in the diaspora, developing links between domestic bases and compatriots abroad. The 1980s' drop in oil prices and cuts in government spending precipitated a crime wave in Nigeria and left numerous Nigerian students stranded overseas when their funding was terminated, turning many of them to fraudulent activities (Stares 1996, 42).

So, too, transnational organized crime groups heighten uncertainty, contributing to a larger trend of what James Rosenau (1990) conceptualizes as turbulence in the global political economy. New hubs of global organized crime—with Johannesburg and Cape Town linked to the Nigerian chain and rapidly emerging as regional centers—are key nodes in these networks. In fact, Nigerians—no longer parvenus in their profession—have penetrated the entire subregion of Southern Africa, and are involved in heroin and cocaine trafficking, various types of fraud, car theft, alien smuggling (aided by illegals who work as couriers), and gang activities, prompting U.S. officials to refuse to train Nigerian police and central bankers because antifraud instruction is deemed only to increase the sophistication of Nigerian criminals (Barber 1997). Now, the Nigerian trafficking groups fan out beyond Africa and have become major actors in drug smuggling in Southeast and Southwest Asia, with increasing involvement in Latin America as well.

Global cities, more than states, are the main loci of transnational criminal organizations. Some cities—such as Hong Kong and Istanbul—have formed a second tier and serve as transshipment points. However, it is global cities—especially New York, London, and Tokyo—that offer agglomerations of financial services (which provide vast opportunities for disguising the use and flow of money), sources of technological innovation, and advanced communications and transportation systems (Sassen 1991, 1996). In these locales and elsewhere, a new breed of cybercriminals can exploit inherent vulnerabilities in the electronic infrastructure of global finance through computer intrusions for the purposes of theft, blackmail, and extortion. Given the vast scope of the Internet, cybergangs can assault a global city from virtually anywhere and remain anonymous, thus crippling the capacity of the state to apprehend and prosecute perpetrators. Yet these cities are epicenters of globalization.

Home to large, diverse populations, global cities allow criminals, and even entire criminal organizations, to blend into legitimate institutions in ethnic neighborhoods. These shelters pose a problem for the police insofar as they do not know the many languages and diasporic cultures harboring criminals or are not trusted by segments of society outside the mainstream. Nigerian criminal gangs in London and Asian criminal gangs in New York are among those able to exploit these advantages, which is testimony to the embeddedness of transnational organized crime in neoliberal economic globalization.

## GLOBAL ORGANIZED CRIME AND NEOLIBERALISM

Thus far, we have argued that transnational organized crime groups act like TNCs, which engage in profit maximization, rational decision making, product innovation, risk reduction, R&D, and technological development. (Even forms of bribery are common to both organized crime groups and many businesses: Until a recent OECD treaty went into force, "side payments" were tax-deductible in several European countries.) Beyond these characteristics, what bears emphasis is that both of these transnational actors, crime groups and corporations, follow the logic of neoliberalism and design innovative strategies to do so. They are engaged in head-on competition with one another. Against Claire Sterling's (1994) description of a major shift in the 1990s toward a global consortium in which the world's great crime syndicates have joined forces to form a "Pax Mafiosa," Louise Shelley (1995, 467) counters that the hegemony of global organized crime is in no way consolidated and is constantly contested by rivals who seek control. Although they are engaged in fierce competition with one another, organized crime groups, like legitimate businesses, cooperate through the formation of strategic alliances or subcontracting, but only when it is to their advantage.

The place to enter this debate between criminalists over collusion versus competition is to stress that the move toward opening markets, liberalizing trade, lifting regulations, and privatizing formerly public holdings has presented criminal groups with unprecedented opportunities. There are more spaces for illegal activities, including those that involve capital and financial instruments, and states respond by using new computerized technologies to augment surveillance, provoking counteractivities by both civil libertarians and organized criminal groups. The new permeability thus provides the conditions for the globalization of organized crime. Just as neoliberalism entails mergers between large concerns, so too have cross-border alliances developed between organized crime groups. Surely cooperation is evident among them in the GDLP: Russians specialize in business scams and frauds; Chinese triads, in credit card counterfeiting and human smuggling; Colombians, in narcotics and money laundering; Nigerians, in bank and credit card fraud; and so on (Lupsha 1996, 28). The Colombian cartels work with Russian organized crime groups to open heroin and cocaine markets in Eastern Europe, with Colombians supplying the product and Russians attending to distribution. Taking collusion one step further, the Russian groups in New Jersey even pay so-called license fees to the Cosa Nostra for permission to operate fuel tax scams in their territory (Burke and Cilluffo 1997).

Yet forms of hypercompetition are also evident. For instance, to cut overhead costs, "snakeheads" (professionals who smuggle émigrés) seek to maximize dividends by using cargo vessels that are not fully seaworthy and by subjecting passengers, each of whom pays between $15,000 and $35,000 for a journey from China to the United States, to severe overcrowding and squalor (Bolz 1995, 148–49). To compete ever more effectively requires developing strategic options. One is venue shopping, touching down where opportunities for crime are greatest. Like other transnational firms, organized crime groups make locational decisions on the basis of a mix of considerations. Increasingly important in this calculus is the permissiveness of regulatory regimes. Frequently, it is vulnerable parts of the developing world that offer the most auspicious conditions. Hence the link between criminality and marginalization.

Crime-exporting states—such as Russia, China, and Mexico—flush out some of their marginalized population. Moreover, as states adopt neoliberal policies, marginalized people are further driven into underground economies. What warrants more attention than it has received heretofore is the criminalization of the state.

## CRIMINALIZATION AND THE RISE OF THE STATE AS A COURTESAN

The state is most often understood in the Weberian sense of exercising a monopoly over the legitimate use of force. Building on this foundation, pluralists have regarded the state as an arbiter, a neutral referee, among different interests in society. In this tradition, pluralists hark back to *The Federalist Papers*, whose authors—John Jay, Alexander Hamilton, and James Madison—developed the idea that the role of the state is to balance and restrain the passions of its citizens. More recently, political scientists from David Easton (1965) to present-day writers have built a concept of the state based on the notion that its major function is the authoritative allocation of values. The role of the public sphere as an allocator of material values is a theme pursued by both conventionally and critically minded social scientists.

Although the foregoing notation about a complex literature is but a conceptual benchmark, one need not explore the subtleties of theories of the state more fully to demonstrate that the globalization of organized crime weakens the very basis of government and constrains its capacity. On the one hand, criminal elements do not seek to take over the state; they are obviously not revolutionary movements seeking to seize its apparatuses. On the other hand, transnational and subnational criminal groups contest the rationale of the state, especially in terms of its legitimate control over violence and the maintenance of justice. These groups are central to the recurrent problem in what Joel Migdal (1988, 22) terms maintaining "state social control": "the successful subordination of people's own inclinations of social behavior or behavior sought by other social organizations in favor of the behavior prescribed by state rules." To be sure, criminal groups are alternative social organizations that, in some respects, challenge the power and authority of the state to impose its standards, codified as law. These groups constitute an alternative system by offering commerce and banking in black and gray markets that operate outside the regulatory framework of the state; buying, selling, and distributing controlled or prohibited commodities, such as narcotics; providing swift and usually discreet dispute resolution and debt collection without resorting to the courts; creating and maintaining cartels when state laws proscribe them; and arranging security for the so-called protection of businesses, as well as sheltering them from competitors, the state, and rival criminals (Gambetta 1994).

Adding to the concentration of unaccountable power amassing with economic globalization, organized crime groups are tapping into a global system of arms trade, as well as raising and channeling immense amounts of money for this purpose. Insurgents in different regions rely increasingly on organized crime groups, and their armed forces are now intermingled with Serbs, Croats, and other soldiers of fortune, demobilized at home and seeking new employment opportunities. In a twist, parasitic states such as Mobutu's Zaire (today, Kabila's Democratic Republic of Congo, challenged at home by rebel forces), like their opponents, have drawn on former police officers and a flourishing business of mercenaries with their own corporate organizations, recruiting networks, and journals. (Among the companies selling arms and other forms of military assistance are Sandline International in the United Kingdom; Military Professional Resources Inc. of Alexandria, Virginia; and Executive Outcomes of South Africa, which had two thousand contract soldiers on call and its own fleet of aircraft until the post-apartheid government passed antimercenary laws in 1998.) By hiring these people for protection, some states are privatizing portions of enforcement and defense. Although ex-police officers and mercenaries themselves may not be criminals, their involvement in regional conflicts accentuates the tendency whereby growing connections between the state and organized crime give rise to more state-sanctioned violence.

Many instances of war and conflict mask transnational organized crime. While the media have, by and large, one-sidedly portrayed Somalia's conflict as warfare among clans causing the collapse of the state, surely cross-border drug trafficking in khat (leaves from a shrub, used as a narcotic when chewed) is a major element in that poverty-stricken country's deadly competition over resources. Similarly, in Lebanon, Sri Lanka, Pakistan, and other locales, much of the fighting ostensibly over religious differences and ethnic loyalties is also about drug trafficking, a source of enormous revenues. Put differently, the violence and urban anarchy in these countries typically melds unlawful, organized arms and drug trafficking, and religious and ethnic cleavages (Lupsha 1996, 27–28).

Heavily laden with the trappings of force, circumscribed but not disempowered, the state is less autonomous, with diminished ability to control borders. Not only is the state porous in terms of flows of knowledge and information, but also, increasingly, transnational criminal elements are entrants. In the face of such cross-border flows, the traditional notion of jurisdiction based on territoriality is progressively brought into question. New forms of criminality infringe on the principle of sovereignty, the centerpiece of the Westphalian interstate system.

The link between the restructuring of the state and development is patent: To combat crime, the state must divert funds from development.

Insofar as transnational organized crime groups transfer income from high-quality to risky investments, economic growth may suffer. Further draining the development budget, criminal activities such as money laundering evade tax collection. Moreover, there is a clear relationship among the weak state, development, and democratization. Transnational organized crime groups often corrupt state authorities, who redirect monies from public coffers and undermine democratic institutions. The infiltration of state offices effectively limits the capacity of states to fight crime in their home territories, thus sapping the legitimacy of democratic initiatives. (And if corruption fails, other options are the intimidation or assassination of journalists who report on human rights violations and of government officials such as judges, whose positions remain vacant in some highly crime-ridden countries.) An added pressure for developing countries facing a surge in transnational organized crime is "decertification," imposed when the United States determines that a so-called source country (i.e., an exporter of crime) is not meeting U.S. standards for bilateral cooperation in stamping out criminal activities, especially in the areas of narcotics and money laundering. Hence, Washington has cut off aid to countries such as Myanmar and Nigeria until they adopt stringent anticrime policies.

Circumstances vary, and the context is important to understanding these dynamics. A telling case that has caught the public eye around the world is that of unprecedented crime and violence since 1990 in South Africa. This surge correlates closely with the demise of long-standing authoritarian state structures—the pillars of apartheid—and the quest for more democratic forms of government to replace them. Against a backdrop of social disintegration (a chronic feature of the contemporary phase of globalization), rapid urbanization, an acute shortage of housing, an unemployment rate estimated at 40 percent of the economically active population, and a paltry system of welfare (Nedcor 1996), there is mounting concern for a culture of crime disembedded from the structures of society and resistant to attempts at eradication. Amid the anti-apartheid campaigns, a culture of violence was created to disable state structures. But today it is the parallel economy throughout the subcontinent and its rampant flow of illicit goods—including an enormous supply of weapons at low cost from demobilized soldiers in adjacent, post-civil war Mozambique—and the movement of criminals across borders that escalate the challenge, this time to an ANC-led state widely regarded as democratic, and to neighboring regimes.

In the face of such pressures, all states are enlisted as tacit partners in market relations but not in the same ways, because they are positioned differently in the GDLP. Currently, notwithstanding programs for crime prevention, the courtesan role of the state is an increasingly prevalent globalizing tendency. Some courtesans seek to ascend from a subaltern to a dominant niche in the GDLP. In restructuring, the state directly promotes entrepreneurship, turns key functions over to technocrats, deregulates at the microlevel if not at the macrolevel, privatizes activities of various bureaus, and adopts legalistic mechanisms to define relations between actors in the marketplace (Howell 1993, 181). In its attempt to move the national economy to higher levels of competitiveness, the courtesan reduces expenditure in the social sector. Often in the face of political protest, it delinks economic reform and social policy. Global organized crime nests in this void. With lowered barriers for cross-border economic flows, and with problems of lawlessness at home, many states qua courtesan become safe havens for global organized crime. In the evolving GDLP, some of them, in turn, evolve as *crime-exporting states*. Their trade in drugs and other contraband confronts the security interests of *law enforcement-exporting states*.

The latter design foreign policies that offer training, financial aid, and technical assistance to law enforcement agencies in the crime-exporting states. But there are conflicts over this issue within the law enforcement-exporting states. Multilateralists emphasize the need to pool resources within organizations such as the EU and the OECD. Other political coalitions stress that the criminal by-products of globalization threaten national security. Hence, Ross Perot links NAFTA to the boom in heroin shipments from Mexico to the United States, and the French right, especially Jean-Marie Le Pen's National Front party, opposes the EU's Schengen accords' allowing the free movement of member states' citizens on the grounds of weakening customs inspections and demeaning national borders. These approaches to curbing crime could of course be combined, but the latter current is a fundamental expression of national security-based resistance to globalizing tendencies.

The *resistant state* shirks the arch features of a courtesan role, but does not reject the market. Surely, only a handful of states are sufficiently recalcitrant to buck the trend of globalization—to hold the course with state programs so as to attempt to address crime at a root level at home through social policies. But even resistant states such as France today, with its heavily regulated economy, large state sector, and emphasis on a distinctive cultural identity, are to some extent courtesans to global market forces: Reluctant courtesans face contestation on a domestic front as well as from without.

Only the most powerful states are in a position to attempt to steer the globalization process, as did the United States in brokering NAFTA over the objections of myriad elements in civil society, including trade unions, environmentalists, and human rights activists. But even then, the state was, and is, less autonomous, subject both to restructuring by politicians who, in keeping with neoliberal ideology, seek to reduce its scope, and to criminalization. Notwithstanding the attempt at ideological rationalization regarding the need for small government, the criminalization of the state is associated with the corruption of civil society in varied ways.

## THE CORRUPTION OF CIVIL SOCIETY

Much has been made of the corruption of government officials, but little notice has been given to the corruption of civil society itself.[3] Many theorists of civil society, from the philosophers of the European Enlightenment to its current-day purveyors, have offered a concept of a sphere of activity in which the people of different classes—the bourgeoisie for some, the proletariat for others—could join together to pursue private or voluntary ends outside the state. But while civil society serves as a countervailing source of power in principle, in fact the very idea of civil society is becoming corrupted, torn away from the theories that spawned it. Today, private foundations, states, and multilateral agencies (interstate entities) seek to develop civil society, to appropriate not only the concept, but also the real activities juxtaposed to the public sphere.

Although in theory, the independent institutions of civil society help to check the state and shape public policy, they often become a fount of corruption symbiotically related to it, evident in the national and global domains. At best, global civil society is a nascent, yet important, normative force for future world order (Cox 1996b, 14). If so, new social movements (such as ecology, human rights, and feminism) are both local and transnational assertions of popular control, constituting a Polanyian backlash against the downside of globalization, and hence a source of counterglobalization. However, the dark side of globalization entails cross-border corruption associated with organized crimes such as smuggling and trafficking in drugs, prostitution, and children. These two seemingly different vectors—embryonic global civil society and the transnational forces that are corrupting it—are not entirely at odds with one another. They both prompt the reconstitution of the state.

In the teeth of globalization, restructuring the state and the recomposition of civil society are concomitant processes. Interacting dialectically, a state in its courtesan role invites global organized crime. The more crippled the state, the greater its susceptibility to global crime. Transnational organized crime groups undercut civil society. With states' immune sys-

---

[3] We are indebted to Şerif Mardin for suggesting the idea "the corruption of civil society."

tems breaking down, there is weakened resistance against infecting civil society with the virus of corruption. Globally, there is a contagion effect. Not only do the pressures on the interstate system allow global crime to thrive, but contempt for the law also catalyzes attitudes and other activities; contravening one law can make it easier to transgress others.

Southern Africa provides a graphic example of the transformation of the state and of conflicts under way in civil society. More than an exemplar, it may prove to be a global harbinger. Since the installation of a popularly elected Government of National Unity in 1994 in South Africa, the police have been unable to stop drug dealers. Frustrated by gangs, the lack of recourse to the violation of women and children, and threats to mosques and Muslim businesses, in 1996 a vigilante group known as People against Gangsterism and Drugs (PAGAD) conducted nightly visits to alleged drug dealers and raided their homes. PAGAD shot and burned to death Rashaad Staggie, a high-profile drug lord, in the Cape Flats near Cape Town. Accused by PAGAD of being ineffective in stopping gangsterism, Justice Minister Dullah Omar fled his home in the Cape Flats. In an ironic twist, the gangs demonstrated publicly, demanding their human rights, insisting that they had voted for Mandela's ANC and were entitled to police protection, suddenly putting aside their own long-standing, intramural feuds.

This event has broad implications, because PAGAD is an alternative to formal structures such as community policing forums and neighborhood watches, and not merely a local phenomenon. The South African media reported that PAGAD has cells in Durban and other cities and has received training from foreign Islamic elements—allegedly part of a growing global trend of militancy and extremism. Although these claims are hard to assess, it is clear that, rooted in religion, race, ethnicity, and poverty, the Muslim-dominated PAGAD and the drug dealers are both armed elements within civil society, locked in violent conflict and facing a state lacking the capacity to provide basic security for its citizens. In such situations, when racial and ethnic groups are marginalized, they forge mechanisms for self-defense tailored to their own political environment.

In South Africa and elsewhere, security is increasingly privatized, whether by private firms for the wealthy, who can pay for these services, or by informal anticrime groups. Private security groups—sometimes criminal themselves—are emerging as a growth industry to perform the role vacated by corrupt officials who do not protect public safety. Increasingly, the beneficiaries of globalization live under conditions—fenced off in enclaves, such as gated communities, disembedded from their surroundings—where sustaining their modes of accumulation and existence requires protection by public and private militias. In poor areas, however, vigilante justice is the order of the day. Plainly, the state does not exercise a monopoly over violence, legitimate or otherwise. Moreover, the bandit is no longer the romantic opponent of hegemonic state power and legitimate authority as traditionally portrayed, because the script has changed. In a globalizing world, the power of the state qua courtesan to control its social and natural environment is highly constrained, and its legitimacy is in question, especially when implicated in systemic crime and corrupt practices. Hence, in South Africa, notwithstanding the aura surrounding the post-apartheid state, the capability and legitimacy of its institutions, including a police force trained to repress popularly based initiatives, is being increasingly contested. At bottom, a form of self-protection (although hardly the one Polanyi had in mind), vigilantism has emerged as an acute response to transnational organized crime.

This phenomenon reflects the dialectical process of *dedifferentiation*, in which the sharply differentiated roles and institutions defined by the apartheid state, such as the police and gangs in the ghettoized townships, have become less distinct as a result of the fall of the minority regime (on the concept of "dedifferentiation," see Crook, Pakulski, and Waters 1992, 229). Without the structural hierarchy of apartheid, including its panoply of laws, old barriers are eased, and access to many roles is somewhat broadened, or some roles are redefined, disrupting the historical patterns of economy, polity, and society in South Africa. The result in post-apartheid South Africa, as we have delineated the global trend, is that gangs provide security, while police engage in crime.

Another response from civil society is to threaten to paralyze the business sector until the state takes steps to curb globalizing crime groups. In Mozambique in 1996, the association representing the business sector indicated that short of effective measures to stop the violence, it would strike ("Mozambique: Businesses Threaten Strike over Failure to Curb Crime" 1996). Transnationally as well, an issue of widespread concern in Southern Africa is the allegation that corrupt customs and immigration officials have helped local gangs to expand smuggling channels across borders so that militarily trained Islamic groups can buttress crime organizations ("South Africa: 'Showdown' Looming between Cape Vigilantes, Drug Dealers" 1996). In these contexts, and in the absence of a viable regional or subregional migration regime, anti-immigrant sentiment is on the rise. Like their counterparts in the West, migrants are subject to random attacks and stereotyped as taking jobs away from citizens, depressing wages, consuming public resources, spreading AIDS, and smuggling arms and drugs. Increasingly, they are marginalized by fear.

While one may hesitate to draw inferences from the specific case of Southern Africa, it does show the dynamic diversity within civil society, some of the impediments to developing it, and a cautionary note about any tendencies to romanticize it. The peril is that the decomposition of civil society provides an opening to demagogues to rally the disaffected masses, including a large segment of the population that does not participate in civil society. Herein is a major danger signal for freedom, an overarching concern registered by Polanyi, who wrote his magnum opus on the basis of lecture notes he prepared at the universities of Oxford and London in the late 1930s and the early 1940s, when the great powers were locked in violent conflict.

Today, there is more of a hint of potentiality. Building on a long history of resistance, ordinary people are beginning to rectify their grievances, organizing to do so, and developing new ideas appropriate for confronting the barriers they encounter. A motivating force is the quest for civility and cultural dignity. On the one hand, there is no mistaking a failure of politics, especially at the state level, given its partnership with transnational organized crime groups and role as a courtesan for the forces of economic globalization. On the other hand, it would be a grave error to write off or underestimate the fledgling responses from above, below, and aside, all of them fundamentally political, to the market-induced processes that are transforming societies, none excepted.

Having dwelled on civil society's reactions to criminalization, it is important to note that from the perspective of business, confidence wanes, because widespread fraud and embezzlement lessen efficiency. Fears of extortion impede investment. Thus, just as criminalization has a corrosive effect on democracy, so, too, does it restrain the opening of markets. The distributional effects of crime are to redirect a sizable share of income to low savers and the marginalized, compounding the loss of confidence. Not surprisingly, capital puts more pressure on the state to stop transnational organized crime, but as noted, the state is permeated by criminal elements. Moreover, anticrime laws undermine efforts to liberalize markets.

## IMPLICATIONS

Our analysis of global organized crime shows the need to push the Polanyian categories of market and nonmarket, first and second phases of the double movement, embedded and disembedded, and so on. These polarities have their parallel in more conventional modes of inquiry—supply and demand—from which we have also derived insights. The problem is that the concepts are too binary. Surely, the dynamics of globalization and transnational organized crime evidence concrete forms of fusion and penetration not captured fully in such dualisms. Transnational organized crime encapsulates both globalization and counter-globalization.

From a theoretical standpoint, there is no reason why the interactions should be twofold rather than multifold. Empirically, global organized crime provides an interval of time and space for multidimensional, globalizing phenomena. Globalizing thrusts are not *either* "from above" *or* "from below," but they can encompass both of these directions, most often disproportionately, or may also represent lateral movements sliding between the two big options. Although the dichotomous distinction is helpful as a heuristic device, there are in fact several globalization projects, including both top-down and bottom-up criminal elements in varied combinations. Moreover, the foregoing analysis of transnational crime groups indicates that Polanyi's fundamental point about re-embedding is suggestive in regard to bringing unfettered globalizing structures under social control, but requires qualification. As argued, the state today is losing control over the monopoly of legitimate coercion that had heretofore been under its aegis. Also, with the novel conjunction of deregulation easing state borders and seismic technological advances spurring transnational flows, it is apparent that market forces are ever more politically unaccountable, bringing the question of democratic governance at a global level to the fore and underlining the important role that civil society may play as a pressure point for greater accountability. But a large segment of civil society itself is undemocratic, if not fundamentally repressive. If so, re-embedding the market in an exploitative social structure in the absence of other conditions would not suffice to secure democratic globalization. Hence, a key research question is, What type of re-embedding, and under what conditions? This is partly a matter of determining an appropriate scale for the organization, or reorganization, of human life.

Surmounting extant categories is the main item on the agenda for studying globalization. A tall order, this would invite different research genres and more grounded inquiry. As demonstrated here, a modest beginning would be to move from simple, two-part interactions to a triad: the globalization of organized crime, the rise of the courtesan role of the state, and the corruption of civil society. This tripartite series could then be supplanted by more complex and nuanced forms of analysis, showing constraints and possibilities. Crucially, it is the structural constraints that frame the possibilities for political intervention. Now let us gauge the global impact of such interventions by drawing the overall balance between globalization's contents and discontents.

# CHAPTER 12

# Conclusion: Contents and Discontents

SEEMINGLY, the sponsors of globalization seek to create a global market in which the peoples of the world increasingly relate to each other only as individuals. In this process, society is being undermined and subordinated to the market. Putting it baldly, Margaret Thatcher declared, "There is no such thing as society, only individual men and women and their families." From this perspective, globalization is an attempt to achieve the utopia of freeing the market from social and political control. It is a utopia in the sense that this condition has never existed.

Not only is the utopia of a free market composed of individual actors ahistorical, but also, in Polanyi's memorable phrase, "*Laissez-faire* was planned; planning was not" (Polanyi 1957, 141). In an earlier century, concerted action by a liberal state in Great Britain gave rise to a supposed self-running economy, but the pressure for ensuing anti-laissez-faire legislation beginning in 1860 started in a spontaneous manner and picked up gradually. Notwithstanding a variety of such enactments, the opening of the so-called free market fomented an "economic earthquake," with severe social dislocation amid apparent economic improvement. However, the consequences of the liberal economy were "primarily a cultural not an economic phenomenon." Whereas the economic process may be a vehicle of destruction, it is not the actual motor of degradation. Rather, cultural contact between societies in different regions "may have a devastating effect on the weaker part," causing cultural disintegration and delivering a "lethal injury to the institutions in which . . . social existence is embodied" (Polanyi 1957, 157). The dispute over cultural debasement marked by symbolic events—e.g., resistance to the loss of ancestral domain—recounted in previous chapters of this book appears to fit this pattern and points toward the rationale for reexamining the utility of a Polanyian framework for understanding contemporary globalizing processes.

## THE CONTENTS OF GLOBALIZATION

### *Polanyi and the Market Paradigm*

A Polanyian perspective provided not only an entry point, but also a template, for this study of the contents of globalization. The contents are a set of systemic changes that generates discontents, something more than a malaise, and may result in active resistance to these interactive processes. A recurrent theme in this book is that globalization research can advance through the critical use of Polanyi's historical method and his concept of the double movement: the expansion of the market and a recoiling in the form of groups seeking self-protection against its jolting effects. Moreover, I have sought to pick up on Polanyi's insights on gender and the environment, using them as a springboard to push into new domains where he did not venture (e.g., global organized crime), and, in so doing, have also identified limitations to his approach.

If I am right in stressing that globalization is a market-induced—not market-determined—phenomenon, then it is fruitful to begin with Polanyi's generative analysis of how the transition from precapitalist systems to capitalism entails the spread of markets as the underlying dynamic of the making of the modern order. He traced the trajectory from social control over the market to a remove of market activities. The market gained autonomy, with the subsequent subordination of society to market forces. Polanyi thus showed the way forward by also indicating the emergence of a protectionist countermovement.

In Polanyi's challenge to the notion of a self-running market—as emphasized, a myth because from its inception, state intervention was a crucial accompaniment—he makes clear that the international market was not regulated by an overarching political authority. If so, the international market cannot draw on the domestic market's basis of legitimacy in the political realm, and is replete with tension. Today, with globalizing factors, it is important to bear in mind the discontinuous nature of market development. The growth and integration of markets are uneven processes. After all, the market is a social institution consisting of interactions between buyers and sellers, and involves hierarchies of different sorts. It is important to de-reify the market and reveal the power relations behind this abstraction. For market forces to be an integral component of a modern economy, there must be a modern society, which entails modern politics.

Polanyi's politics centered on his critique of economic liberalism—an account of the creation of the dystopia of market society—and the need to re-embed market forces in society. What needs to be explicated, however, are the meaning of and strategies for re-embedding. Attention necessarily turns to civil society, which offers promise as a source of democratization, a pressure point on the state, and a seedbed for new ideas. Yet, to varying degrees in different regions and countries, these roles are more a matter of potential than reality. Although civil society may include prodemocracy forces, women's and youth associations, human rights advocates, and environmentalists, there are also religious nationalists, right-wing militias, and neofascists. Additionally, civil society may be a repository of patriarchy and other forms of inequality. Another reason for not glamorizing the emergence of social movements is the problem of accountability: To whom are they responsible, whom do they represent, and how is their leadership constituted? Whereas civil society is defensive and fragmented in some parts of the world, it may not now exist in other parts of the world—do Singapore and Vietnam really have civil societies?—and may represent a Western concept that has traveled to other regions, with far different histories and sociocultural structures. Sponsored by powerful interests as a form of cooptation, the concept of civil society may be promoted as an aspect of neoliberal ideology that constrains the state. Indeed, the corruption of civil society is ambient, as we have seen in the discussion of the globalization of organized crime. Nonetheless, there are also countervailing forces emerging from civil society. To grasp these dynamics, one must venture beyond Polanyi's insights to build the notion of political agency in the context of globalization (Bernard 1997, 80–82).

In exploring the politics of globalization, it is important to identify and then listen to, but not romanticize, the voices of the agents of transformation. In so doing, one may discover more than a double movement. Theoretically, there is no reason why a "great transformation" should be propelled by only two phases, a force and a counterforce. One might posit a series of double movements or a triple movement. In the third phase, the state is an agent responding, partly on a regional basis, to globalizing processes, including both to transnational flows of capital and to the scaling up and thrusting out of grassroots movements. These groups are decidedly protean in their encounter with the integration of market forces. Emerging is a multiplicity of phases, not closure in a twofold thrust and a counterthrust, but continuing synergy that marks the historical transformation known as globalization.

### The Globalization Syndrome

I have tried in this book to develop four core arguments, briefly recapitulated below. First, the point of departure was that at the bottom of the hierarchy of wealth and power, the dominant form of globalization is experienced as a historical transformation of a collectivity's livelihoods and modes of existence, a lessening of political control, and a devaluation of its cultural achievements and perceptions of them. In this sense, globalization is not a single phenomenon but *a syndrome of processes and activities*. Contrary to the case made by observers who claim that globalization is a fiction, the contention here is that the scope and nature of the changes involved are systemic; they are not random or piecemeal but interconnected. There are both a heightened level of familiar interconnections and new relations among political, economic, and social actors. Before citing them, it seems fair to ask, What does globalization leave out? It bears repeating that globalization is a partial process that pertains only to those entities, individual and corporate, that interact with global structures. There are many phenomena, especially on a local level, that are either outside globalization or mingle only indirectly with global processes.

Next, globalization is a triangulated structure, each side represented as the object of study in a separate part of this book. There are, of course, other aspects of globalization (such as global arms sales) hard at work, but they are beyond the scope of this discussion. The first axis is the *global division-of-labor and power*. This construct springs from the conventional Smithian/Ricardian division of labor, which centers on the foundational concept of specialization in the production process and trade; however, the GDLP interpretation advanced here rejects the economism in classical division-of-labor theories in order to account for the multiple cross-border flows and myriad redivisions explicable in terms of social power relations and cultural practices. The notion of the GDLP also builds on the new international division-of-labor thesis introduced by Fröbel and his associates in 1977 (in German, and in 1980 in English), and later amplified by other researchers, to account for the spatial reorganization of production—i.e., the shift of manufacturing from advanced capitalist countries to developing countries. Going beyond the latter, however, the GDLP construct stresses that hegemonic power—a combination of concentrated physical force and subjective elements that together comprise consensual domination—is a key feature of the evolving division of labor and produces the forms of discontent delimited in the foregoing chapters. Incorporating the power component, and adding more complexity and structural depth to division-of-labor theories, the GDLP may then be understood as consisting of a series of interrelated processes: a restructuring among world regions; large-scale transfers of population within and between them; chains that interlink multiple production processes, buyers, and sellers in a variety of ways; and emerging transnational cultural networks that shape and facilitate these flows.

Integral to these evolving processes are technological innovations, particularly in the transportation and communications industries, as well as new information technology. While becoming worldwide, their scope is asymmetrical among regions, and new features of global inequality are rife. For example, the most recent survey of the estimated 112.75 million Internet users in the world indicates the following distribution by region: the Middle East, .525 million; Africa, 1 million; South America, 7 million; Asia/Pacific, including Australia and New Zealand, 14 million; Europe, 20 million; and Canada and the United States, 70 million (Nua Internet Surveys 1998). Data on the percentage of users by race and gender are incomplete, but the racial disparity in access to the Internet in the United Sates is suggestive of the global asymmetry: Whites are six times more likely than African-Americans to have access to the Internet (Nua Internet Surveys 1998, reporting telephone surveys by Nielsen Media Research). The magnitudes are striking and show that *globalization is not really global.* The skewed distribution of technology illustrated in the survey of Internet users directs attention to the linkage between globalization and the world's regions.

*The new regionalism*—the second dimension—is both a component of and a response to globalization. Regionalism today is new insofar as it is more multifaceted than regional alliances in the interwar period, is implanted in a multipolar and more fluid geopolitical context after the Cold War, and includes some degree of impetus from the bottom up. The dominant power, the United States, employs regionalism as an instrument for attempting to sustain hegemony; in parts of the developing world, regional processes are also a means of seeking greater access to global capital. These processes sometimes take the form of subregional projects entailing the design of new geometric shapes and the invention of metaphors or new categories, such as "growth triangles" and "polygons" in Eastern Asia, and "transfrontier parks" in Southern Africa. Such initiatives transcend national boundaries and infringe on sovereignty, even if they have been sparked by the state in the competitive drive to facilitate capital accumulation.

These forces—a GDLP and the new regionalism—beget *resistance to globalization,* the final dimension, which comes in different measures, variably latent and cultural or more open, declared, and formally constituted. There is no denying the appearance of globalizing impulses on the ground: fledgling but in many instances organized, to some extent transnational, efforts letting loose opportunities for creative experimentation and strategies for re-embedding the economy in society. Yet, due to varieties of capitalism, splits among capitalists or with the state, and strategic differences, resistance to globalization from above may emerge not only from below, but also from above. And not surprisingly, globalization from below typically meets resistance from above. Given extensive fragmentation, varied conditions, and attempts to localize in the face of globalizing structures, another possibility is resistance from below to globalization from below, exemplified by the oft-violent conflicts within civil society in South Africa, which are tied into both cross-border religious nationalist movements and transnational criminal organizations (chapter 11). Even if these strategies and movements are diverse and nascent, it would be wrong to mistake the ongoing shifts by either neglecting or exaggerating their potential consequences for world order.

Moving to the third argument advanced in this book, if globalization is a multidimensional process, then a multipronged approach is warranted. But it is often heard that globalization is a market-based, a state-based, or a socioculturally based phenomenon. Claims that economics, politics, or culture are primary implicitly hold that it is possible to split these spheres apart. On the contrary, primacy arguments that posit a division of, say, politics and economics are misleading, because it is the interactions between them that are crucial. Indeed, in the shift toward globalization, there is a reciprocal relationship among economic processes, the state, and society. This is not to engage in circular logic by saying that everything is interdependent. Context and empirical studies are, of course, necessary for explaining these linkages and the variation. Drawing on business school and management literature, a central claim in this book is that hypercompetition is a root cause of globalization. Changing conditions for the accumulation of capital entail an intensification in its inner workings, and the growth mechanisms of capitalist economies are directed more toward external markets, less to the needs of domestic markets. Given the parametric nature of the changes involved, it thus seems reductionist to argue that globalization is market-determined, or for that matter, state-led, or socioculturally driven. On the basis of theoretical analysis and empirical exploration, my contention is that globalization is a product of changes in market relations, and its effects are decidedly manifest in terms of cultural integration and disintegration as well as environmental degradation.

If the market is a social institution, then globalization has been made by humans, and also is being sustained and undermined by them. Humankind can speed up or slow down this phenomenon, as well as remake it in different spatial and temporal scales or even unmake it. Notwithstanding the structural constraints, there are very real choices to be made about the temporal and spatial dimensions of globalizing projects. If indeed these choices exist, globalization is a political process: Its politics is of preeminent importance. Yet, compared to economic and cultural globalization, many aspects of globalization as a congeries of political processes are understudied. Surely, with the rush toward market integration and cultural convergence (dialectically accompanied by divergence), a certain depoliticization has set in. Globalization can be politically disempowering, if one regards it as a juggernaut—i.e., a totalizing or inevitable force governing history. The sublimation of politics is evident in many concrete ways—e.g., a preoccupation with economic growth rather than balanced development or equity in parts of Eastern Asia, a dumbing down of young minds in school systems where critical thinking is either impermissible or not encouraged, and an overall disillusionment with leaders who cannot really lead because globalization compresses the time and space in which they seek to maneuver (abundantly evident in Eastern Asia's economic crisis of the late 1990s).

The fourth point has been to demonstrate that although the contemporary globalization architecture is cast in a neoliberal framework, there are different political strategies for redesigning it. Indeed, there are myriad globalization projects. The foremost form of globalization, neoliberalism, which is not singular but has its own variants, is an ideology justifying the freeing of markets. Employed by governments and international organizations such as the IMF, the World Bank, and the WTO, neoliberalism is also a set of policies centering on deregulation, liberalization, and privatization. It is being advanced by both states and international agencies in economic reform packages that take neoliberalism down to penetrate the grassroots level. For example, in negotiations that began in 1995 under the auspices of the OECD, the industrial nations sought to convince the trade and commerce ministers of more than one hundred WTO countries to establish a Multilateral Agreement on Investment (MAI), with the effect of guaranteeing "national treatment" to global corporations as well as barring governments from providing incentives for local companies and discriminating against foreign ones. Globally, restrictions against foreign corporations in host countries were to be eliminated in the interest of enhancing "competitiveness." The MAI would have proscribed the option—important for developing countries—of constraining foreign ownership of land and property in order to build the national economy, and would have fundamentally changed the legal framework (as embodied, for example, in NAFTA) in which national and local communities exercise some control over the behavior of foreign investors. However, at the OECD in Paris in 1998, a transnationally coordinated action of civil society, led by environmental groups and trade unions, pressured states, and blocked the MAI—although it could resurface again—partly in a spinoff of the (unsuccessful) mobilization to stop NAFTA.

As resistance to the MAI exemplifies, and despite the constraints on the political responses to globalization, there are growing challenges to the neoliberal formula. Not all states are in the same position, and a noteworthy trend is civil-society precipitated and state-enacted resistance to "the Washington consensus": the wave of government deregulation that began in the United States in the 1970s, reductions in spending on health and education, denationalization of the ownership of business, direct and indirect measures to quell the power of trade unions, and frequent devaluation of currencies. It is access to IMF financing that drives many countries to subscribe to this consensus, but other multilateral institutions embrace the same logic and offer incentives. These international organizations are double-edged swords, instilling neoliberal programs, but in other instances, establishing venues for organizations within civil society and delimiting political space for agents of counterglobalization. Few such groups within civil society totally reject a process as broad and multidimensional as globalization, but many of them seek to reconstitute select aspects of it, some in more fundamental ways than others. Chapters of this book document concrete indications of this transnational trend—for example, the development integration model of regionalism, transformative regionalism including its institutional expressions (PP21, the São Paulo Forum, and so on), and an alternative form of trade directly linking consumers in Japan and producers in the Philippines.

Integral to all such experiences is the implicit notion that however great the benefits of advancements in technology, gains in productivity, and the spread of information and knowledge, there is a price to be paid for globalization, for hypercompetition fosters winner-take-all situations. A global redistribution of economic power coincides with a global reconcentration of political power after the Cold War, and the winners win big while the losers suffer heavy losses. Globalization has yet to deliver on its promoters' promises of a win-win scenario. Indeed, when it comes to people's livelihoods, there are no data to support the thesis of job-multiplier effects at the global level. While many transnational corporations are realizing higher profits, the GDLP, especially with its new production systems and technological innovations, means less job security. For the many, particularly in impoverished countries (as illustrated in the case studies), there is scant evidence that globalization means an increase in *real wages*. Furthermore, in both developed and developing countries, with few exceptions, the *social wage*—provisions for public goods such as education, health care, and old age—has been reduced.

This much meets the eye, but the underlying dynamic is that the price of globalization is not openly negotiated on the market. Recall that classical political economists established that markets are opaque. To disclose that the inner workings of the market are hidden from view, Adam Smith detailed what lies behind the "invisible hand," and Karl Marx sought to lift the veil off what he regarded as the fiction of commodities. But globalization is doubly opaque. As well as following the logic of basic market relations, inclusion in globalization requires paying a price not once nor at agreed-upon intervals for a fixed term. Instead, inclusion carries a lasting cost that must be borne in ways that were perhaps never fully contemplated at the outset. The price is the suppression or repression of what is distinctive to a culture or civilization, the reduction of political and economic control, and the increasing polarization of the rich and poor. Faced with this prospect, some countries enthralled by the attractions of globalization have deliberately opted for a fast track and have forsaken all but a modicum of braking or balancing. Notwithstanding that their cultural dignity is at risk, these countries, spearheaded by interests within them that stand to benefit, persist in attempting to gain admittance and become globalizers, but in some cases their fate is exclusion, not inclusion.

### The Current Phase of Globalization as an Interregnum

Just as there are no simple binary choices between the local and the global, it is misleading to think in terms of two ideal types: an open international economy based on exchanges between processes derived from the national level versus a totally globalized economy, even for heuristic purposes. (Among others who construct such dichotomous models are Hirst and Thompson 1996, 7.) Rather, the current period is marked by globalizing structures, which fit Gramsci's felicitous sense of an interregnum between an old order that is dying and the birth of a new one, with many "morbid symptoms." Of course, globalization is not totally new. It is an epochal transformation, not an overnight rupture, that took a turn in the 1970s (Cox 1996c): a long process and part of the history of capital accumulation, which consists of markedly different periods. As indicated, from a historical perspective, globalization may be understood as the contemporary phase of capitalism, which exhibits strong continuities to prior eras, as well as identifiable discontinuities with them. In other words, globalization is a hybrid of historical continuities and discontinuities, an integrating yet disintegrating structure.

In terms of the contradictory forces of integration and disintegration, the geopolitics of globalization are constructed around a shift from Cold War rivalries toward macroregions. Partly based on the regional hegemonies of the United States, Germany, and Japan, these vectors are represented by NAFTA, the EU, and APEC. The activities of this triad are predominant in cross-border flows of capital. The participation of developing countries is increasing, but their inflows and outflows of capital are concentrated in about ten countries in Asia (apart from Japan, and led by China) and Latin America (UNCTAD 1997). The evolving interregional division of labor and power reflects time horizons and spatial scales that are far different from those in the old order. Major features of the globalizing order are heightened competition between regions and new polarities. A chief concern regarding economic competition is that commodity production has become highly fragmented, to the point that components are made and assembled in the countries offering the most profitable combinations of capital and labor, leaving other countries and even regions or subregions, especially their subaltern classes, in a changed, often more unprotected, position in the globalization matrix. The whole concept of security has thus been expanded in the wake of the Cold War from the traditional military-strategic sphere to become more multidimensional, encompassing economic competition and other issues such as migration, poverty, gender, the environment, and organized crime (chapters 3, 4, 5, 10, and 11). This redivision of global labor and power presents new opportunities and constraints, some of them challenging contemporary forms of global governance and exposing the deficiencies.

A leitmotif throughout the preceding eleven chapters is that global governance is in flux and remains a contested proposition. The old formulas no longer work and are being disputed. However, some analysts, notably in the predominant tradition of realpolitik, continue to believe that states are unchanging structures, that histories are enveloped in national territorial containers. On the contrary, if anything, the economic crisis that jolted Eastern Asia beginning in Thailand in 1997, with strong repercussions in other regions, strikingly shows, more than ever, the vulnerability of national actors vis-à-vis global pressures, especially capital flows. Indeed, globalization calls into question the ability of the interstate system to cope with certain fundamental transnational problems. After all, the Westphalian model of governance is a relic of the seventeenth century, established in the West and grafted onto other parts of the world, which are based on different social structures and distinctive historical realities. Contesting the interstate system are the properties of new technologies—interconnectivity and lightning speed—as well as massive concentrations of power, particularly in the global capital market, dwarfing the resources of many national units as well as challenging the principles of sovereignty and territorial jurisdiction.

Of course, the state does not remain idle. Those who hold the reins of power try to adjust by accommodating global flows and turning them to national and local advantage. Not all states suffer from power deflation. So, too, it would be a mistake to portray global processes and the state as locked into a zero-sum relationship, for with globalization, some elements within the state gain power, while others lose. Among the winners are the economic portfolios and the administrative agencies dealing with the external realm, while the offices charged with responsibility for social policy are reduced in scope. Nevertheless, to varying degrees, all states are losing autonomy in a multilevel system. The interstate system is durable, but despite its persistence, when are states free to act independently of market constraints? Increasingly, market power disciplines the state, as with IMF conditionalities and currency speculation.

No doubt when conservatives in the U.S. Congress, as well as renowned neoliberal economists such as Nobel laureate Milton Friedman and Jeffrey Sachs, director of Harvard's Institute for International Development, make common cause with groups on the left, including the 50 Years Is Enough Network, a coalition of more than 200 U.S. organizations seeking fundamental transformation of the IMF and World Bank, in expressing dismay over the workings of the international market, the marketplace of ideas is signaling that something fundamental in the system is amiss. Putting it bluntly, Friedman contended that if there was no IMF, there would have been no crisis in the Asian economies in the late 1990s ("Is It Doing More Harm or Has the IMF Cured Asia?" 1998). Also underscoring the failings of international financial institutions, Sachs argued that an international capitalist revolution has created the world's first truly global market economy and that no one knows how to manage it (Sachs 1997). Indeed, there have been calls for a second Bretton Woods convention, this time including different constituents, because the colonized and civil societies were not invited to the first founders' meeting in 1944. Undergirding the discontents and proposals for revamping the system are the searching questions: Who manages the managers of globalizing institutions? Who actually governs globalization?

In this uncharted expanse, the state is reconstituting itself, attempting to be proactive in order to shape the globalization process. In this regard, the capacities of states differ markedly. What is nevertheless common in the power differentials are the reduction of regulatory activity, the easing of borders, and the lowering of barriers. The restructuring of the state means that it is becoming more of an administrative mechanism of and for globalizing activities insofar as they are localized within the domain of a "sovereign" entity.

To aggregate their power, states have established a highly institutionalized system. Not only has there been a proliferation of international organizations in recent decades, but also, when faced with new problems of globalization such as transnational organized crime, the holders of state power seek a higher level of institutionalization in the interstate system. They create agencies such as the United Nations Interregional Crime and Justice Research Institute, and seek to gain consensus for novel rules like the MAI or plan to launch a "new financial architecture." There are also many rounds of summitry in forums such as the G-7 for the most powerful countries, and the Group of 15 in the developing world. Another formula, increasingly evident, is informal attempts at global governance, for example in the WEF, an annual gathering in Davos, Switzerland, which brings together CEOs of the one thousand largest corporations in the world, central bankers, presidents, prime ministers, and some scholars. Another informal mode of governance is the Trilateral Commission, which consists of corporate, political, and intellectual leaders from the advanced capitalist countries. In addition, privatized forms of governance are becoming more prominent. The structural power wielded by legal and financial services firms (Sassen 1996) and credit-rating agencies, such as Moody's and Standard and Poor's, is based on evaluations that enable borrowers to raise money, or prevent them from doing so, and influences the terms of loans (Sinclair 1994a, 1994b). This power can make or break some developing economies.

The nub of the problem is that the interstate system synergizes institutional forms at a level that does not correspond to an increasing portion of the world's political and economic activities. Incongruity between the cage of the nation-state and actual global flows today is cause for trial and error and reason to use the political imagination more fully. Globalization involves a quest for an appropriate temporal and spatial scale for governance (Jessop 1997). Although moral hazards are nothing new, emphasis in this book has been given to how this search places stress on the cultural environment. The spread and deepening of the market have undermined a sense of community, even transferring millions of people to other parts of the world in magnitudes and directions that differ radically from migratory flows in prior historical eras. We have examined the impact of these shifts in terms of remittances and influences on sexual mores, family structures, and consumption habits.[1] It is not necessary to rehash the preceding analysis to show that the trauma of globalization—its social and cultural intrusions—is caught up with the environmental ethic whereby diverse peoples seek to protect their own ways of life against the quickening of market forces. These attempts at self-protection suggest dismissing the prevalent dualism in thinking of the environment as humans versus nature, and rather framing the discussion of globalization in terms of evolving global structures—a bridging and more encompassing ontology.

## GLOBALIZATION'S DISCONTENTS

### Expressions of Discontent

Polanyian responses to global markets and free trade zones emanate not only from the losers in globalization—as argued, trade union movements, those on the fringes of society who support populist politicians such as

---

[1] The linkage between globalization and migration is immediately apparent to a visitor to small towns in the Philippines, Mexico, and many other developing countries. The center of social activity is no longer the church or the town plaza, but the telephone office, where operators place hundreds, if not thousands, of collect calls to the United States and other overseas destinations each month. The new technologies transmit images of Western culture, which range from sports to music and family life, and convey neoliberal values, highlighted in earlier chapters of this book.

Jean-Marie Le Pen in France and Pauline Hanson of Australia, the unemployed and undertrained in various parts of the world, and the marginalized in developing countries—but now, boosters of this set of processes themselves are distressed about globalizing tendencies. For example, in an article titled "Start Taking the Backlash against Globalization Seriously," Klaus Schwab, founder and president of the Davos forum, and Claude Smadja, its managing director, warn:

> Economic globalization has entered a critical phase. A mounting backlash against its effects, especially in the industrial democracies, is threatening a very disruptive impact on economic activity and social stability in many countries. The mood in these democracies is one of helplessness and anxiety, which helps explain the rise of a new brand of populist politicians. This can easily turn into revolt. (Schwab and Smadja 1996)

An important sign of the mounting discontent with globalization is that its purveyors, at least some of the vanguard, have come to recognize that if important adjustments are not made, globalization is going to become "a brakeless train wreaking havoc" (Schwab and Smadja 1996).

A case in point is the market turbulence of the late 1990s in Eastern Asia, which can be seen as a paradigmatic moment in an extraordinary crisis in global governance. In a dramatic rift, the beneficiaries of the dominant script of globalization, portrayed by financier George Soros and his most vociferous critic, Malaysian Prime Minister Mahathir, alike, have expressed alarm and frustration over the absence of order—a deficiency in rule, or a clash of "spheres of authority" (Rosenau 1997, 39–41)—at the global level. Indeed, Soros cautioned that it is wrong to claim that markets, left to their own devices, tend toward equilibrium. Markets, he held, are unstable, and the global system urgently requires a new form of regulation (as reported in "Who Guards the Guardians?" 1997). For his part, Mahathir repeatedly lamented that in just a few weeks, primarily as a result of the lack of regulation and the ways in which global capital has spun out of control, Malaysia lost the economic gains achieved during forty years of political independence. He verbally attacked "the present rules in which we had no say in their formulation, i.e., if there are rules at all" (as quoted in Abdul and Syed 1997). At loggerheads amid the vitriolic rhetoric, these adversaries' reasoning ultimately converged about root causes, even if they became entangled in a fruitless debate about a conspiracy by currency speculators.

Although it was not put in these terms, the underlying dynamic is the ascendancy of the structural power of capital to discipline the state. This historical turn has far-reaching implications for other parts of the developing and developed worlds. The disciplinary power of capital is evident in IMF conditionality, an economic reform package that may either be adopted de jure, as in Indonesia and a host of African countries, or introduced de facto and presented as a national program, as in Malaysia (until capital controls were established) and South Africa. Either way, the big losers in the economic downturn of the late 1990s are the vast majority of working-class people and an underclass in the countries most directly affected, where the distributional impacts have been profound (see Ishak 1998). Globally, the balance of social forces has shifted. There are the new poor subject to downward mobility, more women than men, and mostly in the developing world, but also in economically advanced countries. The chief beneficiaries of neoliberal globalization are transnationally mobile capital in trade, industry, and finance, as well as domestic firms positioned to enter a strategic alliance with overseas partners. Although capital and holders of state power would like to have it both ways—to reap large profits from globalization and avert the failings of the system—but cannot, there is an important point here about the instability and capriciousness of globalization: No one is in charge.

### The Discontented in Eastern Asia and Southern Africa

In this contestation, would-be globalizers encounter very different conditions in Eastern Asia and Southern Africa, where, in both cases, subregional hegemons, Japan and South Africa, represent major centers of power. Compared to the West, few countries in these subregions have strong civil societies. Relatively robust civil societies exist in the Philippines and Thailand, and some are emerging elsewhere. Such thickening is to be found only in South Africa in the African subcontinent, although Botswana, Namibia, and Zimbabwe are developing a web of NGOs that influence public policy. In the other countries, channels for the inclusion of the civil-society sector remain weak. In both subregions, a lively dialectic of inclusion and exclusion is at work in the relations between state and civil society. Eastern Asia, of course, has much stronger states, with greater capacity, than do the countries of Southern Africa. Generally speaking, civil society in Eastern Asia is also more vibrant than that in Southern Africa, though, in many cases, weak in relation to the state.

In each of these two internally diverse subregions, the level of resistance, the degree of organization, and the efficacy of the movements can be explained in terms of facilitating and inhibiting factors. Without overworking the comparison, what leaps out from this two-by-two matrix—the two sets of factors in the two subregions—are the constraints in Southern Africa relative to those in Eastern Asia. In a fundamental sense, material conditions have retarded self-organizing in Southern Africa. What the playwright Ken Saro-Wiwa, executed in an environmental struggle in eastern Nigeria, said there applies equally in Southern Africa: "In the end the real difficulty was having to cope with the debilitating poverty of the people. It stymied organization, and stopped people from doing what they would like to do" (1995, 214). The lack of technological development, especially in advanced communications, also hampers and thus localizes civil society in Southern Africa. Compared to access in Eastern Asia, the availability of computers, use of the Internet, and the growth of information technology in Southern Africa are negligible. In addition, racial ideology has deflected attention from other issues and has slowed organizing around critical social problems. Although Eastern Asia has also experienced ethnic and racial tensions—sometimes violent ones—as in Malaysia and Indonesia, they have not reached the level or transnational scope endemic to the history of Southern Africa, especially when white minority regimes held power. For many years, racism was given stark expression in the form of protracted military and economic destabilization, waged in the subcontinent by the apartheid regime and its aides-de-camp.

Now, the liberation movements hold, or share, state power in Angola, Mozambique, Namibia, South Africa, and Zimbabwe, and the main resistance groups had supported them in the drive to dismantle white rule. In South Africa, civil society has undoubtedly declined since 1994, when apartheid ended (Asmal 1996), and, to some extent, given economic and political constraints, the ANC-led government supports popular causes. The ANC is the premier case of a resistance movement that commands state power. This presents a complex set of dilemmas for the organs of civil society; many of their members belong to, and even shed blood for, the ANC. Elsewhere in the subregion, single party-dominant systems— e.g., the Zimbabwe African National Union-Patriotic Front—have sought to legitimize themselves by claiming the banner of liberation and donning the mantle of resistance. They are known to use the tactics of intimidation on environmental movements. But as Gramsci pointed out, coercion need not be applied in appreciable measure if consent is secured. As we have seen, ideologies, as well as paradigms, provide the syntax and a substructure of power.

## Deep Tensions

The altered correlation of integration and disintegration is evident in a series of deep tensions. In other words, globalization has become an uneasy coexistence of disjunctures. Four of these seem to be most fundamental, and identifying them helps to both sum up and push the preceding discussion.

First, economic globalization entails an acceleration of cross-border flows—capital, technology, information, migration, and the like—that slice across territorial states. However, the Westphalian, territorial model of political organization requires that sovereign states attempt to control these flows and affirm the logic of the interstate system. The horizontal connections forged in the world economy and the vertical dimensions of state politics are two different vectors of social organization, with the latter seeking to accommodate changing global structures. Although it may be an exaggeration to say that the state is declining, today it should be seen as but one of several tiers in a multilevel world order consisting of interstate and nonstate actors: the global economy itself; macroregions such as the EU, NAFTA, and APEC; subregions such as Eastern Asia and Southern Africa; microregions within states (e.g., EPZs); global cities; and social movements. These units often reach out independently of the national context from which they are becoming disembedded. In this uncertain environment, the state is not dwindling, but rather restructuring in its role as an agent in—not merely the object of—globalization processes.

Second, and closely related, is the clash between the seemingly remote and largely unaccountable forces of economic globalization and demands for greater accountability. Although the global economy is marked by instantaneous transactions of enormous magnitudes that can easily upset national economies, the trend, now attenuated in some instances, has been toward more deregulation and greater liberalization. The system of economic governance may be described as one dollar, one vote. Vast wealth is convertible into power over people's livelihood and welfare across the globe. In our time, the main shareholders in large corporations are investing in institutions run by trustees and salaried administrators. CEOs are answerable not only to individual investors, but also increasingly to banks and brokerage houses, mutual and pension funds, insurance companies, and sometimes other firms owning shares in their companies. A pertinent example is Time Warner, the media giant involved in the production of movies and television programs, magazines and books, and music, marketed and sold in many parts of the world. Who owns this conglomerate? Two of its chief owners are banks, Wells Fargo and Bankers Trust, which mobilized depositors' funds to buy shares in Time Warner. These banks are obligated to look after their depositors' money, but are not required to obtain consent to buy a large part of Time Warner or any other concern (Hacker 1997, 119).

While the global economy is, for the most part, unaccountable to a citizenry and, for all practical purposes, even to individual shareholders, growing pressures are being placed on states for more accountability. There seems to be emerging a global (though not universal) trend to embrace democratization, with impetus building from below. Although the situation varies markedly among and within regions, there is an overall recomposition of civil society, with an incipient tendency toward the globalization of bottom-up movements. However, there are a variety of pressures, some of them countervailing, as shown concretely in the discussion of poverty and gender (chapter 4), environmental resistance politics (chapter 10), and global organized crime (chapter 11). It is true that compared to the concentration of capital in the hands of TNCs and large financiers, the scope of social movements is more localized and, in some cases, microscopic. Yet these groups are beginning to stake the moral high ground and pose searching questions about unregulated globalization and its consequences.

Third, nonetheless spurred by technological advances, especially in communications and transportation, the overarching trend is for global socialization to diffuse the values of modernity, to universalize the norms associated with the idea of neoliberalism. Disseminated by the entertainment industry and the media, and instituted by the national state as well as international organizations through such instruments as structural adjustment programs, the moral standards of consumerism, individualism, and self-aggrandizement are eroding solidary structures, including the family, the village, and neighborhoods. There is an increasing desocialization of hitherto social activities as well as many aspects of work, today electronically linked to the privacy of the home.[2]

For millions of people in the West, home work on the computer and the Internet have replaced face-to-face communities in the office, as have laptop computers used anywhere. Long-distance family relationships are facilitated by the scanner, which sends family snapshots, and "chat" sessions on the Internet phone (a recorded voice-messaging facility), giving new meaning to the notion of "extended families." So, too, teleshopping and increasingly popular cybermalls mean that fewer consumers visit shops. The competitive battle over service is redefining space. The global drive to trim costs, lower payrolls, and be "lean and mean" is now a strong pressure in all sorts of institutions beset by "strategic planning" and "restructuring" exercises. University degrees may be earned in remote locations by "distance learning" via electronic mail, rather than in the traditional classroom with one's peers and instructors. Sports events

---

[2] In my own lifetime, I remember the simple ritual of having a newspaper route as a boy, delivering house-to-house, placing the paper inside the front door or wherever the customer wanted it, and ringing doorbells and socializing with my neighbors when I collected payment on the weekends. This simple ritual connecting families, reproduced for millions of Americans across the country, has become a moribund tradition. Now, I, like others subject to the atomizing effects of neoliberalism accelerated by new technologies, consult the Internet for much of my newspaper information, and one can pay online for such services.

and films are viewed safely at home and on television and the VCR, not in the milieu of a stadium or even at the cinema. From South Africa to northern points in America and Europe, gated communities and condominiums secured by guards are emblematic of larger spatial patterns of segmentation and separation, certainly by social class and often by race. These privatized housing enclaves, typically walled, are symptomatic of a shrinkage of public space. Similarly, developers are narrowing the formerly green space occupied by public parks and for recreation. Increasingly, people of means join private social clubs for these pursuits, especially in locales where an old city or other historical and cultural amenities have been decimated to make way for rapid economic growth.

What is being abandoned is a sense of responsibility—Aristotle emphasized that citizenship is first a matter of duty, rather than rights—as people discard aspects of their cultures and seek to promote what they regard as modern life. Actually, this mode of existence resembles that of the Middle Ages, with its moats, drawbridges, and knights to protect against the violence that loomed outside enclaves known as manors (on the prospects of a "new medievalism," see Strange 1995, 56, recalling Bull 1977). The modern-day equivalent of medieval violence outside the home is systemic crime, currently globalized in the form of transborder drug cartels, irregular migration, the sex industry, and even trafficking in nuclear materials, sometimes involving collusion between a corrupt state and criminal gangs. However, as in the feudal period in Western Europe, when power was parceled out among lords who controlled their vassals and the productive sectors of the economy, the main trends now are not entirely within state control.

Some politicians recognize these limitations. President Fernando Henrique Cardoso has candidly said that he does not rule Brazil, because globalization is swallowing national states. He also noted that the "increase in inequality and exclusion that globalization fuels is intricate and difficult to counter." Moreover, according to Cardoso, "globalization is inevitable, as are its consequences, its disasters, exclusion and social regression" (as quoted in Leite 1996, 25). He has rightly grasped that the state is increasingly constrained, although one might dispute whether globalization is unstoppable for, it is worth repeating, this is a combination of processes made not by accident or nature but by humans and, if so, can be shaped by human agency. Tellingly, Cardoso's views reveal that globalization can be appropriated by political actors and used as an excuse for the lack of a project for political reform, a mark of the failure of the holders of state power to contest evolving global structures and to craft a political solution. Rather, in terms of desocialization, both the state and corporations rely increasingly on computerized monitoring and impersonal surveillance via computer networks, which can involve the invasion of privacy. With desocialization, hypercompetition and abstract arguments about the virtues or inevitability of corporatization displace existing accommodations among social interests.

Fourth is the tension between globalization (at least the neoliberal variant) and marginalization. The primacy ascribed to the neoliberal policy framework and its social Darwinian values polarizes more than did their antecedents. Globalization has furthered marginalization in the sense that it excludes certain groups from playing a central role in the growth mechanisms of the world economy and achieving meaningful participation in decision making (to the extent that political control is being exercised at all). Under globalization, marginalization is a pattern of differentiation characterized by spatial exclusion, yet not limited to it. Entire zones of the global political economy, except for their dominant strata, and pockets in the developed world are left out. The boundaries of marginalization are also being redrawn in nonterritorial forms of distinction based not only on ethnicity, race, gender, and age, but also increasingly on access to information between those who are networked and those who are not—although for Africa, the two forms of exclusion, spatial and nonspatial, coincide.

The mosaic of globalization reflects a shift in the incidence of poverty from when three continents were most adversely affected by globalization to the marginalization primarily of a single region—Africa—and of enclaves in other regions. In other words, there are holes in the global mosaic. Although the data point to a worldwide net reduction of poverty-stricken people, polarization is evident among regions: Truncated globalization combined with local dynamics bar the bulk of Africa from gaining access to the world's productive processes. For the countries of Africa, the greatest challenge is to demarginalize when national options are severely constrained by the forces of globalization. With 265 million people on the African continent mired in poverty, and with little hope for escape in sight, a major contradiction of our time is the conflict between the zones of humanity integrated in the GDLP and those excluded from it.

But is the problem actually globalization or not-globalization? Is the difficulty being part of the system or not being part of it? How can globalization be the source of problems for those excluded from it? In dissecting this vexing matter, one must proceed historically by analyzing the specific and varied processes by which different units were inserted into the global political economy, such as colonialism and which species of colonialism, a top-down and cooptive nationalism or a bottom-up mobilization leading to political independence, and so on. Next, one must determine precisely how, in the contemporary era, a collectivity is tethered to the global political economy, and derive the nature of those links. As the case study of Mozambique demonstrates, it then becomes evident that some units are included in globalization in the sense that they are tied into such structures as debt and transnational arms sales, while being excluded from the pivotal mechanisms of economic and political governance to which they have been trying to gain access. Such are the dynamics of marginalization. Mozambique also shows that a marginalized country may attain, perhaps temporarily, aggregate economic growth elevated by external infusions of capital without internalizing a self-sustaining dynamic; the price is a loss, even more than before, of control over its national economy, the sacrifice of erstwhile egalitarian ideals, and, some would add, forfeiting cultural dignity.

These deep tensions are engines of change, and may eventually transform or even destroy the system, inaugurating a period of postglobalization. But are there alternatives to globalization?

### After Neoliberal Globalization

Trumpeting the virtues of neoliberalism, Margaret Thatcher said with aplomb: "There is no alternative." Although it is true that neoliberalism is predominant and may not have run its course, there are grounds for questioning this expression of triumphalism. And it is important to ask whether the neoliberal way of ordering the world will stay or wane. Like prior forms of capitalism, neoliberalism has a history, and histories have their beginnings and ends. Certainly, neoliberalism will not simply peter out of its own accord. Rather, faced with myriad discontents and countervailing power, neoliberalism is being challenged by various forces that are inchoate but, arguably, mounting. Especially noteworthy is the drive, rapidly picking up speed, toward *reregulation*, particularly apparent in Latin America and evident elsewhere as well (Snyder 1999; also see Kapstein 1994 and Helleiner 1994). Among the reasons for this trend are the spread of the Asian economic crisis to other regions and the buildup of social problems linked to neoliberal policies.

Indeed, the evidence points to a range of efforts to imagine alternative syndromes and convert them into practice. They fall into the basic categories of inclusion and exclusion (or inside/outside, as formulated by Walker 1993), a binary that lends order to the alternatives but also must be exploded to allow for a range of options. The first involves modifications in globalization without challenging its underlying structures, and the second calls for the destruction of this paradigm, or counterglobalization, which entails an attack on the ideas and type of policies that form the bedrock of neoliberalism.

The first category takes as axiomatic the proposition that within the globalization syndrome itself, there are real choices. Notwithstanding structural constraints, especially the rise of hypercompetition and the trend toward the "Washington consensus," the choice is essentially a political one. It is held that the market can benefit society while, to some extent, being kept at bay by innovative state policies. In the vortex of enormous pressure to globalize more, France, as noted, exemplifies a resistant state, one that maintains much regulation, generous welfare provisions (in schooling, health care, vacations, retirement, and unemployment entitlements), and a large government-run infrastructure, such as its reliable subways and rail networks. Its critics point to an unemployment rate currently near 13 percent; a mounting government deficit; frequent strikes and demonstrations impeding daily life, if not rendering it chaotic; and labyrinthine labor legislation, banking codes, and an educational system that discourages innovation. Faced with the Anglo-American model of neoliberalism, and urged to adopt "the American solution," President Jacques Chirac responded that his country has a global sense of itself and will fight to maintain a way of life: "France," he said, "intends to remain France" (as quoted in Trueheart 1997). In the face of unpopular changes to meet intensifying global economic pressures, a nationalist backlash is thus emerging not only from the disadvantaged segments of society, but also from some states themselves.

France's resistance, of course, is atypical, far different from the courtesan role played by the state in serving interests embodied in neoliberal globalization, in some cases linked to global organized crime as well (chapter 11). These varied policy orientations are based on diverse historical patterns and constellations of interests, including those in their respective domestic political economies. Still, there are several modes of adaptation to globalization, and no dearth of proposals for institutional reform. In the domestic arena, important adjustments in administrative agencies and legal procedures—say, in the field of immigration—can alleviate some of the problems brought on by globalization. In the realm of finance, proposed national reforms include tougher bank standards, curbs on hedge funds, an "exit tax," which would penalize investors for quickly withdrawing their money from a country, and other forms of reregulation. The idea behind these proposals is to emphasize investment in the real economy, rather than to encourage short-term speculative capital.

Crucially, social policy may blunt the sharp edges of the market, especially the global trend toward increased income inequality (Teeple 1995). Advocates of safety nets and social clauses are pushing in this direction, but skeptics contend that these may serve merely as public relations devices, deflecting attention from more fundamental issues. To be sure, there is debate about the proper role of the state in the provision of public goods: specifically, in eliminating absolute poverty, dispensing piped water as well as electricity and modern sanitation for all citizens, protecting the environment, supporting the family as a unit, alleviating congested cities, curbing escalating crime, stopping corruption and cronyism, and promoting the equality of women and the rights of children. If there is a political will for such measures, then the appropriate scale for these interventions may not only be national but regional as well. However, my empirical findings on regionalism in Eastern Asia and Southern Africa point to little actual initiative in these domains.

Globally, calls for reform include some of the basic conditions on which the IMF insists, notably transparency and greater accountability by government, aspects of structural adjustment that even the fund's critics find laudable. (However, some of them add that the IMF practices double standards by maintaining secrecy in its operations and opine that the fund should follow its own prescription.) In practice, adopting the formula of transparency and accountability requires that regimes confront the political economy of domination, often the very basis of their political support. Hence, many leaders, as was the case in Suharto's Indonesia, have found themselves in the dilemma of desperately needing foreign capital and yet reluctant or unwilling to commit political suicide by dismantling the structures of dominance that sustain the state.

Another proposal for international reform is the Tobin tax, which would place a small charge on cross-border capital flows in order to discourage the rapid transfers by speculators that upset vulnerable economies. Suggestions also include the creation of an "early warning system" to alert the world to approaching economic trends, actions to keep private losses private (instead of state intervention across borders to cover the losses incurred by private investors and speculators), a global central bank, and semifixed exchange rates among leading currencies. There can be little doubt about the need for institutional reform, but for the foreseeable future, it is difficult to conceive of heads of state galvanized to agree on and implement a new architecture for global governance, let alone wield the wherewithal to rein in corporate power, which, after all, is transnationally constituted and thus largely escapes the jurisdiction of sovereign entities. More fundamentally, these alternatives cannot work if they fail to come to grips with the power relations inscribed in globalization.

The second order of alternatives calls for structural change, and seeks to rewrite the script of globalization. On the right of the political spectrum, practitioners and intellectuals have sought to reassert identities based on membership in religious, racial, ethnic, or linguistic communities subject to globalizing forces, often personified by the immigrant, a representation of the Other. Movements based in religion have reacted sharply to the convulsive processes of globalization, partly a recognition of the anomie associated with the ways in which globalizing tendencies are undermining the values of community and ripping the social fabric. Inasmuch as neoliberal globalization facilitates cross-boundary flows, challenges national culture, and tolerates immigration, right-wing movements, especially in Europe and the United States, have opposed major elements in this structure, though not market society per se. Not only have xenophobic groups invoked a sense of nativism, but there has also been opposition to regional schemes, such as NAFTA, on the grounds that they weaken sovereignty and are a precursor to world government. The right's political project embraces the principle of sovereignty, and would build a fortress around territorially bound notions of the state, thereby implicitly calling for the downfall of globalization.

In the search for alternatives, there is a third, also structural, yet even more embryonic project that similarly poses the question, Is globalization indefinitely sustainable? The torchbearers involved in this effort represent a broad constellation of social forces, generally the victims of globalization, elements in civil society, some politicians, and organic intellectuals. They do not advocate a status quo ante; there is no going back to pre-globalization conditions, and the Keynesian welfare state of bygone decades is not the solution. Unlike the right, this group would promote the relaxation of sovereignty in favor of identities at other levels, which would involve redrawing the boundaries of political economy. This project affirms the importance of engaging yet localizing the global, and of bottom-up processes. If anything, the latter entails a greater diffusion of power. It includes new venues for experimentation and reinventing the relations among the market, state, and society. It is an effort to redefine politics, to expand the space for nonstate politics. It calls for participatory democratic control of market forces, which ultimately is a matter of political agency. It is also a matter of asserting, relative to globalizing structures, greater autonomy, a political and moral precept used by ancient Greek writers, in a somewhat different sense by social contract theorists, and in Kantian ethics.

The core of autonomy is self-determination—a tenet that resonates with contemporary liberalism, as illustrated by aspects of John Rawls' theory of justice (1993). The principle of autonomy implies that agents have the capacity for critical reflection and, notwithstanding structural pressures, the right to choose among options. Exercising this right requires some control over conditions and actions. The principle of autonomy thus means political and economic self-governance by the majority, and allows for freedom and equality in pursuit of the "common good" (Held 1995, 146–47; and on the coupling of globalization and democratic theory, Rosow 1999). Building autonomy from below should not be confused with fencing off and attempting to erect a fortress against the world, actions that could disable civil-society responses to globalization, which in fact often gain strength from their transnational elements. And an assertion of autonomy from below eventually requires topping up: initiatives within the arena of state politics to bring about greater accountability. After all, the netherworld below the state can be a perilous place, usually marked by fragmentation, and sometimes by intolerance and authoritarian forms of identity politics at odds with democratic life. In the face of the drive by neoliberalism to limit the scope of the state (both its activities and budget) and enforce market discipline, a strong state permitting broad access to power and a vibrant civil society pressing for democratic politics, as exemplified by the new environmental and feminist movements, stand to augment one another and possibly serve as a counterpoint to globalization from above (Walzer 1999). Although there is no reason to believe that the nation-state is eternal, at present the state and civil society, with their many joint members, seem to need each other in the quest for *democratic globalization.*

### A Normative Way Forward?

One response to globalization is to pose the question: Is it ethically sustainable? Morally and politically, is it possible to maintain a global system in which the world's 225 richest people have a combined wealth equal to the annual income of 2.5 billion people, the poorest 47 percent of the world's population? In which the three richest people have assets that exceed the combined GDP of the forty-eight least developed countries (UNDP 1998, 30)? Is it ethically defensible to claim that this is the price paid for the gains that accompany expanding market forces? Or would it be better to attempt to reduce the cost by searching for a democratic solution, which, is, above all, a normative preference? Surely this would not be a panacea; there are different versions of democratic theory, and normative preferences cannot be realized without countervailing power. Knowing my own limitations, and given the scope of this undertaking, I can offer only points for further consideration, not a full-blown analysis. These points are principles, not policies, for the latter must be devised for different conditions, which is to say that the principles may not converge on one best answer for all times and places.

To clear the path for examining the nexus between globalization and democratization, it is important to assess the argument that economic globalization is an emancipatory political force. This thesis is "out there"—being discussed—in scholarly forums and now and again appears in popular writings (e.g., Friedman 1997, 1999). According to this contention, globalization emanates from neither above nor below, but from beyond. In this view, globalization—a lateral movement crossing state borders in the form of capital, technologies, tourism, information, and knowledge—spreads norms and values that penetrate the state. China and some other states have tried to block these forces, but have found that the values accompanying global flows are unstoppable. It is therefore argued that economic globalization brings democracy: "[G]lobal markets today are demanding, in return for their investments, the rule of law, transparency, predictability, cooperation and pluralism in financial affairs" (Friedman 1997).

True, neoliberalism is prevalent, but its correlation with liberal democracy is more varied and problematic than this interpretation suggests. While free market reforms and liberal democracy have taken root in some Latin American countries, such as Paraguay, there are also signs, overwhelmingly reflected in polls, that people are discontented with the impact of this combination: basic failings in the banking system and a major drop in the value of the currency, accompanied by large increases in unemployment, crime, poverty, and income inequality. Indeed, the argument that market liberalism fosters liberal democracy fails to allow for reverses and nondemocratic change: the erosion or downfall of democracy brought on, at least in good part, by economic reforms. For example, in 1997, a time of great economic tribulation, Bolivians returned their former dictator to the country's highest office. In Africa, there is wide variation: diverse patterns of economic reform and very different types of democratization reflecting distinctive conjunctions of precolonial, colonial, and postcolonial systems as they encounter globalizing structures. Clearly, the conjecture that economic globalization is a source of democratic politics does not account for Africa's collapsed states, which, after incorporation into the Westphalian system and long contact with world markets, have taken a nondemocratic course.

More basically, the problem with the claim that economic globalization generates democracy is that it misses the point that economic markets themselves lack accountability. It also misspecifies the linkage between wealth and power. Markets exercise structural power, including the power to punish the state if it strays too far from the neoliberal path. This often entails coercion, as with the implementation of the structural adjustment programs that have triggered IMF riots in several countries. Adhering to the logic of a market system, the economically powerful, after all, seek to maximize profits and beat their competitors. Although liberal democracy may prove convenient or preferable to other methods of governance, the beneficiaries of globalization have no inherent interest in promoting democracy. The logics of markets and democracy clash over the issue of liberty versus equality, depending on the meaning attributed to these constructs. Then, too, there is the question of the caliber of different versions of democracy.

Democracy in its several variations revolves around the notion of accountability. The Western liberal variant detaches democracy from one sphere of human activity to another: political governance from economic governance. Emphasis is accorded to institutional forms, especially electoral mechanisms. Equity among social strata—reducing inequality in the economic realm—is not the priority in a system whose cardinal feature is a rotation of political power among those who usually represent the interests of the privileged segments of society. Hence the tension between globalization and democratization. How, then, can democracy be an antidote for a form of globalization that has spun out of control to the extent that its discontents are expressed by holders of state power, financiers, preeminent neoliberal economists, and the marginalized alike? In other words, how can the contents of globalization be revised so as to maintain its many important achievements and relieve the discontents?

To approach this compelling question, if only in a preliminary and schematic manner, one must grasp the properties of what democratic control in the context of globalization would mean. Put briefly, democracy is a contested concept; different and competing forms are appropriate for varied social and historical structures, although accountability remains a central criterion of democratic rule. Additionally, democracy is not a final state of affairs, but unfolds with changing dynamics. Democracy heretofore has been framed for territorially bounded states that purportedly can contain the movement of people, ideas, and technologies. However, many states, especially the ones with large concentrations of diasporic populations and citizens employed by firms based in other regions, are now subject to deterritorialization and denationalization. With globalization, democracy must be reterritorialized—strengthened both within and across state borders—as a method of governance for regions and, indeed, for solving global problems.

Indeed, there are signs that in an intersubjective sense and in objective ways as well, the national state is becoming a transnational state. In a transnational state, citizens imagine their identities in terms of more than one state—e.g., as is the case with some diasporic populations—and actively participate in the politics of two or more countries, which is permitted by the laws and voting procedures in certain contexts. The challenge, then, is to rethink the concept of national democracy and bring it in line with a form of politics in which boundaries are not eradicated, but are blurred or complicated by transborder arrangements, some of them authored by the state, and others rooted in economy and culture and either sanctioned by a reluctant state or not at all legitimated by the state.

In this transformation, a vital issue is the matter of access. How can global governance be recast so that civil society may participate meaningfully in the steering processes and economic growth mechanisms of a powerful structure—globalization—that has the potential to deliver to the many—not merely the few—aggregate economic gains (including a cornucopia of consumer goods), technological advances, greater information, new knowledge, and an escape from long-established forms of social control? There cannot be much assurance of the eventual outcome of an open-ended, historical process, but making clear the dynamics, knowing the constraints, and imagining the possibilities, if only a glimmer of the prospects, mark the direction that may help to put humankind on the right path.

# Appendix

## Interview Questionnaire

1. How and why did your organization form? What is its history?
2. How have the goals evolved and shifted?
3. Is there a secretariat? What is the size of the staff? Its functions and scope?
4. How many members are there? From what sectors of the population are they drawn? In what proportions?
5. How is the leadership determined?
6. To what extent are the leaders accountable to the rank-and-file? What are the forms of interaction between them?
7. What are the strategies of organization and mobilization?
8. What are the impediments to achieving the goals?
9. What is your organization's relationship to the state?
10. What alliances has your organization formed?
11. Practically speaking, how do such organizations work together? On a single issue? Multiple issues?
12. To what extent is action between rural and urban movements coordinated? Between local or national and overseas affiliates? Donors?
13. Who is opposed to your group and why? What are the different strands of the environmental movement?
14. How are differences resolved?
15. How would you map the ties among environmental movements in the region? How dense are the interactions?
16. Is there coordination at the regional level?
17. Are there different conceptions of regionalism?
18. Are there efforts to induce greater regional consciousness?
19. What are the facilitating factors?
20. What are the constraints?
21. To what extent does globalization affect ecology in your locality, and how does your organization prioritize global issues?
22. To what degree does your organization participate in global environmental networks? How useful and effective are they?
23. What are the factors that facilitate your work on a global level?
24. What are the constraints?
25. In light of your organization's goals, what are its chief accomplishments? Failings? How would you evaluate the overall results?

- Is there anything you would like to add?
- Are there other people whom you suggest I see? Who would be most helpful?
- Do you have literature or documents on these matters that I might review?

# References

Abdul Kadir Jasin, and Syed Nadzri. 1997. "No Choice but to Accept Globalisation." *New Straits Times* (Kuala Lumpur), 25 October.

Adas, Michael. 1986. "From Footdragging to Flight: The Evasive History of Peasant Avoidance Protest in South and South-east Asia." *Journal of Peasant Studies* 13, no. 7 (January): 64–86.

Addleton, Jonathan S. 1992. *Undermining the Centre: The Gulf Migration and Pakistan*. Karachi: Oxford University Press.

*Africa Research Bulletin: Economic, Financial and Technical Series*. 1996. "Mozambique." 4 June: 12557–58.

Akamatsu, Kaname. 1962. "A Historical Pattern of Economic Growth in Developing Countries." *The Developing Economies* 1 (March–August): 3–25.

Akrasanee, Narongchai. 1993. "Economic Regionalism: Which Way Now?" Paper presented at the international conference on "Southeast Asia: Challenges of the 21st Century." Singapore: Institute of Southeast Asian Studies, August–September.

Albaran, Francisco T. 1996. Agriculturalist, MUCARD. Interview by author. Cagayan de Oro City, Mindanao, Philippines, 4 March.

Albertyn, Chris, and Coworkers. 1996. National Coordinator, Environmental Justice Networking Forum. Interview by author. Braamfontein, South Africa, 2 August.

Albrow, Martin. 1996. *The Modern Age*. Stanford, CA: Stanford University Press.

Amsden, Alice. 1989. *Asia's Next Giant: South Korea and Late Industrialization*. New York: Oxford University Press.

"APEC: The Opening of Asia." 1994. *The Economist* (London) 333, 7889. 12 November.

Appelbaum, Richard P., and Jeffrey Henderson. 1992. *States and Development in the Asian Pacific Rim*. Newbury Park, CA: Sage.

Arlacchi, Pino. 1986. *Mafia Business: The Mafia Ethic and the Spirit of Capitalism*. Trans. Martin Ryle. London: Verso.

Arthur, John A. 1991. "International Labor Migration Patterns in West Africa." *African Studies Review* 34, no. 3 (December): 65–87.

Asheim, Björn. 1992. "Flexible Specialisation, Industrial Districts and Small Firms: A Critical Appraisal." In *Development and Contemporary Industrial Response: Extending Flexible Specialisation*, ed. Huib Ernste and Verena Meier, 45–63. London: Belhaven.

Asmal, Kader. 1996. Minister of Water Affairs and Forestry, Republic of South Africa. Interview by author. Pretoria, South Africa, 31 July.

Augelli, Enrico, and Craig N. Murphy. 1988. *America's Quest for Supremacy and the Third World: A Gramscian Analysis*. London: Pinter.

———. 1997. "Consciousness, Myth and Collective Action: Gramsci, Sorel and the Ethical State." In *Innovation and Transformation in International Studies*, ed. Stephen Gill and James H. Mittelman, 25–38. Cambridge: Cambridge University Press.

Bach, Robert L. 1993. *Changing Relations: Newcomers and Established Residents in U.S. Communities: A Report to the Ford Foundation by the National Board of the Changing Relations Panel.* New York: Ford Foundation.

Barber, Lionel. 1995. "Delors Speaks Up for an EU Integration Led by Core." *Financial Times* (London), 24 February.

Barber, Simon. 1997. "Lessons for SA from Nigeria's Example." *Business Day Online—Comment & Analysis,* 20 February. http://www.bday.co.za/96/0917/comment/cs.htm.

Baum, Richard. 1982. "Science as Culture in Contemporary China: The Roots of Retarded Modernization." *Asian Survey* 22, no. 2 (December): 1166–86.

Berger, Peter, and Hsin-Huang Michael Hsiao, eds. 1988. *In Search of an East Asian Development Model.* New Brunswick, NJ: Transaction Publishers.

Berger, Suzanne, and Ronald Dore, eds. 1996. *National Diversity and Global Capitalism.* Ithaca, NY: Cornell University Press.

Berman, Jessica. 1996. "Bike-Aid: Focus on Environment and Development." *Global Links: Newsletter of the Overseas Development Network* (Spring): 9.

Bernard, Mitchell. 1997. "Ecology, Political Economy and the Counter-movement: Karl Polanyi and the Second Great Transformation." In *Innovation and Transformation in International Studies,* ed. Stephen Gill and James H. Mittelman, 75–89. Cambridge: Cambridge University Press.

Bernard, Mitchell, and John Ravenhill. 1995. "Beyond Product Cycles and Flying Geese: Regionalization, Hierarchy, and the Industrialization of East Asia." *World Politics* 47, no. 2 (January): 171–209.

Berresford, Susan V. 1997. "President's Message: 1997 Ford Foundation Annual Report." New York: Ford Foundation.

Bienefeld, Manfred. 1988. "The Significance of the Newly Industrializing Countries for the Development Debate." *Studies in Political Economy* 25 (Spring): 7–39.

Block, Fred, and Margaret R. Somers. 1984. "Beyond the Economistic Fallacy: The Holistic Social Science of Karl Polanyi." In *Vision and Method in Historical Sociology,* ed. Theda Skocopl, 47–84. Cambridge: Cambridge University Press.

Boland, Vincent. 1997. "Earnings from Organised Crime Reach $1,000bn." *Financial Times,* 14 February.

Bolz, Jennifer. 1995. "Chinese Organized Crime and Illegal Alien Trafficking: Humans as a Commodity." *Asian Affairs: An American Review* 22, no. 3 (Fall): 147–58.

Braganza, Braggy. 1996. Research Scientist, Environmental Research Division of the Institute of Environmental Science for Social Change (formerly the Manila Observatory). Interview by author. Quezon City, Philippines, 2 March.

Braudel, Fernand. 1980. *On History.* Trans. Sarah Matthews. Chicago: University of Chicago Press.

Broad, Robin. 1993. *Plundering Paradise: The Struggle for the Environment in the Philippines.* With John Cavanagh. Berkeley: University of California Press.

Broad, Robin, and John Cavanagh. 1988. "No More NICs." *Foreign Policy* 72 (Fall): 81–103.

Brosius, J. Peter. 1997. "Endangered Forest, Endangered People: Environmentalist Representations of Indigenous Knowledge." *Human Ecology* 25, no. 1 (March): 47–69.

Buchler, Michelle. 1995. "Community-based Environmentalism in Transitional South Africa: Social Movements and the Development of Local Democracy." Master's thesis, Department of Sociology, University of the Witwatersrand, Johannesburg.

Bull, Hedley. 1977. *The Anarchical Society: A Study of Order in World Politics.* London: Macmillan.

Burbach, Roger, Orlando Nunez, and Boris Kagarlitsky. 1997. *Globalization and Its Discontents: The Rise of Postmodern Socialisms.* London: Pluto.

Burke, Gerard P., and Frank J. Cilluffo, eds. 1997. *Russian Organized Crime Task Force Report.* Washington, DC: Center for Strategic and International Studies.

Butler, Judith, and Joan W. Scott, eds. 1992. *Feminists Theorize the Political.* New York: Routledge.

Buzan, Barry. 1991. *People, States and Fear: An Agenda for International Security Studies in the Post-Cold War Era.* Boulder, CO: Lynne Rienner.

Canadian International Development Agency. 1989. *Mozambique Country Report.* Quebec: CIDA Briefing Centre.

Canadian Security Intelligence Service. 1994. "Immigration by Sea to North America: More Golden Ventures?" *Commentary* 43 (April). http://www.cisisscrs.gc.ca/eng/comment/com43e.html.

Carnoy, Martin. 1993. "Multinationals in a Changing World Economy: Whither the Nation-State?" In *The New Global Economy in the Information Age: Reflections on Our Changing World,* ed. Martin Carnoy et al., 45–96. University Park: Pennsylvania State University Press.

Carruthers, Jane. 1995. *The Kruger National Park: A Social and Political History.* Pietermaritzburg, South Africa: University of Natal Press.

Castaneda, Jorge. 1995. *The Mexican Shock: Its Meaning for the United States.* New York: W. W. Norton.

Cerny, Philip G. 1990. *The Changing Architecture of Politics: Structure, Agency, and the Future of the State.* London: Sage.

Chia Siow Yue, and Lee Tsao Yuan. 1993. "Subregional Economic Zones: A New Motive Force in Asia-Pacific Development." In *Pacific Dynamism and the International Economic System,* ed. Fred Bergsten and Marcus Noland, 225–69. Washington, DC: Institute for International Economics.

Chin, Christine B. N. 1998. *In Service and Servitude: Foreign Female Domestic Workers and the Malaysian "Modernity Project."* New York: Columbia University Press.

Ching Kwan Lee. 1995. "Engendering the Worlds of Labor: Women Workers, Labor Markets, and Production Politics in the South China Economic Miracle." *American Sociological Review* 60, no. 3 (June): 378–97.

"Chissano Says Stop." 1989. *The Economist* 311, 7607, 17 June.

Chossudovsky, Michael. 1998. "Global Poverty in the Late 20th Century," 27 October. http://www.interlog.com/~cjazz/chossd.htm.

Chow, Peter C. Y. 1987. "Causality between Export Growth and Industrial Development: Empirical Evidence from the NICs." *Journal of Development Economics* 26 (June): 55–63.

Cohen, Robin. 1987. *The New Helots: Migrants in the New International Division of Labour.* Brookfield: Gower.

Commission of the European Communities (CEC). 1990. "Policies on Immigration and the Social Integration of Migrants in the European Community" (Sec [90] 1813). Brussels: CEC, 28 September.

———. 1991. "Commission Communication to the Council and the European Parliament on Immigration" (Sec [81] 1855). Brussels: CEC, 23 October.

Cornelius, Wayne A. 1995. "Nafta Costs Mexico More Job Losses Than U.S." *New York Times,* 17 October.

Costy, Alexander. 1995. "Donor Dollars and Mozambique's NGOs." *Southern Africa Report* 10, no. 5 (July): 15–19.

Cottrell, Robert. 1986. "The Silent Empire of the Kuok Family." *Far Eastern Economic Review* 134, 44 (30 October): 59–63.

Cox, Robert W. 1982. "Production and Hegemony: Toward a Political Economy of World Order." In *The Emerging International Economic Order: Dynamic Processes, Constraints and Opportunities,* ed. Harold K. Jacobson and Dusan Sidjanski, 37–58. Beverly Hills: Sage.

———. 1986. "Social Forces, States and World Orders: Beyond International Relations Theory." In *Neorealism and Its Critics,* ed. Robert O. Keohane, 204–54. New York: Columbia University Press.

———. 1987. *Production, Power, and World Order: Social Forces in the Making of History.* New York: Columbia University Press.

———. 1991. "Programme on Multilateralism and the United Nations System, 1990–1995." Tokyo: United Nations University. Unpublished.

———. 1996a. *Approaches to World Order.* With Timothy J. Sinclair. Cambridge: Cambridge University Press.

———. 1996b. "Economic Change and Civil Society." Paper presented at the International Symposium on Prospects for Civil Society in Asia." Tokyo, September.

———. 1996c. "A Perspective on Globalization." In *Globalization: Critical Reflections,* ed. James H. Mittelman, 21–30. Boulder, CO: Lynne Rienner.

———. 1998. Letter to author. 5 November.

———. 1999. "Civil Society at the Turn of the Millennium: Prospects for an Alternative World Order." *Review of International Studies* 25, 1 (January): 3–28.

Crane, George. 1990. *The Political Economy of China's Special Economic Zones.* Armonk, NY: M. E. Sharp.

Crompton, Rod, and Alec Erwin. 1991. "Reds and Greens: Labour and the Environment." In *Going Green,* ed. Jacklyn Cock, 78–91. Oxford: Oxford University Press.

Crook, Stephen, Jan Pakulski, and Malcolm Waters. 1992. *Postmodernization: Change in Advanced Society.* London: Sage.

Crone, Donald. 1993. "Does Hegemony Matter? The Reorganization of the Pacific Political Economy." *World Politics* 45, no. 4 (July): 501–25.

Crossette, Barbara. 1998. "Worldwide Tourist Industry Takes Off." *International Herald Tribune* (Paris), 13 April.

Curry, Robert L. 1991. "Regional Economic Co-operation in Southern Africa and Southeast Asia." *ASEAN Economic Bulletin* 8, no. 1 (July): 15–28.

Dacumos, Victor. 1996. Chairman, Guardians of the Environment for the Future of Youth. Interview by author. Gabaldon, Nueve Ecija, Philippines, 9 March.

Dahl, Robert A. 1971. *Polyarchy: Participation and Opposition*. New Haven, CT: Yale University Press.

D'Aveni, Richard. 1994. *Hypercompetition: Managing the Dynamics of Strategic Maneuvering*. With Robert Gunther. New York: Free Press.

Davies, Robert. 1992. "Integration or Co-operation in a Post-Apartheid South Africa: Some Reflections on an Emerging Debate." Belville, South Africa: University of the Western Cape Centre for Southern African Studies Working Paper Series, October.

———. 1996. "New Sources for Growth and Hope: Prospects for Southern Africa." *Development* 2: 24–28.

de Guzman, Apollo. 1996. Parish priest and President, Confederation of Nueva Ecijanons for the Environment and Social Order, Inc. Interview by author. Cabanatuan City, Nueva Ecija, Luzon, Philippines, 9 March.

del Castillo, Romulo A. 1996. Professor of Forest Resources and Director, University of the Philippines, Los Banos Agroforestry Program. Interview by author. Los Banos, Laguna, Philippines, 11 March.

dela Torre, Edicio. 1996. President, Folk Philippine-Danish School. Interview by author. Quezon City, Philippines, 12 March.

De Melo, Jaime, and Arvind Panagariya. 1992. "The New Regionalism." *Finance and Development* 29, no. 4 (December): 37–40.

DePalma, Anthony. 1995. "For Mexico, Nafta's Promise of Jobs Is Still Just a Promise." *New York Times*, 10 October.

Deron, Francis, and Phillipe Pons. 1997. "Les triades au secours." *Le Monde* (Paris), 2 July.

Deyo, Frederic C., ed. 1987. *The Political Economy of the New Asian Industrialism*. Ithaca, NY: Cornell University Press.

Dicken, Peter. 1998. 3rd ed. *Global Shift: The Internationalization of Economic Activity*. New York: Guilford Press.

Dicken, Peter, Philip F. Kelly, Kris Olds, and Henry Wai-Chung Yeung. 1999. "Chains and Networks, Territories and Scales: Towards a Relational Framework for Analyzing the Global Economy." Faculty of Arts and Social Sciences, National University of Singapore. Unpublished.

Dilima, Nomtha. 1996. Director, Tsoga Environmental Centre. Interview by author. Langa, Cape Town, South Africa, 23 July.

"Disquieting Signs in Mozambique One Year On." 1995. *Southern Africa Report* 13, no. 44 (November): 11–12.

Dixon, Chris. 1991. *South East Asia in the World-Economy*. Cambridge: Cambridge University Press.

Doner, Richard F. 1991. *Driving a Bargain: Automobile Industrialization and Japanese Firms in Southeast Asia*. Berkeley: University of California Press.

Drozdiak, William. 1995. "Regions on the Rise: As European Borders Become More Porous, Cities Replace Countries in Transnational Economic Alliances." *Washington Post*, 22 October.

Drysdale, Peter, and Ross Garnaut. 1993. "The Pacific: An Application of a General Theory of Economic Integration." In *Pacific Dynamism and the International Economic System*, ed. C. Fred Bergsten and Marcus Noland, 183–223. Washington, DC: Institute for International Economics.

Duke, Lynne. 1996. "Rural Mozambicans Waiting for a Train: Derailed by War, Key Routes Still in Ruins." *Washington Post*, 21 June.

Durfee, Mary, and James N. Rosenau. 1996. "Playing Catch-Up: International Relations Theory and Poverty." *Millennium: Journal of International Studies* 25, no. 3 (Winter): 521–45.

Durkheim, Emile. 1984. *The Division of Labor in Society*. Trans. W. D. Halls. New York: Free Press.

Earthlife Africa, Toxics Group. 1996. Meeting, Brixton, Johannesburg, South Africa, 15 July.

Easton, David. 1965. *A Systems Analysis of Political Life*. New York: John Wiley and Sons.

Eccleston, Bernard. 1996. "Does North-South Collaboration Enhance NGO Influence on Deforestation Policies in Malaysia and Indonesia?" *Journal of Commonwealth and Comparative Politics* 34, no. 1 (March): 66–89.

Eccleston, Bernard, and David Potter. 1996. "Environmental NGOs and Different Political Contexts in South-East Asia: Malaysia, Indonesia and Vietnam." In *Environmental Change in South-East Asia*, ed. M. Parnwell and R. Bryant, 49–66. London: Routledge.

Economist Intelligence Unit. 1989. *Tanzania/Mozambique: Country Report No. 1 1989*. London: EIU.

———. 1996. *Country Report: Mozambique, First Quarter 1996*. London: EIU.

Egerö, Bertil. 1987. *Mozambique: A Dream Undone: The Political Economy of Democracy, 1975–84*. Uppsala, Sweden: Nordiska Afrikainstitutet.

Elson, Diane. 1994. "People, Development and International Financial Institutions: An Interpretation of the Bretton Woods System." *Review of African Political Economy* 21, no. 62 (December): 511–24.

Emmerij, Louis. 1992. "Globalization, Regionalization and World Trade." *Columbia Journal of World Business* 27, no. 2 (Summer): 6–13.

Engel, Charles, and John H. Rogers. 1996. "How Wide Is the Border?" *American Economic Review* 86, no. 3 (December): 112–25.

Environmental Justice Networking Forum. 1996. "Proceedings of the Conference on Regional Cooperation in Environmental Governance." Broederstroom, South Africa, November.

"Europe's Immigrants: Strangers inside the Gates." 1992. *The Economist* (U.S. edition): 322, 7746, 15 February.

Evans, Peter B., Dietrich Rueschemeyer, and Theda Skocpol, eds. 1985. *Bringing the State Back In*. Cambridge: Cambridge University Press.

Eviota, Elizabeth Uy. 1992. *The Political Economy of Gender: Women and the Sexual Division of Labor in the Philippines*. London: Zed Press.

Falk, Richard. 1993. "The Making of Global Citizenship." In *Global Visions: Beyond the New World Order*, ed. Jeremy Brecher, John Brown Childs, and Jill Cutler, 39–50. Boston: South End Press.

———. 1997. "Revisiting 'Globalisation-from-above' through 'Globalisation-from-below.'" *New Political Economy* 2, no. 1 (March): 17–24.

Fernández Kelly, Maria Patricia. 1989. "International Development and Industrial Restructuring: The Case of Garment and Electronic Industries in Southern California." In *Instability and Change in the World Economy*, ed. Arthur MacEwan and William Tabb, 147–65. New York: Monthly Review Press.

Fiorentini, Gianluca, and Sam Peltzman, eds. 1995. *The Economics of Organised Crime*. Cambridge: Cambridge University Press.

Fishlow, Albert, and Stephan Haggard. 1992. *The United States and the Regionalisation of the World Economy*. Paris: OECD.

Foucault, Michel. 1980. *Power/Knowledge: Selected Interviews and Other Writings, 1972–77*. Trans. and ed. C. Gordon et al. New York: Pantheon Books.

Fourth ACP-EEC Convention. 1990. *Internationales Umweltrecht—Multilaterale Verträge* BZUB7/I.92, 989:93/11.

Frank, Robert H., and Philip S. Cook. 1995. *The Winner-Take-All Society*. New York: Free Press.

Freedom from Debt Coalition, Women's Committee. 1996. Interview by author. Manila, 13 March.

French, Howard W. 1992. "Caribbean Exodus: U.S. Is Constant Magnet." *New York Times*, 6 May.

Friedman, Thomas L. 1997. "Berlin Wall, Part 2: Asia's New Route to Democracy." *New York Times*, 22 December.

———. 1999. *The Lexus and the Olive Tree*. New York: Farrar, Straus and Giroux.

Friman, H. Richard, and Peter Andreas, eds. 1999. *The Illicit Global Economy and State Power*. Lanham, MD: Rowman and Littlefield.

Fröbel, Folker, Jürgen Heinrichs, and Otto Kreye. 1980. *The New International Division of Labour: Structural Unemployment in Industrialised Countries and Industrialisation in Developing Countries*. Trans. Pete Burgess. Cambridge: Cambridge University Press.

Fukuyama, Francis. 1989. "The End of History?" *The National Interest* 16 (Summer): 3–18.

Gambetta, Diego. 1994. *The Sicilian Mafia*. Cambridge: Harvard University Press.

Gamble, Andrew, and Anthony Payne, eds. 1996. *Regionalism and World Order*. New York: St. Martin's.

Garnaut, Ross. 1993. "The Changing International Environment and Its Challenges for the Asian Market Economies." Paper presented at the international conference on "Southeast Asia: Challenges of the 21st Century." Singapore: Institute of Southeast Asian Studies, August–September.

Geertz, Clifford. 1983. *Local Knowledge: Further Essays in Interpretive Anthropology*. New York: Basic Books.

Geertz, Clifford. 1995. *After the Fact: Two Countries, Four Decades, One Anthropologist.* Cambridge: Harvard University Press.

George, Susan. 1992. *The Debt Boomerang: How the Third World Debt Harms Us All.* Boulder, CO: Westview Press.

Gereffi, Gary. 1988. "Rethinking Development Theory: Insights from East Asia and Latin America." *Sociological Forum* 4, no. 4 (December): 505–33.

———. 1990. "Paths of Industrialization: An Overview." In *Manufacturing Miracles: Paths of Industrialization in Latin America and East Asia,* ed. Gary Gereffi and Donald L. Wyman, 3–31. Princeton: Princeton University Press.

Gereffi, Gary, and Stephanie Fonda. 1992. "Regional Paths of Development." *Annual Review of Sociology* 18: 419–48.

Gereffi, Gary, and Miguel Korzeniewicz. 1990. "Commodity Chains and Footwear Exports in the Semiperiphery." In *Semiperipheral States in the World-Economy,* ed. William Martin, 46–77. Westport, CT: Greenwood Press.

———, eds. 1994. *Commodity Chains and Global Capitalism.* Westport, CT: Greenwood Press.

Gersony, Robert. 1988. "Summary of Mozambican Refugee Accounts of Principally Conflict-Related Experience in Mozambique." Report submitted to Bureau for Refugee Programs, U.S. Department of State. Washington, DC. Unpublished.

Giddens, Anthony. 1990. *The Consequences of Modernity.* Cambridge: Polity Press.

Gilley, Bruce. 1996. "Irresistible Force: Migrant Workers Are Part of a Solution, Not a Problem." *Far Eastern Economic Review* 159, no. 14 (4 April): 18–20.

Glick Schiller, Nina. 1999. "Citizens in Transnational Nation-States: The Asian Experience." In *Globalization and the Asia Pacific: Contested Territories,* ed. Kris Olds, Peter Dicken, Philip Kelly, Lily Kong, and Henry Wai-chung Yeung, 202–18. London: Routledge.

———. Forthcoming. "Transmigrants and Nation-States: Something Old and Something New in the U.S. Immigrant Experience." In *The Handbrook of International Migration: The American Experience,* ed. Charles Hirschman, Josh DeWind, and Philip Kasinitz. New York: Russell Sage Press.

Goldblatt, David. 1996. *Social Theory and the Environment.* Boulder, CO: Westview Press.

Goodman, David S. G. 1994. "The PLA and Regionalism in Guangdong." *Pacific Review* 7, no. 1: 29–39.

Goodman, Edward, and Julia Bamford, eds. 1989. *Small Firms and Industrial Districts in Italy.* London: Routledge.

Gordon, David. 1988. "The Global Economy: New Edifice or Crumbling Foundations?" *New Left Review* 168 (March/April): 24–64.

Government of Denmark. 1997. *Conditions for Social Progress: A World Economy for the Benefit of All.* Copenhagen: Ministry of Foreign Affairs.

Government of Mozambique National Executive Commission for the Emergency, and Department for the Prevention and Combat of National Disasters. 1988. *Rising to the Challenge: Dealing with the Emergency in Mozambique.* Maputo:

Government Printer. As cited in Prakish Ratilal. 1988. "Mozambique—Overview of the Economy in the Last Ten Years." Maputo. Unpublished.

Government of Mozambique National Planning Commission. 1984. *Economic Report*. Maputo: Government Printer.

Government of Mozambique and World Bank. 1988. *Mozambique: Policy Framework Paper, 1988 to 1990*. Washington, DC: World Bank.

Gramsci, Antonio. 1971. *Selections from the Prison Notebooks*. Trans. and ed. Quintin Hoare and Geoffrey Nowell Smith. London: Lawrence and Wishart.

Greenaway, David, and Chong Hyun Nam. 1988. "Industrialisation and Macroeconomic Performance in Developing Countries under Alternative Trade Strategies." *Kyklos* 41, no. 3: 419–35.

Griffin, Keith, and Azizur Rahman Khan. 1992. *Globalization and the Developing World: An Essay on the International Dimensions of Development in the Post-Cold War Era*. Geneva: United Nations Research Institute for Social Development.

Grinberg, Ruslan, Boris Shmelev, and Leonid Vardomsky. 1994. "New Regionalism in the Post-Soviet Space." Paper presented at the workshop on "Regionalism and Globalism." Berlin: United Nations University/World Institute for Development Economics Research, August.

Guillén, Mauro F. Forthcoming. *Diversity in Globalization: Organizational Change in Argentina, South Korea, and Spain*. Princeton: Princeton University Press.

Gumende, Antonio. 1998. "Mozambique: The Art of Managing Dependence." Harare, Zimbabwe: Southern African Research and Documentation Centre. 29 January. Unpublished.

Habibul Haque Khondker. 1997. "Globalization Theory: A Critical Appraisal." In *ASEAN in the Global System*, ed. H. M. Dahlan et al., 109–25. Bangi, Malaysia: Penerbit Universiti Kebangsaan Malaysia [National University of Malaysia Press].

Hacker, Andrew. 1997. *Money: Who Has How Much and Why*. New York: Scribner.

Haggard, Stephan. 1990. *Pathways from the Periphery: The Politics of Growth in the Newly Industrializing Countries*. Ithaca, NY: Cornell University Press.

———. 1994. "Thinking about Regionalism: The Politics of Minilateralism in Asia and the Americas." Paper presented at the annual meeting of the American Political Science Association. New York, September.

Halliday, Fred. 1990. "The Crisis of the Arab World: The False Answers of Saddam Hussein." *New Left Review* 184 (November/December): 69–74.

Hamilton, Gary, ed. 1991. *Business Networks and Economic Development in East and Southeast Asia*. Hong Kong: University of Hong Kong Centre of Asian Studies Occasional Papers and Monographs No. 99.

Hamilton, Gary, and Cheung-Shu Kao. 1987. "Max Weber and the Analysis of East Asian Industrialization." *International Sociology* 2, no. 3: 289–300.

Hamzah, B.A. 1991. "ASEAN and the Remilitarisation of Japan: Challenges or Opportunities?" *Indonesian Quarterly* 19, no. 2 (Second Quarter): 141–67.

Hanlon, Joseph. 1997a. "Can Mozambique Make the World Bank Pay for Its Mistakes?" http://www.igc.org/afjin. October.

———. 1997b. "Success Story? Bretton Woods Backlash in Mozambique." *Southern Africa Report* 13, no. 1 (November): 26–29.

———. 1998. "Paris Club to Debate Mozambique Debt Relief." *Mozambique Peace Process Bulletin.* 20 January.

Harries-Jones, Peter, Abraham Rotstein, and Peter Timmerman. 1992. "Nature's Veto: UNCED and the Debate over the Earth." Unpublished.

Hart, Jeffrey. 1995. "Maquiladorization as a Global Process." In *Foreign Direct Investment in a Changing Political Economy,* ed. Steve Chan, 25–38. London: Macmillan.

Hart-Landsberg, Martin. 1994. "Post-NAFTA Politics: Learning from Asia." *Monthly Review* 46, no. 2 (June): 12–21.

Harvey, David. 1990. *The Condition of Postmodernity.* Oxford: Basil Blackwell.

Hasenau, Michael. 1991. "ILO Standards on Migrant Workers: The Fundamentals of the UN Convention and Their Genesis." *International Migration Review* 25, no. 4 (Winter): 687–97.

Hefner, Robert W., ed. 1998. *Market Cultures: Society and Morality in the New Asian Capitalisms.* Boulder, CO: Westview Press.

Held, David. 1995. *Democracy and the Global Order: From the Modern State to Cosmopolitan Governance.* Cambridge: Polity Press.

Held, David, Anthony G. McGrew, David Goldblatt, and Jonathan Perraton. 1999. *Global Transformations: Politics, Economics and Culture.* Stanford, CA: Stanford University Press.

Helleiner, Eric. 1990. "Fernand Braudel and International Political Economy." *International Studies Notes* 15, no. 3 (Fall): 73–78.

———. 1994. *States and the Reemergence of Global Finance: From Bretton Woods to the 1990s.* Ithaca, NY: Cornell University Press.

Henderson, Jeffrey. 1989. *The Globalization of High Technology Production: Society, Space and Semiconductors in the Restructuring of the Modern World.* London: Routledge.

Heng Pek Koon. 1992. "The Chinese Business Elite of Malaysia. In *Southeast Asian Capitalists,* ed. Ruth McVey, 127–44. New York: Cornell University Southeast Asia Program.

———. 1994. "Asia's New Dynasties: The Sino-Capitalist Network." *Japan Scope* (Autumn): 24–28.

———. 1997. "Robert Kuok and the Chinese Business Network in Eastern Asia: A Study in Sino-Capitalism." In *Culture and Economy: The Shaping of Capitalism in Eastern Asia,* ed. Timothy Brook and Hy V. Luong, 155–86. Ann Arbor: University of Michigan Press.

Hessler, Stephan. 1994. "Regionalization of the World Economy: Fact or Fiction?" Paper presented at the annual meeting of the International Studies Association. Washington, DC, March.

Hettne, Björn. 1994. "The New Regionalism: Implications for Development and Peace." In *The New Regionalism: Implications for Global Development and International Security,* ed. Björn Hettne and András Inotai, 1–49. Helsinki,

Finland: United Nations University/World Institute for Development Economics Research.

Hewitt, Tom, Hazel Johnson, and David Wield. 1992. *Industrialization and Development*. Oxford: Oxford University Press.

Higgott, Richard, and Richard Stubbs. 1995. "Competing Conceptions of Economic Regionalism: APEC versus EAEC in the Asia Pacific." *Review of International Political Economy* 2, no. 3 (Summer): 516–35.

Hirst, Paul, and Grahame Thompson. 1996. *Globalization in Question: The International Economy and the Possibilities of Governance*. Cambridge: Polity Press.

Ho Hua Chow. 1997a. "A Value Orientation for Nature Preservation in Singapore." *Environmental Monitoring and Assessment* 44: 91–107.

———. 1997b. Senior Lecturer, Department of Philosophy, National University of Singapore. Interview by author. Singapore, 5 December.

Holbrooke, Richard. 1995. "America, a European Power." *Foreign Affairs* 74, no. 2 (March/April): 38–51.

Hooks, Bell. 1981. *Ain't I Woman: Black Women and Feminism*. Boston: South End Press.

———. 1984. *Feminist Theory: From Margin to Center*. Boston: South End Press.

Hopkins, Terence K., and Immanuel Wallerstein. 1986. "Commodity Chains in the World-Economy Prior to 1800." *Review* 10, no. 1 (Summer): 157–70.

Hotta, Masahiko. 1996. President, Alter Trade Japan, Inc. Interview by author. Tokyo, 25 February.

Howell, Jude. 1993. *China Opens Its Borders: The Politics of Economic Transition*. Boulder, CO: Lynne Rienner.

Hughes, Thomas L. 1990. "Pro Patria Per Orbis Concordiam." Remarks presented at the Carnegie Endowment for International Peace Trustees' Dinner. Washington, DC, 18 November.

Huntington, Samuel P. 1993. "The Clash of Civilizations?" *Foreign Affairs* 72, no. 3 (Summer): 22–49.

Hurrell, Andrew. 1995. "Explaining the Resurgence of Regionalism in World Politics." *Review of International Studies* 21, no. 4 (October): 331–58.

Inoue, Reiko. 1996. Director, Pacific Asia Resource Center. 1996. Interview by author. Tokyo, 24 February.

Interim Coordinating Committee for the Maputo Development Corridor. 1996. *Maputo Development Corridor: A Development Perspective*. Maputo: Interim Coordinating Committee.

International Monetary Fund. 1993. *World Economic Outlook*. Washington, DC: IMF, May.

———. 1997. *World Economic Outlook. Globalization: Opportunities and Challenges*. Washington, DC: IMF, May.

Ireland, Patrick. 1991. "Facing the True 'Fortress Europe': Immigrant and Politics in the EC." *Journal of Common Market Studies* 29, no. 5 (September): 457–80.

"Is It Doing More Harm or Has the IMF Cured Asia?" 1998. *New Straits Times*, 26 April.

Ishak Shari. 1998. "Asian Financial and Economic Crisis and Implications on Poverty and Income Inequality in Malaysia: A Preliminary Observation." Bangi, Malaysia: Institute of Malaysian and International Studies, Universiti Kebangsaan Malaysia. Unpublished.

James, Valentine Udoh, ed. 1995. *Women and Sustainable Development in Africa.* Westport, CT: Praeger.

Jauch, Herbert, Dot Keet, and Leon Pretorius. 1996. *Export Processing Zones in Southern Africa: Economic, Social and Political Implications.* Development and Labour Monographs 2. Cape Town: University of Cape Town Institute of Development and Labour Law.

Jessop, Bob. 1997. Comments at the workshop on "The Logic(s) of Globalization." Singapore: National University of Singapore, December.

Johnson, Chalmers. 1982. *MITI and the Japanese Miracle.* Stanford, CA: Stanford University Press.

———. 1986. "The Nonsocialist NICs: East Asia." *International Organization* 40, no. 2 (Spring): 557–65.

Kabeer, Naila. 1991. "Cultural Dopes or Rational Fools? Women and Labour Supply in the Bangladesh Garment Industry." *European Journal of Development Research* 3, no. 1 (June): 133–60.

Kamm, Henry. 1993. "In Europe's Upheaval, Doors Close to Foreigners." *New York Times,* 10 February.

Kant, Chander. 1992. "Foreign Sector in Singapore's Economic Development, 1980–1991." Paper presented at the Institute of Southeast Asian Studies. Singapore, June.

Kapstein, Ethan B. 1994. *Governing the Global Economy: International Finance and the State.* Cambridge: Harvard University Press.

Keck, Margaret E., and Kathryn Sikkink. 1998. *Activists beyond Borders: Advocacy Networks in International Politics.* Ithaca, NY: Cornell University Press.

Keely, Charles. 1992. "Economic Integration and International Migration." Paper presented at the conference on "Social and Economic Aspects of International Migration." Taipei: Institute of European and American Studies, Academia Sinica, June.

Keller, Bill. 1993. "South Africa's Wealth Is Luring Black Talent." *New York Times,* 10 February.

Kelly, Philip F. 1997. "Globalization, Power and the Politics of Scale in the Philippines." *Geoforum* 28, no. 2 (May): 151–71.

Keohane, Robert O. 1990. "Multilateralism: An Agenda for Research." *International Journal* 45, no. 4 (Autumn): 731–64.

Khan, Farieda. 1990. "Beyond the White Rhino: Confronting the South African Land Question." *African Wildlife* 44, no. 6 (November/December): 321–24.

———. 1994. "Rewriting South Africa's Conservation History—the Role of the Native Farmers Association." *Journal of Southern African Studies* 20, no. 4 (December): 499–516.

Koch, Eddie. 1996a. "SA Still under Fire for Toxic Waste Policy." *Mail & Guardian* (Braamfontein, South Africa), 5 to 11 July.

————. 1996b. Environmental Editor, *Mail & Guardian*. Interview by author. Braamfontein, South Africa, 19 July.

————. 1996c. "SA Still in the Waste Business." *Mail & Guardian*, 26 July to 1 August.

Kofman, Eleonore, and Gillian Youngs, eds. 1996. *Globalization: Theory and Practice*. London: Pinter.

Kondo, Mari. 1996. "Towards Borderless Asia and Beyond: An Overview of Factors Nurturing Asian Growth Polygons." In *Asian Growth Polygons*, ed. Asian Institute of Management. Manila: Proceedings of the Seventh Asian Institute of Management, Management Conference on Asia, March.

Kong, Lily. 1994. " 'Environment' as a Social Concern: Democratizing Public Arenas in Singapore?" *Sojourn* 9, no. 2: 277–87.

Kumar, Sree. 1993. "New Directions for Economic Growth in Southeast Asia." In *Southeast Asian Affairs 1993*, 22–39. Singapore: Institute of Southeast Asian Studies.

Kumar, Sree, and Lee Tsao Yuan. 1991. "A Singapore Perspective." In *Growth Triangle: The Johor-Singapore-Riau Experience*, 1–36. Singapore: Institute of Southeast Asian Studies.

Kurien, Prema. 1992. "Sojourner Migration and Gender Roles: A Comparison of Two Ethnic Communities in Kerala, India." In *Continuity and Change: Women at the Close of the Twentieth Century*, 43–61. Providence: Thomas J. Watson Institute for International Studies, Brown University, Occasional Paper 12.

Kuznets, Paul W. 1988. "An East Asian Model of Economic Development: Japan, Taiwan, and South Korea." *Economic Development and Cultural Change* 36, no. 3 (April): 11–43.

Lal, Deepak. 1983. *The Poverty of "Development Economics"*. Cambridge: Harvard University Press.

Lambert, Rob. 1992. "Constructing the New Internationalism: Australian Trade Unions and the Indian Ocean Regional Initiative." *South African Labour Bulletin* 16, no. 5 (May–June): 66–73.

Lee Tsao Yuan. 1991. *Growth Triangle: The Johor-Singapore-Riau Experience*. Singapore: Institute of Southeast Asian Studies.

Lee Yok-shiu F., and Alvin Y. So. 1999. "Conclusion." In *Asia's Environmental Movements: Comparative Perspectives*, ed. Lee Yok-shiu F. and Alvin Y. So. 287–308. Armonk, NY: M.E. Sharpe.

Legler, John M. 1995. "Come Together: Investment and Trade Links Are Growing Rapidly in Asia." *Far Eastern Economic Review* 158, no. 41 (12 October): 46–52.

Leite, Paulo Moreira. 1996. "Males Globalizados." Trans. Lillian Duarte. *Veja* 29, no. 9 (28 February): 24–25.

Lim, David. 1994. "Explaining the Growth Performance of Asian Developing Economies." *Economic Development and Cultural Change* 42, no. 4 (July): 429–42.

Lim, Linda. 1983. "Chinese Economic Activity in Southeast Asia: An Introductory Review." In *The Chinese in Southeast Asia: Ethnicity and Economic*

*Activity*, ed. Linda Lim and L.A. Peter Gosling, 1–29. Vol. 1. Singapore: Maruzen Press.

Lim, Linda. 1995. "Success through International Openness." In *Global Change, Regional Response: The New International Context of Development*, ed. Barbara Stallings, 238–71. Cambridge: Cambridge University Press.

———. 1996. "ASEAN: New Modes of Economic Cooperation." In *Southeast Asia in the New World Order: The Political Economy of a Dynamic Region*, ed. David Wurfel and Bruce Burton, 19–35. London: Macmillan, and New York: St. Martin's.

Lipietz, Alain. 1985. *Mirages and Miracles: The Crisis of Global Fordism*. Trans. David Macey. London: Verso.

Lipschutz, Ronnie. 1992. "Restructuring World Politics: The Emergence of Global Civil Society." *Millennium: Journal of International Studies* 21, no. 3 (Winter): 389–420.

———. 1997. "The Great Transformation Revisited." *The Brown Journal of World Affairs* 4, no. 1 (Winter/Spring): 299–318.

Lopez, George A., Jackie G. Smith, and Ron Pagnucco. 1995. "The Global Tide." *The Bulletin of the Atomic Scientists* 51, no. 4 (July/August): 33–39.

Lupsha, Peter A. 1996. "Transnational Organized Crime versus the Nation-State." *Transnational Organized Crime* 2, no. 1 (Spring): 21–48.

Machado, Kit G. 1997. *The Growing Complexity of the East Asian Division of Labor: Implications for Regionalism and ASEAN Industrial Development*. Bangi, Malaysia: Institute of Malaysian and International Studies Working Papers, No. 8, Universiti Kebangsaan Malaysia.

Machungo, Mario. 1988. Prime Minister of Mozambique. Interview by *Southern African Economist* 1, no. 4 (August–September): 25–27.

Magane, Pelelo. 1996. Organizer, Chemical Workers Industrial Union. Interview by author. Johannesburg, South Africa, 30 July.

Magno, Francisco A. 1993. "The Growth of Philippine Environmentalism." *Kasarinlan* 9, no. 1 (3rd quarter): 7–18.

Mahathir bin Mohamad. 1989. "Regionalism, Globalism and Spheres of Influence: ASEAN and the Challenge of Change in the 21st Century." Singapore: Institute of Southeast Asian Studies.

Mandaza, Ibbo. 1990. "SADCC: Problems of Regional Political and Economic Cooperation in Southern Africa: An Overview." In *Regional Integration in Africa: Unfinished Agenda*, ed. Anyang' Nyong'o, 141–55. Nairobi: African Academy of Sciences.

Manila People's Forum on APEC 1996. 1996. "Hidden Costs of Free Trade: Statement of the Philippine PO-NGO Summit on the APEC." Quezon City, Philippines, 6 July. Unpublished.

Mansfield, Edward D., and Helen V. Milner, eds. 1997. *The Political Economy of Regionalism*. New York: Columbia University Press.

Marchand, Marianne H. 1994. "Gender and the New Regionalism in Latin America: Inclusion/Exclusion." *Third World Quarterly* 15, no. 1 (March): 63–76.

Marshall, Judith. 1989. "On the Ropes: Socialism and FRELIMO's Fifth Congress." *Southern Africa Report* 5, no. 2 (July): 557–81.

———. 1990. "Structural Adjustment and Social Policy in Mozambique." *Review of African Political Economy* 47 (Spring): 28–43.

Matowanyika, Joseph Z. Z. 1996. Director, ZERO. Interview by author. Harare, Zimbabwe, 11 July.

McCallum, John. 1995. "National Borders Matter: Canada-U.S. Regional Trade Patterns." *American Economic Review* 85, no. 3 (June): 615–23.

McGrew, Anthony. 1992. "A Global Society?" In *Modernity and Its Futures*, ed. Open University, 62–102. Cambridge: Polity Press.

McMichael, Philip. 1996a. *Development and Social Change: A Global Perspective*. Thousand Oaks, CA: Pine Forge Press.

———. 1996b. "Globalization: Myths and Realities." *Rural Sociology* 61, no. 1 (Spring): 25–55.

Melucci, Alberto. 1985. "The Symbolic Challenge of Contemporary Social Movements." *Social Research* 52 (Winter): 789–816.

Migdal, Joel S. 1988. *Strong States and Weak Societies*. Princeton: Princeton University Press.

Minter, William. 1998. Senior Research Fellow, Africa Policy Information Center, Washington Office on Africa. Letter to author. 1 February.

Mittelman, James H. 1981. *Underdevelopment and the Transition to Socialism: Mozambique and Tanzania*. New York: Academic Press.

———. 1990. "The Dilemmas of Reform in Post-Revolutionary Societies." *International Studies Notes* 15, no. 2 (Spring) : 65–70.

———. 1994. "The Globalization of Social Conflict." In *Conflicts and New Departures in World Society*, ed. Volker Bornschier and Peter Lengyel, 317–33. Vol. 3 of *World Society Studies*. New Brunswick, NJ: Transaction Publishers.

———, ed. 1996. *Globalization: Critical Reflections*. Boulder, CO: Lynne Rienner.

———. 1997a. *Globalization, Peace and Conflict*. Bangi, Malaysia: Penerbit Universiti Kebangsaan Malaysia [National University of Malaysia Press].

———. 1997b. "Rethinking Innovation in International Studies: Global Transformation at the Turn of the Millennium." In *Innovation and Transformation in International Studies*, ed. Stephen Gill and James H. Mittelman, 248–63. Cambridge: Cambridge University Press.

Mittelman, James H., and Mustapha Kamal Pasha. 1997. *Out from Underdevelopment Revisited: Changing Global Structures and the Remaking of the Third World*. London: Macmillan, and New York: St. Martin's.

Mohanty, Chandra Talpade, Ann Russo, and Lourdes Torres, eds. 1991. *Third World Women and the Politics of Feminism*. Bloomington: Indiana University Press.

Morales, Horacio "Boy." 1996. President, Philippine Rural Reconstruction Movement. Interview by author. Quezon City, Philippines, 13 March.

Morales, Rebecca, and Carlos Quandt. 1992. "The New Regionalism in Developing Countries and Regional Collaborative Competition." *International Journal of Urban and Regional Research* 16, no. 3 (September): 463–75.

Moreira Alves, Maria Helena. 1988. "Democratization Versus Social Equality in Latin America: Notes for Discussion." Paper presented at the conference on

"Comparative Politics: Research Perspectives for the Next 20 Years." City University of New York Graduate School. New York, September.

"Mozambique: Businesses Threaten Strike over Failure to Curb Crime." 1996. *FBIS Daily Report.* 8 October. http://fbis.fedworld.gov./cgi-bin/retrieve.

Mozambiquefile. 1993a. "Food Aid Rots in Maputo." *Mozambiquefile: A Mozambique News Agency Monthly* 200 (March): 21.

———. 1993b. "Food Aid Stolen." *Mozambiquefile: A Mozambique News Agency Monthly* 201 (April): 21.

Munck, Ronaldo. 1988. *The New International Labour Studies: An Introduction.* London: Zed Books.

Murphy, Craig N. 1994. *International Organization and Industrial Change: Global Governance since 1850.* New York: Oxford University Press.

Mushakoji, Kinhide. 1994. "Japan, the Japanese NIEs, and the Japanese in the Post-Cold War Asia-Pacific Region." *PRIME* 1 (1994): 13–31.

Muto, Ichiyo. 1994. "PP21: A Step in a Process." *AMPO Japan-Asia Quarterly Review* 25, no. 2: 47–53.

———. 1996. Pacific Asia Resource Center. Interview by author. Tokyo, 25 February.

Muto, Ichiyo, and Smitu Kothari. Undated. "Towards Sustainable Systems." Tokyo, discussion paper for PP21.

Naisbitt, John. 1996. *Megatrends Asia: Eight Asian Megatrends that Are Reshaping Our World.* New York: Simon & Schuster.

National Council of Women of the Philippines (NCWP). 1996. "APEC and the Women: Catching the Next Wave." GO-NGO Forum on Women, 16 July. Unpublished.

Naya, Seiji, and Michael G. Plummer. 1991. "ASEAN Economic Co-operation in the New International Economic Environment." *ASEAN Economic Bulletin* 7, no. 3 (March): 261–76.

Nazarea-Sandoval, Virginia D. 1995. *Local Knowledge and Agricultural Decision Making in the Philippines: Class, Gender, and Resistance.* Ithaca, NY: Cornell University Press.

Nedcor. 1996. "The Nedcor Project on Crime, Violence and Investment: Main Report." Johannesburg, South Africa: June. Unpublished.

Nicaso, Antonio, and Lee Lamothe. 1995. *Global Mafia: The New World of Organized Crime.* Toronto: Macmillan.

Nolan, Peter. 1990. "Assessing Economic Growth in the Asian NICs." *Journal of Contemporary Asia* 20, no. 1: 41–63.

Nua Internet Surveys. 1998. http://www.nua.ie/surveys/how many online/index.html.

Nye, Joseph S. 1990. *Bound to Lead: The Changing Nature of American Power.* New York: Basic Books.

Obasanjo, Olusegun. 1988. *Southern Africa: The Security of the Front-line States.* Report of the Security Mission to the Front-line States. London: Commonwealth Secretariat.

Ohmae, Kenichi. 1990. *The Borderless World: Power and Strategy in the Interlinked World Economy.* New York: Harper Business, London: HarperCollins.

O'Laughlin, Bridget. 1995. "Past and Present Options: Land Reform in Mozambique." *Review of African Political Economy* 22, no. 63 (March): 99–106.

Ong, Aihwa. 1987. *Spirits of Resistance and Capitalist Discipline: Factory Women in Malaysia*. Albany: State University of New York Press.

Organization for Economic Cooperation and Development. 1989. *Geographical Distribution of Financial Flows to Developing Countries*. Paris: OECD.

Østergaard, Tom. 1993. "Classical Models of Regional Integration—What Relevance for Southern Africa?" In *Southern Africa after Apartheid*, ed. Bertil Odén, 27–47. Uppsala, Sweden: Scandinavian Institute of African Studies.

Palan, Ronen, and Jason Abbott. 1996. *State Strategies in the Global Economy*. With Phil Deans. London: Pinter.

Palmer, Norman D. 1991. *The New Regionalism in Asia and the Pacific*. Lexington, MA.: Lexington Books.

Papademetriou, Demetrios. 1988. "International Migration in a Changing World." In *Emerging Issues*, ed. Charles Stahl, 237–50. Vol. 2 of *International Migration Today*. Paris: United Nations Educational, Scientific, and Cultural Organization.

Pasha, Mustapha Kamal, and Ahmed I. Samatar. 1996. "The Resurgence of Islam." In *Globalization: Critical Reflections*, ed. James H. Mittelman, 187–201. Boulder, CO: Lynne Rienner.

Peluso, Nancy Lee. 1992. *Rich Forests, Poor People: Resource Control and Resistance in Java*. Berkeley: University of California Press.

"Pointers." 1997. *Jane's Foreign Report* 2448 (22 May).

Poitras, Guy. 1995. "Regional Trade Strategies: U.S. Policy in North America and toward the Asian Pacific." Paper presented at the annual meeting of the International Studies Association. Chicago, February.

Polanyi, Karl. 1945. "Universal Capitalism or Regional Planning?" *London Quarterly of World Affairs* 10, no. 3 (January): 86–91.

———. 1957. *The Great Transformation: The Political and Economic Origins of Our Time*. Boston: Beacon Press.

———. 1968. *Primitive, Archaic and Modern Economies: Essays of Karl Polanyi*. Ed. George Dalton. Garden City, NY: Anchor Books.

———. 1977. *The Livelihood of Man*. Ed. Harry W. Pearson. New York: Academic Press.

Porter, Michael. 1990. *The Competitive Advantage of Nations*. New York: Free Press.

"Proposed Philippine PO-NGO Position." 1996. Executive Summary. Manila People's Forum (MPF) on APEC 1996. Manila.

Puchala, Donald. 1992. Letter to author. 9 June.

Rasiah, Rajah, and Mohd. Haflah Piei. 1998. *Understanding the AFTA Process*. Singapore: Information and Resource Center.

Rawls, John. 1993. *Political Liberalism*. New York: Columbia University Press.

Rebugio, Lucrecio L. 1996. Professor and Dean, College of Forestry, University of the Philippines Los Banos. Interview by author. Los Banos, Laguna, Philippines, 11 March.

Redding, S. Gordon. 1990. *The Spirit of Chinese Capitalism*. Berlin and New York: Walter de Gruyter.

Ricardo, David. 1932. *Principles of Political Economy*. Ed. E. C. K. Gonner. London: G. Bell and Sons.

Robertson, Roland. 1992. *Globalization: Social Theory and Global Culture.* Newbury Park, CA: Sage.

Robinson, William I. 1992. "The São Paulo Forum: Is There a New Latin American Left?" *Monthly Review* 44, no. 7 (December): 1–12.

———. 1996. *Promoting Polyarchy: Globalization, US Intervention, and Hegemony.* Cambridge: Cambridge University Press.

Robison, Richard. 1986. *Indonesia: The Rise of Capital.* Sydney: Allen and Unwin.

Robson, Peter. 1993. "The New Regionalism and Developing Countries." *Journal of Common Market Studies* 31, no. 3 (September): 329–48.

Rodan, Garry. 1996. "Theorising Political Opposition in East and Southeast Asia." In *Political Oppositions in Industrialising Asia*, ed. Garry Rodan, 1–39. London: Routledge.

Rodrik, Dani. 1997. *Has Globalization Gone Too Far?* Washington, DC: Institute for International Economics.

———. 1998. "The Global Fix." *New Republic* 219, no. 18, issue 4,372 (2 November), 17–19.

Roesch, Otto. 1989. "Nampula: What's Left?" *Southern Africa Report* 5, no. 2 (November): 9–13.

Rosa, Kumudhini. 1994. "The Conditions and Organizational Activities of Women in Free Trade Zones, Malaysia, Philippines and Sri Lanka, 1970–1990." In *Dignity and Daily Bread: New Forms of Economic Organizing among Poor Women in the Third World and First*, ed. Seheila Rowbotham and Swasti Mitter, 73–99. London: Routledge.

Rosenau, James N. 1990. *Turbulence in World Politics: A Theory of Change in Continuity.* Princeton: Princeton University Press.

———. 1997. *Along the Domestic-Foreign Frontier: Exploring Governance in a Turbulent World.* Cambridge: Cambridge University Press.

Rosenau, James N., and Ernst-Otto Czempiel, eds. 1992. *Governance without Government: Order and Change in World Politics.* Cambridge: Cambridge University Press.

Rosow, Stephen J. 1999. "Globalization/Democratic Theory: The Politics of Representation of Post-Cold War Political Space." Paper presented at the annual meeting of the International Studies Association. Washington, DC, February.

Ruggie, John Gerard. 1992. "Multilateralism: The Anatomy of an Institution." *International Organization* 46, no. 3 (Summer): 561–98.

———. 1993. "Territoriality and Beyond: Problematizing Modernity in International Relations." *International Organization* 47, no. 1 (Summer): 139–74.

Sachs, Jeffrey. 1997. "Secretive Workings of the IMF Call for Reassessment." *New Straits Times*, 23 December.

Sadler, David. 1992. *The Global Region: Production, State Policies and Uneven Development.* Oxford: Pergamon Press.

Sakamoto, Yoshikazu, ed. 1994. *Global Transformation: Challenges to the State System.* Tokyo: United Nations University Press.

Saro-Wiwa, Ken. 1995. *A Month and a Day: A Detention Diary.* New York: Penguin.

Sassen, Saskia. 1991. *The Global City: New York, London, Tokyo.* Princeton: Princeton University Press.

———. 1996. *Losing Control? Sovereignty in an Age of Globalization.* New York: Columbia University Press.

———. 1998. *Globalization and Its Discontents: Essays on the New Mobility of People and Money.* New York: The New Press.

Sato, Mitsuo. 1996. "Keynote Speech." In *Asian Growth Polygons,* ed. Asian Institute of Management. Manila: Proceedings of the Seventh Asian Institute of Management, Management Conference on Asia.

Scholte, Jan Aart. 1997. "The Globalization of World Politics." In *The Globalization of World Politics: An Introduction to International Relations,* ed. J. Baylis and S. Smith, 13–30. Oxford: Oxford University Press.

Schwab, Klaus, and Claude Smadja. 1996. "Start Taking the Backlash against Globalization Seriously." *International Herald Tribune,* 1 February.

Scott, James C. 1976. *The Moral Economy of the Peasant: Rebellion and Subsistence in Southeast Asia.* New Haven, CT: Yale University Press.

———. 1985. *Weapons of the Weak: Everyday Forms of Peasant Resistance.* New Haven, CT: Yale University Press.

———. 1990. *Domination and the Arts of Resistance: Hidden Transcripts.* New Haven, CT: Yale University Press.

Segal, Aaron. 1992. "International Migration: Conflict and Cooperation." Paper presented at the annual meeting of the International Studies Association. Atlanta, April.

Segal, Aaron, and Linda Marston. 1989. "Maps and Keys—World Voluntary Migration 1500–1980." *Migration World Magazine* 17, no. 1 (1989): 36–41; as cited in Shirley Hune. 1991. "Migrant Women in the Context of the International Convention on the Protection of the Rights of All Migrant Workers and Members of Their Families." *International Migration Review* 25, no. 4 (Winter): 800–17.

Seidman, Ann, and Fredrick Anang, eds. 1992. *Twenty-first-Century Africa: Towards a New Vision of Self-Sustainable Development.* Trenton, NJ: Africa World Press.

Sender, Henry. 1991. "Inside the Chinese Overseas Network." *Institutional Investor* (September): 37–42.

Serrano, Isagani R. 1994. "Civil Society in the Asia-Region." In *Citizens: Strengthening Global Civil Society,* ed. CIVICUS: World Alliance for Citizen Participation, 217–317. Washington, DC.

———. 1996. Vice President, Philippine Rural Reconstruction Movement. Interview by author. Quezon City, Philippines, 13 March.

Shaw, Martin. 1994. "Civil Society and Global Politics: Beyond a Social Movements Approach." *Millennium: Journal of International Studies* 23, no. 3 (Winter): 647–67.

Shaw, Timothy M. 1992. "Revisionist Perspectives on Regionalism in Africa: IGADD & the Horn in the 1990s." Paper presented at the annual meeting of the African Studies Association. Seattle, November.

Shelley, Louise L. 1995. "Transnational Organised Crime: An Imminent Threat to the Nation-State?" *Journal of International Affairs* 48, no. 2 (Winter): 463–89.

Shiva, Vandana. 1992. "Resources." In *The Development Dictionary: A Guide to Knowledge as Power*, ed. Wolfgang Sachs, 206–18. London: Zed Books.

"Siege Survival Tactics." 1987. *South* 79 (May): 27–28.

Silverman, Gary. 1996. "Vital and Vulnerable." *Far Eastern Economic Review* 159, no. 21 (23 May): 60–63.

Sinclair, Timothy J. 1994a. "Between State and Market: Hegemony and Institutions of Collective Action under Conditions of International Capital Mobility." *Policy Sciences* 27, no. 4: 447–66.

———. 1994b. "Passing Judgment: Credit Rating Processes as Regulatory Mechanisms of Governance in the Emerging World Order." *Review of International Political Economy* 1, no. 1 (Spring 1994): 133–59.

Singerman, Diane. 1995. *Avenues of Participation: Family, Politics, and Networks in Urban Quarters of Cairo*. Princeton: Princeton University Press.

Singh, Gurmit K. S. 1997. Executive Director, Centre for Environment, Technology and Development, Malaysia. Interview by author. Petaling Jaya, Malaysia, 15 November. .

Sklair, Leslie. 1994. "Global Sociology and Global Environmental Change." In *Social Theory and the Global Environment*, ed. M. Redclift and T. Benton, 205–17. London: Routledge.

———. 1997. "Social Movements and Global Capitalism: The Transnational Capitalist Class in Action." *Review of International Political Economy* 4, no. 3 (Autumn): 514–38.

Smith, Adam. 1970. *An Inquiry into the Nature and Causes of the Wealth of Nations*. Harmondsworth, Middlesex: Penguin Books.

———. 1976. *The Theory of Moral Sentiments*, ed. D. D. Raphael and A. I. Macfie. London: Oxford University Press.

Smith, Jackie, Charles Chatfield, and Ron Pagnucco, eds. 1997. *Transnational Social Movements and Global Politics: Solidarity beyond the State*. Syracuse: Syracuse University Press.

Snyder, Richard. 1999. "After Neoliberalism: The Politics of Reregulation in Mexico." *World Politics* 51, no. 2 (January): 173–204.

Social Weather Station. 1994. "Social Weather Report Survey." Quezon City, Philippines: Social Weather Station; as cited in Ofreno, Reno. 1995. "Globalization and the Filipino Working Masses," 6. Proceedings of the Sixth Annual Lecture of the Civil Liberties Union. Greenhills, Philippines.

Somers, Margaret R. 1994. "The Narrative Constitution of Identity: A Relational and Network Approach." *Theory and Society* 23, no. 5 (October): 605–49.

Songco, Danilo A. 1996. National Coordinator, CODE-NGO. Interview by author. Quezon City, Philippines, 13 March.

"South Africa: 'Showdown' Looming between Cape Vigilantes, Drug Dealers." 1996. *FBIS Daily Report*. 3 August. http://fbis.fedworld.gov/cgi-bin/retrieve.

South African Institute of Race Relations. 1996. *South Africa Survey 1995/96*. Johannesburg, South Africa: South African Institute of Race Relations.

*Southern Africa Online* (Harare, Zimbawe). 1989. 2, 25 (7 July): 1–9.

Stares, Paul B. 1996. *Global Habit: The Drug Problem in a Borderless World*. Washington, DC: Brookings Institution.

Stein, Howard, ed. 1995. *Asian Industrialization and Africa.* New York: St. Martin's.

Sterling, Claire. 1994. *Thieves' World: The Threat of the New Network of Organized Crime.* New York: Simon & Schuster.

Stewart, Sally, Michael Tow Cheung, and David W. K. Yeung. 1992. "The Latest Asian Newly Industrialized Economy Emerges: The South China Economic Community." *Columbia Journal of World Business* 27, no. 2 (Summer): 30–37.

Stopford, John M., and Susan Strange. 1991. *Rival States, Rival Firms: Competition for World Market Shares.* With John S. Henley. Cambridge: Cambridge University Press.

Strange, Susan. 1995. "The Defective State." *Daedalus* 124, no. 2 (Spring): 55–74.

———. 1996. *The Retreat of the State: The Diffusion of Power in the World Economy.* Cambridge: Cambridge University Press.

Stubbs, Richard. 1989. "Geopolitics and the Political Economy of Southeast Asia." *International Journal* 44 (Summer): 517–40.

———. 1991. "The ASEAN Dimension in US-Japan Trade Relations." Paper presented at the meeting of the Canadian Council on Southeast Asian Studies. Toronto: York University, October.

———. 1994. "The Political Economy of the Asia-Pacific Region." In *Political Economy and the Changing Global Order*, ed. Richard Stubbs and Geoffrey R. D. Underhill, 366–77. New York: St. Martin's.

Sum Ngai-Ling. 1996. "The 'Geo-Governance' and 'Embeddedness' of Cross-Border Regional Modes of Growth: Some Theoretical Issues and the Case of 'Greater China.'" Paper presented at the Karl Polanyi Conference on "Reciprocity, Redistribution and Exchange: Re-embedding the Economy in Culture and Nature." Montreal: Concordia University, November.

Sun, Lena H. 1992. "South China Drives Boom Region." *Washington Post,* 2 December.

Tabb, William K. 1994. *The Postwar Japanese System: Cultural Economy and Economic Transformation.* New York: Oxford University Press.

———. 1999. "Progressive Globalism: Challenging the Audacity of Capital." *Monthly Review* 50, no. 9 (February 1999): 1–10.

Tabbarah, Riad. 1988. "Prospects for International Migration." In *Emerging Issues*, ed. Charles Stahl, 251–65. Vol. 2 of *International Migration Today.* Paris: United Nations Educational, Scientific, and Cultural Organization.

Tanzer, Andrew. 1997. "The Amazing Mr. Kuok." *Forbes* 160, no. 2 (28 July): 90–96.

Taylor, Charles. 1989. *Sources of the Self: The Making of the Modern Identity.* Cambridge: Harvard University Press.

Teeple, Gary. 1995. *Globalization and the Decline of Social Reform.* Atlantic Highlands, NJ: Humanities Press International.

Tengco, Gary James C. 1996. Project Coordinator, Institute of Environmental Science for Social Change (formerly Environmental Research Division of the Manila Observatory). Interview by author. Cabanatuan City, Nueva Ecija, Luzon, Philippines, 9 March.

Thompson, Carol B. 1991. *Harvests under Fire: Regional Co-operation for Food Security in Southern Africa*. London: Zed Books.

Tinley, K. L., and W. F. Van Riet. 1991. "Conceptual Proposals for Kruger-Banhine." Maputo: Government of Mozambique.

Truehart, Charles. 1997. "French Hold Proudly Fast to Benevolent Central Rule." *Washington Post*, 14 July.

Tschirley, David L., and Michael T. Weber. 1994. "Food Security Strategies under Extremely Adverse Conditions: The Determinants of Household Income and Consumption in Rural Mozambique." *World Development* 22, no. 2 (February): 159–73.

United Nations Children's Fund. 1990. "Country Programme Recommendation: Mozambique." E/ICEF/1990/P/L.6.

United Nations Conference on Trade and Development. 1995. "Recent Developments in International Investment and Transnational Corporations." TD/B/ITNC/2. 21 February.

———. 1996. *World Investment Report 1996: Investment, Trade and International Policy Arrangements*. New York and Geneva: United Nations.

———. 1997. *World Investment Report 1997: Transnational Corporations, Market Structure and Competition Policy*. New York and Geneva: United Nations.

United Nations Development Program. 1996, 1998. *Human Development Report*. New York: Oxford University Press.

United Nations High Commissioner for Refugees. 1997. "Mozambique." http://www.unhcr.ch/unhcr/world/afr/mozambiq.htm.

United Nations Population Fund. 1993. *The State of World Population 1993*. New York: United Nations Population Fund.

United States Department of Commerce. 1989. *Foreign Economic Trends and Their Implications for the United States*. FET 89–51. Washington, DC: U.S. Department of Commerce.

Vann, Stephen. 1997. U.S. Department of State Desk Officer for Mozambique. Interview by Juliet Litterer. Washington, DC, 11 December.

Vatikotis, Michael et al. 1991."Building Blocs." *Far Eastern Economic Review* (31 January): 32–33.

Walker, Tony. 1993. "Beijing Fears Grow over Runaway Economy." *Financial Times*, 25 June.

Walker, R. B. J. 1993. *Inside/Outside: International Relations as Political Theory*. Cambridge: Cambridge University Press.

———. 1994. "Social Movements/World Politics." *Millennium: Journal of International Studies* 23, no. 3 (Winter): 669–700.

Walpole, Peter W., S. J. 1996. Executive Director, Institute of Environmental Science for Social Change (formerly Environmental Research Division of the Manila Observatory). Interview by author. Quezon City, Philippines, 12 March.

Walzer, Michael. 1999. "Rescuing Civil Society." *Dissent* (Winter): 62–67.

Wapner, Paul. 1996. *Environmental Activism and World Civic Politics*. Albany: State University of New York Press.

Waters, Malcolm. 1995. *Globalization*. London: Routledge.

Weber, Max. 1947. *The Theory of Social and Economic Organization.* Trans. A. M. Henderson and ed. Talcott Parsons. New York: Free Press.

Wettern, Joern. 1993. "The Place of Guestworkers in the German Political Economy: Continuation of a Failed Immigration Policy." Paper presented at the annual meeting of the International Studies Association. Acapulco, Mexico, March.

White, Gordon, ed. 1988. *Developmental States in East Asia.* New York: St. Martin's.

Whitley, Richard. 1996. "Business Systems and Global Commodity Chains: Competing or Complementary Forms of Economic Organisation?" *Competition & Change* 1: 411–25.

"Who Guards the Guardians?" 1997. *The Straits Times* (Singapore), 5 December.

Williams, Phil. 1994. "Transnational Criminal Organisations and International Security." *Security* 36, no. 1 (Spring): 96–113.

Williams, Raymond. 1977. *Marxism and Literature.* Oxford: Oxford University Press.

Wilpert, Czarina. 1988. "Migrant Women and Their Daughters: Two Generations of Turkish Women in the Federal Republic of Germany." In *Emerging Issues,* ed. Charles Stahl, 168–86. Vol. 2 of *International Migration Today.* Paris: United Nations Educational, Cultural and Scientific Organization.

Women's Forum. 1996. "Women's Forum for the APEC Manila Process." Manila People's Forum on APEC. Manila, 3 July.

World Bank. 1989a. *Trends in Developing Economies 1989.* Washington, DC: World Bank.

———. 1989b through 1999b. *World Development Report.* New York: Oxford University Press.

———. 1993. *Global Economic Prospects and the Developing World.* New York: Oxford University Press.

———. 1996. *Poverty Reduction and the World Bank: Progress and Challenges in the 1990s.* Washington, DC: World Bank.

World Economic Forum. 1997. *The Global Competitiveness Report 1997.* Geneva: WEF. http://www.weforum.org/publications/gcr/ranking.

Wu Yuan-li, and Chun-hsi Wu. 1980. *Economic Development in Southeast Asia: The Chinese Dimension.* Stanford, CA: Hoover Institution Press.

Yamamoto, Yoshinobu. 1993. "Regionalization in Contemporary International Relations." Paper presented at the conference "Regionalization in the World Economy." Tokyo, July.

Yearley, Steven. 1996. *Sociology, Environmentalism, Globalization: Reinventing the Globe.* London: Sage.

Zakaria, Fareed. 1994. "A Conversation with Lee Kuan Yew." *Foreign Affairs* 73, no. 2 (March- April): 109–26.

Zawiah Yahya. 1994. *Resisting Colonialist Discourse.* Bangi, Malaysia: Penerbit Universiti Kebangsaan Malaysia [National University of Malaysia Press].

Zinniker, Laura. 1993. "The Presence of Arab Migrants and the Politics of French 'Nationalism.' " Paper presented at the annual meeting of the International Studies Association. Acapulco, Mexico, March.

Printed in Great Britain
by Amazon.co.uk, Ltd.,
Marston Gate.